Sarah Burkhalter &
Laurence Schmidlin
[eds.]

Spacescapes
Dance & Drawing since 1962

JRP|RINGIER & LES PRESSES DU RÉEL

To Frances

Sarah Burkhalter &
Laurence Schmidlin
[eds.]

Spacescapes Dance & Drawing since 1962

Table of Contents

Introduction
Sarah Burkhalter & Laurence Schmidlin

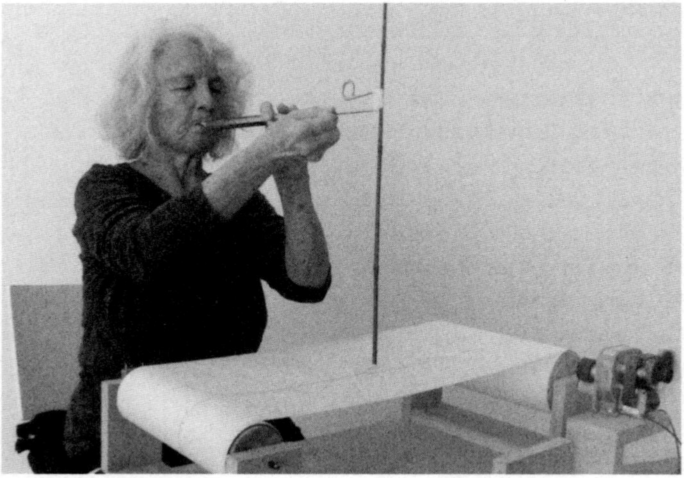

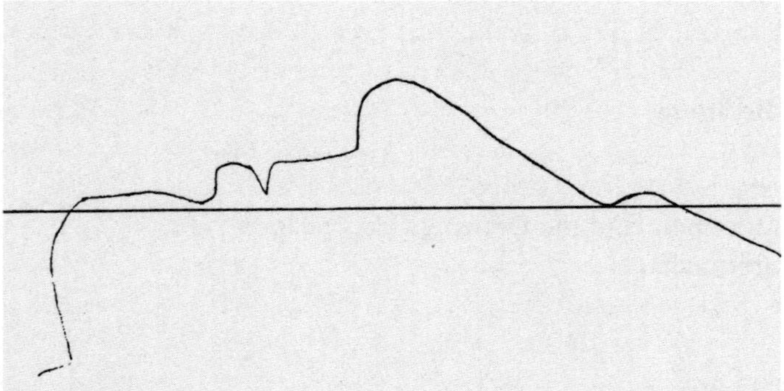

Simone Forti
Face Tunes, 1968/2011
HD video still; camera: Jason Underhill

Face Tunes, 1968
Drawing in Simone Forti, *Handbook in Motion*, The Press of the Nova Scotia College of Art & Design, Halifax 1974 (distribution by Contact Editions)

When Simone Forti performed *Face Tunes* in 1967 at the School of Visual Arts in New York City, she was returning to choreography in an unprecedented way. As if reading a score, she interpreted the profiles of seven faces that she had drawn on a paper scroll, playing a slide whistle to which a stylus was attached. Pointed at a right angle, the instrument followed the tracings, emitting a tune drafted from the various physiognomical contours that were activated by a motor. "As form seemed to be the storage place for presence," Forti explained in *Handbook in Motion* (1974), "I hoped that the act of translating a coherent aspect of a set of faces to a corresponding form might awaken a more primitive level of pattern or ghost recognition."[1] Although *Face Tunes* is musical in nature, the piece carries the imprint of the kinesthetic memory that Forti had nurtured during a decade of dance, performance, and bodily practice. She thus situated herself at the intersection of line and action, form and sound, notation and gesture.

If we begin this volume with *Face Tunes*, it is because the piece is one the most original examples of the correlation between the body's expression and graphic tracing. Seated, almost static, Forti nonetheless acts as the intermediary in a drawing's creation, a drawing that, in turn, produces a melody.

Dance and drawing share many characteristics and often refer to one another. The function of drawing in the conception of dance, the understanding of movement as a fleeting graphic imprint, the spatial reciprocity of the two mediums have thus featured among the questions that motivated this book. Drawing indeed appeared to us to be the most appropriate art to relate to dance. We believed that its economy of means and the role given to the body within its array of materials would enable us to study with precision the issues at stake in the exchanges between a permanent art and an ephemeral art. Space therefore presented itself as the common field of activity, since both configure it by engaging physically with it and by allowing themselves to be marked by its architectural, telluric, or incidental elements. Dance and drawing give shape to space, creating what we have named "spacescapes," and inscribe each other in spatialized places and moments.

Dance and drawing are intimately linked to the gesture that performs them. The dancing body creates a figure in space and leaves a volatile impact on site. The restrained event of gesture on a medium, for its part, sets a point in motion, recalling the description of the line given by Paul Klee in 1920.[2] It captures an ephemeral event, which is reproduced in graphic form.

In reviving the inscription of bodies in space through her breath, Forti adds a respiratory power to the metabolism of drawing as Paul Valéry defined it. "Every single glance at the model, every line traced by the eye becomes an instantaneous element of memory, and it is from memory that the hand will lend itself to the law of movement. A visual tracing transforms itself into a manual tracing," he wrote of Edgar Degas. "The artist moves forward, backward, bends over, blinks his eyes, carries his whole body like an accessory of his eye, totally becomes a device for sighting, aiming, adjusting, fine tuning,"[3] he continued, describing the artist as someone who devoted his whole being to seeing and making visible. It is not a question of form, offering itself as a finite reality, but of "the way of seeing form." Drawing is thus an operative and embodied act, and while it was still anchored in visual mimesis in Degas, it earned its independence from figurative representation throughout the 20th century, ultimately exploring the kinetic and spatial value of line in itself.

The body of the artist—whether a dancer or a visual artist—is thus shared by these practices and has become the instrument of their simultaneous realization. Drawing has indeed collided with dance in opening up to three-dimensional space, incorporating surfaces—floor, ceiling, walls—as well as volumes into its process.

It is these intersections that are the focus of this collection, which took shape following the international symposium *"J'aime penser sur mes pieds." Danse et dessin depuis 1962/ "I love thinking on my feet." Dance and Drawing since 1962*, organized at the University of Geneva on May 31 and June 1, 2012. The texts here are not, however, the literal proceedings of the conference: through the essays and interviews published here for the first time,[4] this collection aims to evaluate and discuss the specific interaction of the two media and how their practices have diversified over the last 50 years. Their interdependence of course exceeds this temporal framework, as Ann Hutchinson Guest and Claudia Jeschke have demonstrated in their work on the history of choreographic drawings and notations.[5] Their correlation, de facto, calls forth the essential questions that Gabriele Brandstetter asks in her essay, which has been translated into English for the first time: "What is the status of notation as document, as score, as pre-script of 'pre-scribed' practices or as autonomous visual form? What are the dynamics that unfold from the tension between notation and performative practice? What are the topographies of temporality that can be deciphered in typographies, notations, or diagrams? And what are the specific forms of spatiality that open up in them?"[6]

The first performance of the Judson Dance Theater took place on July 6, 1962, in Manhattan. This event brought together dancers and choreographers from different backgrounds, many of whom were roused by the research of Anna Halprin in San Francisco, as Sarah Burkhalter reminds us in her essay [see p. 112–129].[7] We leave aside the circumstances that contributed to the renewal of the New York art scene, as well as the paths taken by the individuals who gathered there, over the course of two years of intense interaction (1962–1964), in a church devoted to promoting the arts of its time; Sally Banes, and Pauline Chevalier in this volume [see p. 130–146], have accurately established the issues of the projects undertaken at the Judson Dance Theater.[8] We refer to July 6, 1962 as a milestone in cultural history. From then onward, the performing and the visual arts developed, in particular, as a result of their dialogue.

Postmodern dance emerged first of all from this context. The dancers and choreographers who imagined it—without however turning it into a movement—were opposed to technical virtuosity and a symbolic, even narrative dimension of gesture. The reliance on chance and improvisation, the exploration of new stage spaces, among them the street and the museum, and the primacy of process over content featured among the main characteristics of this fresh way of conceiving and practicing dance. Thus for Rainer, the minimalist art object—devoid of the handmade trace of the artist, of compositional hierarchy or of illusionist effect—provided a paradigm for the performer's absence of phrasing, for the equality and repetition of danced parts or for the daily task completed on a human scale. In an interview conducted for this publication, Catherine Quéloz questions the intersecting uses that Rainer makes of notation, drawing, and spoken score [see p. 16–27]. As for the spatial implementations of written form, including choreographic notation and *écriture corporelle*, Alexander Schwan and Susan Rosenberg explore them in Trisha Brown's work, providing close readings of two pivotal pieces in the Brownian repertoire, *Roof and Fire Piece* (1973) and *Locus* (1975). These readings bring out, on one hand, the graphic dimension of the communicating body, and on the other hand, its role as a conceptual tool [see p. 60–73 and p. 74–87].

Conversely, many artists who took part in the Judson Dance Theater, or who occasionally dipped into it, thoroughly transformed the norms of production and reception of works of art. For example, the minimalist sculpture of Robert Morris was rooted in the experience of the body in space, even though, it should be noted, the artist has always minimized the impact of dance on his work. In 1970 he declared: "To specifically answer your question, I don't think I found anything in dance to apply to sculpture. I've always thought that the materials and problems and possibilities of each were separate,"[9] reasserting in 2014, in an interview with Katia Schneller published here for the first time [see p. 28–36], that each medium relies on its own economy and does not require taking advantage of the other. If dance has not, according to the artist, spearheaded his research in another field of artistic expression, one may at least affirm that the embodied awareness of action has been a creative force and has foregrounded the notion of process. Several murals drawn in the early 1970s and the series of drawings entitled *Blind Time I* (1973) clearly illustrate this.

It is therefore from this perspective that we wish to consider the interactions of dance and drawing, that is, in mobilizing both disciplines from the standpoint of what reunites them—body, figure, gesture, time—and, consequently, beyond the sole question of how the visual arts borrowed from dance or, inversely, from its notation. We believe that the scriptural dimension of both disciplines, for instance, ought to be less literally situated in the graphic encoding of movement than in the imprint of gesture, although we have not sidelined this question. We shall return to it later.

It is important to note that, parallel to the developments in dance, drawing practices densified from the late 1950s onward. Traditional functions of drawing were echoed in artistic practices that renounced, deliberately or for technical reasons, the materiality of the work of art. Simultaneously, performance art staged the medium of drawing, and sculpture shifted it into tangible space. Three-dimensional spatialization was therefore typical of the development of drawing.[10]

Instances of the convergence of the performing and visual arts can be found throughout the 20th century. While visual artists investigated the embodied and energetic value of form, dancers and choreographers experimented with the interfaces between sign and action, between notation and improvisation, between a spatial sense of self and an architectural configuration of movement. The hybridization of dance and drawing accelerated from mid-century onward, as performance art introduced innovative practices, and boundaries between disciplines were worn thin. Intermedial forms became ever more frequent. Laurence Schmidlin examines, in particular, how photography highlighted the graphic nature of a body, and at the same time revealed the stages of a drawing [see p. 192–206]. Moreover, through photography and digital visualization, the point of contact between dance and drawing unfolds itself. In the middle of their sequencing into fixed images, their temporal and spatial essence is made all the more manifest, as Robin Rhode points out in his conversation with Anna Lovatt [see p. 208–216].

Photography participates not only in the production of documents. Its technical parameters contribute to the definitive work beyond its form and function: it reveals, through image, a state of dance and of drawing. In comparison, a mechanical device—when it is used in the same context as these disciplines—harnesses the temporal and spatial characteristics of these media so as to lead them further still, to the edge of chance and disorder. Paul Kaiser, a member of the American collective OpenEndedGroup, explains to Nadia Peručić the creative purpose that technology can serve in human motion capture and in the production of new movements, sometimes unexpected [see p. 218–225]. From Jean Tinguely to Rebecca Horn, there have been numerous mechanical drawing devices throughout the 20th century. Those constructed by Alan Storey rely on the influence of extraneous forces (shipping, hygrometric variations, etc.). In an interview with Katrin Gattinger [see p. 88–98], he recalls that the autonomy granted to these devices is a modality that simply shifts the implications of an intentional body to a programmed yet free body, a modality the only clue to which appears through unpredictable tracing. Finally, Laetitia Legros uses the camera as a means of reproducing space through its digital transcription, as she explains to Magali Le Mens [see p. 100–109]. There are of course further uses of technology in the context of dance and drawing. For instance, Sidi Larbi Cherkaoui in *TeZuKa* (2011), and Mathilde Monnier and François Olislaeger in *Qu'est-ce qui nous arrive?!?* (2013) with whom she has been working since 2008,[11] use drawing as a backdrop: the dancers interact with sketches, nascent and animated graphic shapes. Although it would have complemented our exploration, this type of interaction between dance and drawing has not been considered in the essays gathered here. Likewise, cartoons and mangas, which inspired both these choreographic pieces, would have offered counterparts to contemporary forms of drawing.

A distinctive feature of recent decades has been the growing presence of dance in art museums and art centers. Dance is necessarily subject to an "expositional intermediality"[12] since it is not a priori intended for such venues, except when these act as a stage or performance space. As with cinema, music, or fashion—and bearing in mind that visual artworks are not all destined to be exhibited as we see them—the content must then be adapted to a framework that is usually unfamiliar, and which consequently transforms it.[13] There are numerous examples of expositional intermediality. One of them is spontaneous or intentional movement facing an artwork: for instance, the performative sequence of *Da inventare sul posto* (1972) by Jannis Kounellis, in which a violinist and a ballerina performed in front of a painted canvas, or the four dancers whom Mollyne Karnofsky invited to interact with her drawing, entitled *Paper Environment March 1978*, at the New Orleans Contemporary Arts Center (1978).

The implications, in terms of exhibiting dance, have therefore become more radical than ever. In addition to learning how to dance in a museum, how to conceive a piece in situ, and how to perform it—*Walking on the Wall* by Trisha Brown, which premiered at the Whitney Museum of American Art in New York in 1971 is a remarkable example—a recent area of exploration has been how to transmit dance as archive and cultural memory, not only evidenced by all its documents, but also by its actual performance. Xavier Le Roy[14] and Anne Teresa De Keersmaeker[15] have conceived projects from their repertoire that are specifically tailored for the exhibition space and time, wherein the dancing occurs during the opening hours of the host institution; these are examples of attempts to answer such an impasse. They bear witness to the fact that no literal adaptation is possible, that on the contrary, it is a question of reinventing gesture, movement, and choreography to conform to the parameters of the exhibition format, including the time span (approximately three months). Dance therefore leads us to think differently about exhibiting.

The history of dance in the museum begins with its notation. Indeed, drawn notes are often the first documentation of dance, a fragmentary type of document since they do not represent dance as it is, and, moreover, rarely offer sufficient information for reinterpretation. In the 1970s, along with the increasing recognition of drawing and the significance given to notes—as a result of conceptual art, which at times amounted to an idea jotted down on a sheet of paper—numerous dance scores were exhibited, although they were not always meant for public viewing in this capacity. Janet Kardon included scores and other sketches in the "Language" section of the American Pavilion at the 39th Venice Biennale in 1980.[16] Fascination with the visual materialization of thought and the expression of creative genius disregarded the often obscure nature of these sheets.

The incursion of dance into the museum space has, on the other hand, deeply altered the sensorial awareness of the public. It has challenged the way we see and look at visual art works, extending them with body figures or decoding them with the same movements that gave rise to them. In contrast to a place of static contemplation, in touch with a network of mobile activity and intersubjective communication, dance performances now regularly inhabit the museum and reshape the curatorial tenets of such an institution.

The intermediality of drawing and dance was precisely the point of *Tracking, Tracing, Marking, Pacing. Movement Drawings*, an exhibition held at the Pratt Institute in Brooklyn in 1982,[17] and *Danses tracées: dessins et notations des chorégraphes*, at the Centre national de la danse in Marseille in 1991. Works exhibited in *On Line. Drawing through the Twentieth Century* at The Museum of Modern Art in New York in

2010–2011 connected the drawn line with other types of lines.[18] The hem of the dress of a Loïe Fuller-style dancer performing the serpentine dance (1892), was thus seen as a vibrant contour, a first representation of the reciprocal ontology of the two media, via textile in this case. In 2012, at the Centre Pompidou in Paris, the exhibition entitled *Danser sa vie*—in reference to the memoirs of Isadora Duncan—studied the 20th century in light of the dialogue between the visual and the performing arts in the West[19]; at the Institute of Contemporary Arts in Boston, *Dance/Draw* examined the three-dimensionality of drawing and the graphic summarization of dance, alongside other questions, in the work of American and Latin American artists, many of whom are still active today.[20]

Among the monographic exhibitions that have offered surveys since the early 2000s of the subject we are exploring here, as well as of the works of dancers and choreographers, the following are of note: *Trisha Brown: Dance and Art in Dialogue 1961–2001*, at the Addison Gallery of American Art, Phillips Academy in Andover, Massachusetts, in 2002[21]; *Merce Cunningham. Drawings and Videos*, at the Margarete Roeder Gallery in New York in 2007[22]; *Trisha Brown: So That The Audience Does Not Know Whether I Have Stopped Dancing*, at the Walker Arts Center in Minneapolis in 2008[23]; *Simone Forti. Thinking with the Body*, at the Museum der Moderne in Salzburg in 2014[24]; *Yvonne Rainer: Dance Works*, at Raven Row in London the same year[25]; and finally *William Forsythe. The Fact of Matter*, at the Museum für Moderne Kunst in Frankfurt-am-Main in 2015.[26]

Therefore the intermedial relations between dance and drawing can be observed from multiple perspectives. They are primarily at work in choreographic notation, when movements, shifts, or any other element that is conducive to the performance of dance are codified. Such notations are not necessarily autonomous. They often require instructions on behalf of the choreographer who conceived them, of a dancer who has performed them, or even of complementary video footage. Their heuristic value, thus made contingent, magnifies their graphic value. As Catherine Wood explains, Channa Horwitz began by drawing on graph paper to conceive movement sequences, before devising a composition system named *Sonakinatography* [see p. 182–190].[27] Anne Teresa De Keersmaeker describes her commitment to representing abstract motifs that transcend time and culture, and the use of drawing as a measuring device in her choreographic scores to Julie Enckell Julliard [see p. 148–162]. Cindy Van Acker writes rather than draws, as she explains to Nolwenn Mégard, even though she sometimes outlines the dancers' figures, so as to avoid coding the movements [see p. 164–171].

Drawings made by choreographers or dancers—a category that is distinct from notation—are the matter of another form of intermediality. The artists do not seek to conceive a language that may translate a series of movements. They seize a given space—generally a sheet of paper—in order to leave traces made by the body. As in certain performances, they create a drawing that is at once the means and the aim of a succession of movements, and their memory once the body has disappeared. Mark Franko thus invites us to observe the various defigurations that are underway in *Retranslation/Final Unfinished Portrait (Francis Bacon)* (2006), an installation by Peter Welz and William Forsythe; playing on the different meanings of "defiguration," the author likewise points to the varying degrees of drawing within a dance work [see p. 174–181].

The correlation as well as the divide between dance and drawing can be experienced and conceived, we believe, through three modalities—"Writing," "Exploring," and "Expanding." The essays and interviews that compose this book have been arranged according to the most salient interaction, or the most fruitful drift.

May the authors, dancers, artists, and choreographers find here the expression of our deepest gratitude. Their ideas, imagination, and practice have shaped the space that we have mapped and now offer to the reader, a *space* that ultimately *escapes* words at the stroke of a line.

[1] Simone Forti, *Handbook in Motion*, The Press of the Nova Scotia College of Art and Design, Halifax 1974, p. 76. The work of Simone Forti has recently been presented at the Museum der Moderne Salzburg: *Simone Forti. Thinking with the Body: A Retrospective in Motion*, curated by Sabine Breitwieser (July 18–November 9th, 2014).

[2] Paul Klee, "Schöpferische Konfession," in Kasimir Edschmid (ed.), *Tribüne der Kunst und der Zeit. Eine Schriftensammlung*, vol. XIII, Reiss, Berlin 1920, p. 28–40.

[3] Paul Valéry, *Degas Danse Dessin*, Gallimard, Paris 2008, p. 81–82 [1st ed.: 1938].

[4] The essay by Gabriele Brandstetter ("The Figurative Scripts of Dance: Between Notation, Diagram, and Ornament," p. 40–59) is the only reprint of an article that predates this project. Its insight prompted us to commission a translation into English.

[5] See especially Ann Hutchinson Guest, *Choreographics: A Comparison of Dance Notation Systems from the Fifteenth Century to the Present*, Routledge, London 1998; Claudia Jeschke, *Tanzschriften. Ihre Geschichte und ihre Methode. Die illustrierte Darstellung eines Phänomens von den Anfängen bis zur Gegenwart*, Comes Verlag, Bad Reichenhall 1983.

[6] Gabriele Brandstetter, "The Figurative Scripts of Dance: Between Notation, Diagram, and Ornament," see this volume, p. 40–59.

[7] Concerning Anna Halprin's practice of drawing, see the exhibition *Mapping Dance: The Scores of Anna Halprin* at the Museum of Performance + Design, San Francisco, curated by Elliot Mercer and Muriel Maffre (March 17–May 31, 2016).

[8] See Sally Banes, *Democracy's Body. Judson Dance Theater 1962–1964*, "Studies in Fine Arts: The Avant-Garde," no. 43, UMI Research Press, Ann Arbor, Michigan 1980.

[9] E. C. Goossen, "The Artist Speaks: Robert Morris," in *Art in America*, vol. 58, no. 3, May–June 1970, p. 105.

[10] For a detailed survey of these questions, see Laurence Schmidlin, "'The Drawingness of Drawing.' La spatialisation du dessin dans l'art américain des années 1960–1970," PhD dissertation, Université de Genève, 2016.

[11] They have also published a graphic novel, *Danser après tout*, Denoël Graphic, Paris 2013.

[12] Johanne Lamoureux, "L'exposition comme produit dérivé: *Marie-Antoinette au Grand Palais*," in *Intermédialités: histoire et théorie des arts, des lettres et des techniques/Intermediality: History and Theory of the Arts, Literature and Technologies*, no. 15, "Exposer/Displaying," Spring 2010, p. 77.

[13] Ibid., p. 73.

[14] *Rétrospective* was an exhibition that consisted of a series of actions taken from solos that were choreographed by Xavier Le Roy between 1994 and 2010. Laurence Rassel invited Xavier Le Roy to conceive the exhibition, which first ran at the Fundació Antoni Tàpies, Barcelona, from February 24–April 22, 2012. It traveled widely until 2015.

[15] The exhibition *Work/Travail/Arbeid* reconfigured the choreographic piece *Vortex Temporum* (2013) over a nine-week period. It was conceived by Anne Teresa De Keersmaeker in collaboration with Rosas, following a proposal by Elena Filipovic, and opened at the Wiels arts center in Brussels (March 20–May 17, 2015) before heading to the Centre Pompidou in Paris (February 26–March 6, 2016) and The Museum of Modern Art in New York (March 25–April 2, 2017).

[16] June 1–September 30, 1980. The exhibition toured, with a renewed selection of artworks, to the Institute of Contemporary Art, University of Pennsylvania, Philadelphia (October 4–November 9, 1980), and to the Museum of Contemporary Art, Chicago (May 29–June 26, 1981). It was also presented as *Desenhos: Década Pluralista* at the Fundacão Calouste Gulbenkian, in Lisbon (April and May, 1981).

[17] Curated by Ellen Schwartz ([dates unknown], 1982).

[18] Curated by Cornelia H. Butler and Catherine de Zegher (November 21, 2010–February 7, 2011). See in particular Cornelia H. Butler, "Walkaround Time. Dance and Drawing in the Twentieth Century," in Cornelia H. Butler and Catherine de Zegher (eds.), *On Line. Drawing through the Twentieth Century*, exh. cat., The Museum of Modern Art, New York 2010, p. 137–203.

[19] Curated by Emma Lavigne and Christine Macel (November 23, 2011–April 2, 2012).

[20] Curated by Helen Molesworth (October 7, 2011–January 16, 2012).

[21] Curated by Hendel Teicher (September 27–December 31, 2002). The exhibition toured to Skidmore College, Saratoga Springs (NY), the Contemporary Arts Museum, Houston (TX), the New Museum of Contemporary Art, New York (NY), and the Henry Art Gallery, University of Washington, Seattle (WA).

[22] June 13–September 22, 2007. See especially Merce Cunningham and David Vaughan, *Merce Cunningham: Other Animals*, Aperture, New York 2005.

[23] Curated by Peter Eleey (April 18–July 20, 2008). See especially Peter Eleey, "If You Couldn't See Me: the Drawings of Trisha Brown," in Philip Bither and Peter Eleey (eds.), *Trisha Brown: So That The Audience Does Not Know Whether I Have Stopped Dancing*, exh. cat., Walker Arts Center, Minneapolis 2008, p. 18–35.

[24] Curated by Sabine Breitwieser and Katja Mittendorfer-Oppolzer (July 18–November 9, 2014).

[25] Curated by Catherine Wood (July 11–August 10, 2014).

[26] Curated by William Forsythe and Mario Kramer (October 17, 2015–January 31, 2016). For a survey of how choreography and exhibitions articulate each other, see Mathieu Copeland and Julie Pellegrin (eds.), *Chorégraphier l'exposition/Choreographing Exhibitions*, Les presses du réel, Dijon 2013. The publication follows *A Choreographed Exhibition*, curated by Mathieu Copeland at the Kunst Halle Sankt Gallen (December 1, 2007–January 13, 2008) and reiterated as *Une Exposition Chorégraphiée* at La Ferme du Buisson in 2008 (November 8–December 21).

[27] The practice of drawing by Channa Horwitz has been analyzed in a recent exhibition, *Channa Horwitz*, held at Raven Row in London (March 10–May 1, 2016).

Language and Politics as a Driving Force An Interview with Yvonne Rainer

Catherine Quéloz

This interview took place by email between January 11 and February 15, 2014.
The author wishes to thank Denis Pernet for his suggestions.

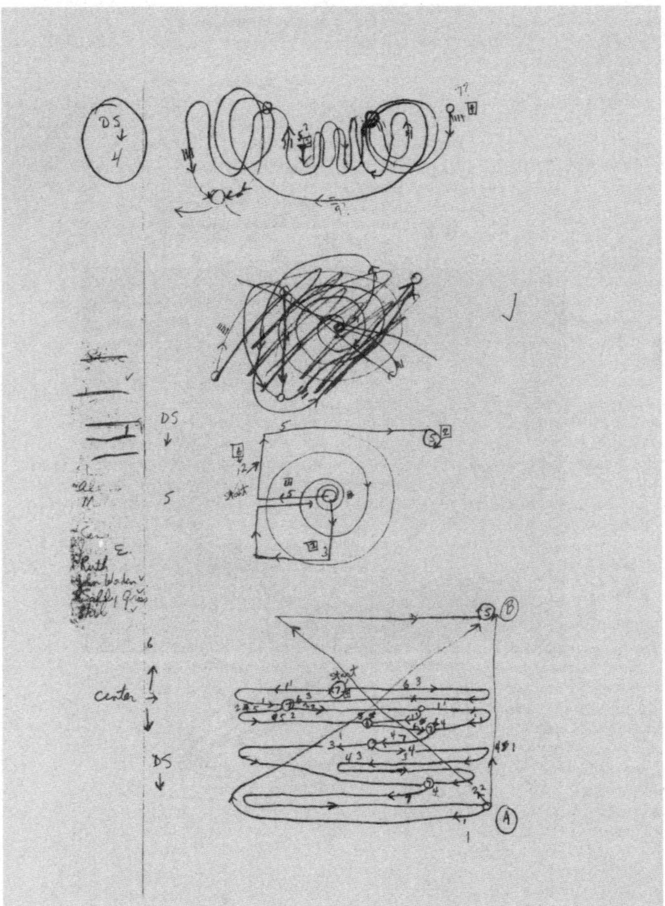

Yvonne Rainer
Drawing for *We Shall Run*, 1963, in Yvonne Rainer, *Work 1961–1973*, The Press of the Nova Scotia College of Art and Design, Halifax 1974, p. 292
Originally performed by Trisha Brown, Lucinda Childs, Philip Corner, Juke Ekman, Malcolm Goldstein, Ruth Emerson, Alex Hay, Deborah Hay, Tony Holder, Carol Scothorn, John Worden and Arlene Rothlein; music: *Tuba Miram* from Hector Berlioz' *Requiem* (1837)

Yvonne Rainer's work adjusts manifold discursive mediums to specific situations in time and space, involving personal history with political and critical issues. Her cultural references are often unusual, and she resorts to distancing strategies such as humor, montage, and *dérive*, thus giving them shape and meaning in choreographies, performances, essays, narratives, and films. Her complex research develops alongside her everyday life, and she discusses the radical, artistic sensibilities of the past few decades while conveying her commitment and a strong independent position. She studied acting with Lee Grant and dance with Merce Cunningham for eight years, and was one of the founding members of the Judson Dance Theater. The structure of her early dances was based on John Cage's random composition, close to ordinary Fluxus gestures and involved in thoughts about process and minimal art. From using narrative in her choreography, and slides and films as props in her dances, her work slowly moved toward filmic narratives in which biographical elements met with political issues and theoretical discourse. Since the beginning of the 2000s, Rainer has again been commissioned to choreograph many projects, a sign that the core of her work is not a matter of medium.

In the following conversation, Rainer explores issues around the specific and diverse formats she has used to communicate self-expression, and political commitment to her collaborators, dancers, and actors, as well as to the spectators.

* * *

CATHERINE QUÉLOZ We could start with the observation you made in one of our first email exchanges regarding the "Dance and Drawing since 1962" project: "I haven't made graphic notations for choreography for a very long time. Most of my notes are now in verbal language." Is this a way to emphasize the live performance and the "teaching-of-a-dance as dance," i.e. *Continuous Project–Altered Daily* (1969–1970) where rehearsal and teaching are part of the performance?[1]

YVONNE RAINER I should correct that quote: most of my notes are now in written language. My drawing ability has become so limited that even stick figures are inadequate for conveying movement. As for "teaching-of-a-dance as dance," that was something that was of use to me in the 1960s and early 1970s, not so much now. I've broadened my resources for movement as I age, that is, as my own body becomes a more limited source of movement, I have looked for the "found object" equivalent, purloining movement from Laurel and Hardy, Robin Williams, Jacques Tati, and other sources.

CQ You mention "written language" as your main means for conveying movement today, but it seems that in your works from 1961 to 1973, written language was already important (list of verbs, description of movements, manifestoes, etc.). So what is so different today?

YR The sources of movement are different, so the referents are linked to those sources, like *Berth Marks* (1929), a film starring Laurel and Hardy.

CQ What attracts you to these sources—the cinematic, the everyday situation, humor, misunderstandings?

YR The last three plus the possibilities for pantomime.

CQ You refer to actors' gestures and behaviors as "found objects" to convey movements. The actors you quote are popular, male, comic, and burlesque comedians. What about the gender of your role model? Has the comic register a gender?

YR Consistent with my early work, there is very little gender differentiation in my current choreography. I guess that is still a reaction to the classical hauling around of women by their male partners.

CQ In the 1960s in "Some nonchronological recollections of *The Mind is a Muscle*"[2] you wrote: "When I first began teaching *Trio A* [1966] to anyone who wanted to learn it —skilled, unskilled, professional, fat, old, sick, amateur— and gave tacit permission to anyone who wanted to teach it, […] Well, I finally met a *Trio A* I didn't like. It was fifth generation, and I couldn't believe my eyes."[3] Could you talk about the balance between control and surrender in these two situations?

YR I rely on much input from my performers. For instance, just prior to a recent show, Pat [Catterson] came over to me and said, "I don't think Patricia [Hoffbauer] should be wearing those knee socks. It looks creepy." I had to agree with her and asked Patricia to take them off. The dancers are encouraged especially to bring in their own textual material, which I sometimes edit but rarely censor.

CQ In an excerpt of *Rainer Variations* (2002),[4] a video work edited by Charles Atlas, you teach Martha Graham (the role is played by Richard Move[5]) your signature solo, *Trio A*. But she/he seems to be unable to reproduce the model or she/he resists doing it and tends to develop her/his own choreography. Is it an excess of subjectivity or desire to transgress?

YR That is the tactic Richard and I agreed on and that contributed to the comedy of that section. Martha refuses to cooperate with my refusal to be dramatic. It was a way of pointing out the difference between the Graham and Rainer aesthetics.

CQ In your book *Work 1961–73* (1974), which records your main choreographies, the complex scores are transmitted through various means—graphic notations, schemas, drawings, dialogues, notes, and comments. Can dancers today read your choreographies according to these indications? Would you allow that?

YR A great many of those notations are indecipherable to me today. I give young choreographers permission to interpret them, as they will, as a fresh source of movement and actions that will probably have no relation to the originals.

CQ The preparatory material for *Terrain* (1963)[6] is composed of a few diagrams, four small schematic drawings of dancers' movements, a written score, and a handwritten/drawn page of a notebook of the individual score distributed to each performer. The notebook page is pretty sophisticated though, with ten colors, different types of lines pointing out the speed and figures and indicating the length of stillness following a particular movement. Were the different components of the score important for the dancers?

YR The diagrams with colored graphics were distributed to the dancers. The colored lines corresponded to descriptions of movement, which was interpreted and executed by each dancer.

CQ Did you consider them "drawings"?

YR I didn't in 1968, but since then artist friends have referred to them as such.

CQ In dance, sound/music can also be a solid support for the choreography and also be considered part of the score. Could you tell us about the choice of the sound accompanying the different sections of the choreography of Spencer Holst's *Thirteen Essays. Sixty Drawings* (1960) in *Terrain*, or the diary of William Bentley (1905; written between 1784 and 1819) in *Parts of Some Sextets* (1965)?[7] How were they chosen and what was their role?

YR The two Holst stories were assigned to three dancers, each of whom recited one of the stories while executing a sequence of movements that had been choreographed and learned independently of the stories. In other words, the texts and movements constituted two simultaneous autonomous trajectories. Excerpts from the diary of William Bentley were read in continuous voice-over on the sound track during the dance with particular words serving as cues for changes in the spatial field and actions. I chose the excerpts for their drama and extremity, such as those dealing with an elephant or sea monster or cancer "eating away half" of a villager's face.

CQ Some scores (i.e. the chart in *Parts of Some Sextets*) seem very precise and controlled and do not leave much space for improvisation except—as you write—for "the physical space of the dance [that] was to be decided by necessity and whim as rehearsals progressed." Was the rehearsal a moment of sharing with the dancers and discussing the score?

YR As I recall, the score was already set before the first rehearsal. There is a Peter Moore photograph of Robert Morris, one of the performers, consulting the score that is tacked on the wall, so what remained to be decided was the spacing of the particular actions.

CQ The program notes of *Continuous Project–Altered Daily*[8] give information on the construction process of the work. Why did you write: "it is not necessary to read this program prior to the performance"?

YR I left it up the individual spectator as to how much information he/she desired beforehand.

CQ Spoken language is also central in your work, not only in the soundtrack of the dance (found texts, biography as found object, dialogues). In short your dances are very verbal. Is there a link with the important use of language in the arts (more particularly the visual arts) at the time?

YR I have continued to use language to add an extra dimension and meaning to abstract movement. The ambiguity of dance movement has always challenged me to enrich it with language. In a recent work I have a performer go up to another performer and ask: "What does that mean?" I am easily bored by choreography that piles on movement for its own sake—unless the performers or the choreography are extraordinary, as in Merce Cunningham or George Balanchine.

CQ Has this attraction for language had the opportunity to develop further?

YR Yes. In my last dance, *Assisted Living: Do You Have Any Money?* (2013), the dancers recite news reports, stories, and political analyses while executing intricate steps. For instance, in a duet, Keith Sabado explains Keynesian economics while performing a balletic adagio with his partner, Emily Coates.

CQ In your performances you use a lot of objects and materials (stairs, mattresses, pillows, a white screen, balls, food). Are they mainly props or do they have another function?

YR They are props that often contain inherent associations, like the mattress with sleep, illness, death. The stairs functioned both surreally and athletically.

CQ Is everyday life the link between the task-oriented movements of the dance and the acting techniques of movie actors?

YR That's one of them, certainly. Lifting a mattress or a heavy object would tax an actor in the same way as a dancer.

CQ The performance *Carriage Discreteness* (1966)[9] was a collaboration with artists (Carl Andre for the props and material, Hollis Frampton for the slides projection, and Robert Morris as a performer). How was the collaboration organized?

YR I asked Carl Andre to lend me his Styrofoam beams, which he did. That dance was just the opposite of a collaboration, which I regret. I was stationed on a high balcony and ordered the performers around like puppets.

CQ *Carriage Discreteness* is an example of the use of a spoken score, as you and Morris transmitted the movements to the dancers by walkie-talkie. Was the Morris version different from yours?

YR I have no idea. He replaced me because I was taken ill in hospital for the second show.

CQ In *Grand Union Dreams*, a choreography of 1971, you name your score a "script" and write: "The plot thickens." Progressively from 1972 on, your scores are increasingly formatted like scripts. Is there a difference between a score and a script?

YR A script suggests a predominant reliance on language, whereas a score can be anything from stick figures to abstract drawings or imperfections on a piece of paper (Cage), or verbal instructions.

CQ Did your transition from choreography to film (1972–1975) change your use of words/language?

YR Yes. It was through language that I could address issues broader than dance.

CQ What kind of issues?

YR Racism, sexual ambivalence, urban gentrification, oil pollution, political violence, illness …

CQ When you changed medium and went from dance to film, did you change your way of communicating instructions to the performers?

YR My instructions to actors were very minimal, as I have never really understood what acting is about. In other words, I usually communicated to them that I didn't want them to act, just "do." I was much more comfortable dealing with the nuances of movement and was glad, finally, to return to it.

CQ Can you talk about the role of film in some of your performances of the 1960s?

YR *Volleyball* (1977) was the only film out of what I like to call my "early, short, boring films" that had a central place in a section of choreography. A screen was placed downstage center and raised on a stand so that when the migrating clump of dancers arrived to stand behind it, only their legs were revealed to create a contrast in scale between the live legs and those in close-up on the screen. The other films were either shown independently or sometimes projected on one side of the proscenium or the other.

CQ Was the choreography and the dance present in the filmmaking?

YR Do you mean, "Was there dance in those early films?"? You might call the movement in *Trio Film* (1968) dance, or the movement of the chickens in *Rhode Island Red* (1968).

CQ From 1972 (*Lives of Performers*) to 1996 (*MURDER and murder*), you shot seven feature films. Does your dance today borrow from the filming experience, for example when you conceived of *Assisted Living: Do You Have Any Money*?

YR If you mean the production process, I would say no. I remain a sort of techno dummy or hysteric. I was never comfortable with either the technical or social aspects of making films. I feel much more at home dealing with the materiality and immediacy of dancers and their bodies.

CQ You said that the film as a medium is more appropriate to talk about emotions. Why?

YR I meant specific emotions. I never made movement that was meant to represent or convey specific emotions. As Merce Cunningham has indicated, the dancer's body is intrinsically emotional. There is no need to add on or overlay emotion. So when I began to think about specific emotions such as anger, ambivalence, sexual conflict, fear, etc., again it was language that led the way and film that seemed the more appropriate vehicle, for me at least.

CQ It is interesting to note that several of your performances are included in others, or reinterpreted as if they were flexible enough to adapt to different situations or performers. *Trio A*, for example, is the performance that has traversed your work, and that you still perform. What is your relationship to *Trio A* like today?

YR At 79, I no longer perform it. It's just too difficult to get down and up from the floor in the manner that *Trio A* requires. There are now five dancers who are authorized by me to teach and perform it. I sometimes go in at the end of the process to fine-tune it.

CQ How did you decide to come back to dance over the last decade?

YR Mikhail Baryshnikov commissioned a dance in 2000 (*After Many a Summer Dies the Swan*). It was an offer I couldn't refuse.

CQ Since 1999 several revivals of your main choreographic works have been performed. How do you respond to that? Are you still involved in staging them?

YR Sometimes, sometimes not. Pat Catterson is the primary "emissary" of my work.

CQ Dance seemed very appropriate to the 1960s context of collaborative and live activism. How do you see it now?

YR In the 1960s and early 1970s the Vietnam War was the main catalyst for arts activism. I can't say I keep up with the current dance activity in the US and Europe, but from the little I see, issues such as globalization, voting rights, the incarceration system, and economic inequality in the US are not mustering protests in the arts with as much ferocity as that war once did. But maybe that's just my old fogey talking.

CQ In the appendix of the anthology you wrote on your dance performances, there is a heading that reads "Important Moments as a Viewer,"[10] a list of eight entries among which is "1959 Agon, George Balanchine." In 2005 you created *AG Indexical, with a Little Help from H.M.*, based on George Balanchine's *Agon* (1957).[11] Could you tell us the specific link you have with this piece and your relationship to Balanchine's work?

YR *Agon* has always been my favorite Balanchine ballet. When I was invited to contribute a dance to a program on Igor Stravinsky, *Agon* was the first thing that sprang to mind. I revisit the Balanchine programs at the New York City Ballet every couple of years. The sparseness, clarity, humor—also the back story of *Agon* relating to Balanchine's dealing with the polio of his wife, Tanaquil LeClerc—all make that particular work very meaningful for me.

YR Which of "passion" or "politics" is the driving force of your work?[12]

YR I don't know about passion, although I can't deny that I am ambitious, maybe even driven. *Assisted Living: Do You Have Any Money?* has given me an impetus to bring other political material into my next project. The contrast between abstract movement overlaid with facts and history continues to be a challenge.

[1] “Rehearsal: Performance of previously learned material that is not in polished condition [...] thereby necessitating verbalization, repeats, arguments, etc.” and “Teaching: A performer teaches previously learned material to one or more performers who do not know it [...].” Yvonne Rainer, “Rudimentary Notes Toward a Changing View of Performance,” facsimile reprinted in Yvonne Rainer, *Work 1961–73*, The Press of the Nova Scotia College of Art and Design/New York University Press, Halifax/New York 1974, p. 130–131.

[2] Yvonne Rainer, “Some Nonchronological Recollections of *The Mind is a Muscle*,” in Yvonne Rainer, *Work 1961–73*, p. 77–83.

[3] Ibid., p. 77.

[4] Charles Atlas, *Rainer Variations*, 2002, video, 41’30, b&w and color, sound. Produced as part of the retrospective exhibition *Yvonne Rainer: Radical Juxtapositions 1961–2002*, Schmidt Center Gallery, Boca Raton (FL), November 4, 2005–January 21, 2006.

[5] New York-based performer Richard Move is a choreographer, performing artist, and filmmaker internationally known for his interest in Martha Graham and the ability to recreate her performances.

[6] *Terrain*, a 1 ½ hour work in five sections for six people, first performed at Judson Memorial Church in New York City, April 28 and 29, 1963. See Yvonne Rainer, *Work 1961–73*, p. 12–43.

[7] *Parts of Some Sextets*, a dance for 10 people and 12 mattresses, performed at the Wadsworth Atheneum, Hartford, and the Judson Memorial Church, New York, in March 1965. See Yvonne Rainer, *Work 1961–73*, p. 45–61.

[8] The performance was held at the Whitney Museum of American Art, New York, on March 31, April 1 and 2, 1970. Yvonne Rainer, “[Continuous Project–Altered Daily],” facsimile reprinted in Yvonne Rainer, *Work 1961–73*, p. 129–131.

[9] The performance was held on October 15–21, 1966, during the event *9 Evenings: Theater and Engineering*, at the 69th Regiment Armory in New York.

[10] Yvonne Rainer, *Work 1961–73*, p. 333.

[11] Editor’s note: *Agon* (1957) is a ballet for 12 dancers, with choreography by George Balanchine and music by Igor Stravinsky. In 2006, New York-based Dance Theater Workshop invited six choreographers—Yvonne Rainer, Dayna Hanson & Linas Phillips, Cynthia Hopkins, David Neumann, and Rennie Harris—to work on Stravinsky’s legacy. The project, entitled *Sourcing Stravinsky*, was curated by Annie-B Parson (New York, April 19–22, 2006).

[12] In reference to Yvonne Rainer, “Where’s the Passion? Where’s the Politics? or How I Became Interested in Impersonating, Approximating, and End Running Around My Selves and Others, and Where Do I Look When You’re Looking at Me?” the title of a lecture given at *Cinematic Migrations: A Symposium and Lecture Series*, MIT Program in Art, Culture, and Technology, Cambridge (MA), April 7, 2014.

“Life Doesn’t Make Sense as a ‘Whole.’ Why Should Art?” An Interview with Robert Morris

Katia Schneller

This interview took place by email in January 2014. The quote in the title is from Robert Morris in an interview with Penelope Curtis, April 26, 1997 (Robert Morris Archives, Gardiner, NY).

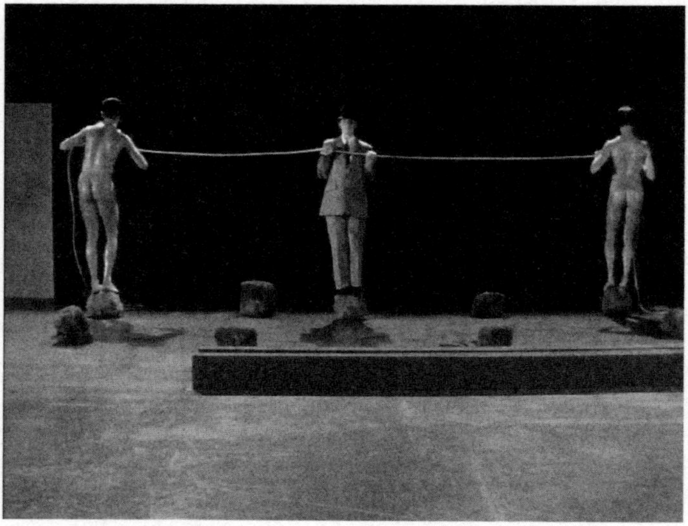

Robert Morris
Waterman Switch, 1965
Originally performed by Lucinda Childs, Robert Morris, and Yvonne Rainer, presented for the first time at the Judson Memorial Theater, New York, March 23, 1965; here as performed and filmed for the retrospective exhibition *Robert Morris: The Mind/Body Problem*, Solomon R. Guggenheim Museum, New York, 1994

Robert Morris is often mentioned as one of the most prominent figures of what has been called Minimalism since the 1960s, but his work has always exceeded this label by concurrently investigating various mediums like dance and drawing.

While living in San Francisco at the end of the 1950s, he distanced himself from painting and started working with a group of musicians, artists, and dancers such as Simone Forti to whom he was then married, and who was a student of Anna Halprin's.[1] Morris sometimes attended Halprin's classes and workshops—such as the one during the summer of 1960—before he moved to New York City. He then participated in evenings organized by major Fluxus figures like La Monte Young. He was one of the performers of the famous *Five Dance Constructions and Some Other Things* (1961) that Forti presented at Yoko Ono's Chambers Street loft in May 1961. Her task performances using props had a deep impact on

Morris' work in which experiencing the work process was of great importance, as is evident in *Card File* (1962), *Box with the Sound of Its Own Making* (1961), or *Morris Prints* (1962–1963).

Morris' involvement with dance became more significant when he started working with the Judson Dance Theater group in 1963. He danced in the pieces created by other dancers like Yvonne Rainer and Judith Dunn, but also choreographed six dance pieces. The first one, entitled *War*, is a duo with Robert Huot developed from a discussion about urban violence in 1963. That same year he performed *Arizona* at the Judson Dance Theater where he executed slow gestures for 20 minutes while a recording of the reading of the text "A Method for Sorting Cows" (1961)[2] played. In 1964, he titled his piece *21.3* after one of the classes he was teaching at Hunter College, and in which he acted like a scholar giving a talk for 10 minutes until a disruption between the voice uttering Erwin Panofsky's text and the performer's gestures occurred. He also choreographed *Site* (1964), where for 17 minutes he moved plywood slabs around Carolee Schneemann who was reclining naked in a posture reminiscent of Édouard Manet's *Olympia* (1863). Morris toured with Rainer to present his last two dance works in Düsseldorf and Stockholm, where he created *Check*, a 30-minute piece for the Moderna Museet: 40 performers carried out various actions around seven hundred chairs, while the audience remained standing. His last dance, *Waterman Switch* (1965), is a 20-minute trio: after having rolled stones onto the stage, the three performers—Morris and Rainer, both naked, and Lucinda Childs, in a suit—used the boulders as pedestals. Rainer and Morris tried to roll the stones over with their feet while wrenching away a rope held by Childs, and, locked into an embrace, walked along a wooden beam. After this last piece, Morris left the Judson Dance Theater and published "Notes on Dance"[3] about his dance work and "Dance"[4] and "Dance, Part 2"[5] about the Judson Dance Theater.

As Morris has pointed out in his texts, and articulates here, it has always been important for him to carry out several lines of research simultaneously, as each medium provides him with different possibilities for investigation.

* * *

KATIA SCHNELLER Your dance work seems to have been a crucial moment in your path to so-called minimalist sculpture. Why did you choose not to include your texts about dance in your book *Continuous Project–Altered Daily: The Writings of Robert Morris* (1993)?[6]

ROBERT MORRIS I consider the works I choreographed quite separate from the sculptural efforts. There may be some overlapping concerns between the two areas, but I think the issues involved in dance are quite different from those of sculpture.

Working Process

KS In "Notes on Dance" you mention Simone Forti's influence on your choreographic work, especially her exploration of "the possibilities inherent in a situation of 'rules' or game-like structures which required the performer to respond to cues."[7] I wondered if you used the same type of working process?

RM I don't think I was very focused on "systems" in the few works I choreographed. The dance works I made allowed me to exploit a kind of imagery that was unavailable in sculpture at the time. Javelin throwing, lights circling in the dark, and so on in *Arizona*, the workman in white in *Site*, the costume in *War*, etc. Each dance presented a different persona by means of images fashioned from costumes and props. I didn't rely much on rules for the dance works. I made no charts or scores. I worked in my notebook jotting things down about props and the kinds of movement I had in mind, and then worked out the movement details in rehearsals.

Conception of the Body

KS In "Notes on Dance" you said that you used tasks and objects in your choreography to generate movement, which was not executed for its own sake, but resulted from the accomplishment of a task, to reduce performance to action. Many dancers of the Judson Dance Theater apprehended the body as an object, in terms of its material qualities of mass and volume, and were then rethinking the concept of body. For example, instead of representing the dancer as a persona, Yvonne Rainer considered that the dancer's body could be "handled like an object, picked up and carried—and that objects and bodies could be interchangeable."[8] However, in your dance works, objects are still controlled by the body. How would you describe your approach to the physicality of the body?

RM The possibilities and limitations of the moving body (and sometimes challenging these limits) were a concern. But the body was not just an "object." I treated it as a charged psychological identity that was different in the different works. The dances offered the possibility of exploring imagery and/as identities not available in the sculpture. I see no "discrepancy." I did not seek in sculpture what I explored in dance.

KS At the same time, you realized different series of drawings, like the *Memory Drawings* (1963) or *Ruler Drawn from Memory after 5 Minutes Observation and Actual Ruler Traced* (1962), by following a preestablished protocol (regularly writing the same text or reproducing the same shape from memory in a given time frame). Would you say that this proceeded from the same impulse as blocking the "dancer's performing 'set'"[9]?

RM In the *Blind Time Drawings*[10] I followed strict rules. But I see no very direct connection here to the impulse of the dancer to "block a performance set." In some (not all) of Forti's *Five Dance Constructions* her instructions were so explicit and taxing that the dancer was hard put to "express" herself. This might resonate with my task-following in the *Blind Time Drawings*, but the connection seems tenuous.

One of the things the *Memory Drawings* dealt with was the decay of memory over time. *Ruler Drawn from Memory ...* dealt with image discrepancies. I find no parallels here to anything in Forti's *Five Dance Constructions*.

Anti-Humanism

KS Concerning the minimalist sculptures, you have stated: "When I sliced into the plywood with my Skilsaw,

I could hear, beneath the ear-damaging whine, a stark and refreshing 'no' reverberate off the four walls: no to the transcendence and spiritual values, heroic scale, anguished decisions, historicizing narrative, valuable artifact, intelligent structure, interesting visual experience."[11] In these lines, your purpose is close the *No Manifesto* (1965)[12] by Yvonne Rainer. Would you say that it was the same anti-humanist motivation that nourished your dance and drawing work? Were you rejecting the humanism and the anthopocentrism usually associated with dance and drawing until then?

RM Possibly there was some rhetorical rejection of "humanism" in various statements made by a number of artists at the time. But looking back this seems like a rather honorific gesture.

KS Rainer has stated that her reading of the essay *Pour un nouveau roman* (1963) by Alain Robbe-Grillet was a sheer revelation to her.[13] Just like Robbe-Grillet, whose writing is characterized by the meticulous object descriptions and its refusal of humanism, Rainer was interested by description in her dance work: in *Parts of Some Sextets* (1965), she included the sound recording of the tales of banal events happening in Salem in the 18th and 19th century as recounted by Reverend William Bentley. Were you also attempting to apprehend the body from the outside in *Arizona* when you used a sound recording of the reading of your text "A Method for Sorting Cows" in which you carefully describe cowboys' movements?

RM I had little interest in the writings of Robbe-Grillet. I was reading Beckett in the late 1950s–early 1960s. The recorded text of "A Method for Sorting Cows" lasted something like 10 minutes or maybe longer. This time length allowed me to rotate my upper body so slowly through 90-degrees that the movement was not perceptible. To show movement that could not be perceived was one of the reasons for using the text.

KS As Simon Grant noted,[14] in your autobiographical text "Indiana Street" (1993)[15] you have described the movements of workers' bodies, such as that of your father in the Kansas stockyards, or of an iceman,[16] as reminiscent of elements of your dance pieces *Arizona* and *Site*. Could you please elaborate on the relation between those movements and your dance pieces?

RM I came from the working class and had observed the various physical bodily motions and abilities of coworkers when I worked as a horse wrangler, a railroad switchman, a semi-pro ball player, a carpenter. So I had a repertoire of movements to draw upon.

Focusing on Process

KS In "Notes on Dance" you explain that, like Simone Forti, you used preestablished tasks and objects in your dance work. But you add that your need for structural systems was "for syntactical rather than methodological bases."[17] Could you explain what you meant and what is different between your approach and Forti's in *Five Dance Constructions and Some Other Things*?

RM Forti's *Five Dance Constructions* were works of genius that shifted the premise of dance from expression to task performance. By imposing rule-following or the negotiation of objects, Forti eliminated the trained dancer and replaced that kind of narcissism with workman-like "ordinary movement." My dance works would not have been possible without this ground-breaking shift in presuppositions for dance.

KS You explained in "Notes on Dance" that it was important for you to work with the coexistence of the static and the mobile, as in *Waterman Switch* when ten Eadweard Muybridge slides of a nude man lifting a stone (1887) were followed by a nude performer carrying out some of the same actions. Is this what you are referring to when you speak about syntactical bases to address specific problems?

RM The temporal factor was always of significance in the sculpture, and different works relied on different strategies. *Box with the Sound of Its Own Making* uses time very differently than the large early plywood works where it is factored into phenomenological perception. But these uses are different from the extreme slowness of some phases of *Site* or *Arizona*, or the contrast of sequential images with continuous motion in *Waterman Switch*, or the freezing of bodies in motion via camera flashes in *Check*.

KS Your research into the process of working has also been present since the beginning of the 1960s in your object work, such as *Box with the Sound of Its Own Making*, and in your drawing and print work. But in your print work, such as *Morris Prints*, or *On Wheels* (1962), where the same image is repeated and progressively fades because of ink exhaustion due to the fact that the same plate is reprinted, one of the main issues is your interest in entropy. Were your dance works also related to this research?

RM I don't think entropy was much of a concern for the dance works. Of course the Leonardo quote in *Waterman Switch* makes reference to it.

KS In *Waterman Switch*, while you are balancing on the boulders, your taped voice can be heard reciting a fragment of Leonardo da Vinci's notebooks dealing with the erosive effects of rivers on stones, which is the entropic condition of all objects and beings. The last words pronounced are: "With time, everything changes." The reference to da Vinci is recurrent in your work. For example, you made a wheel in 1963 that refers to da Vinci's *Vitruvian Man* (c. 1490), a lead relief with his name on it in 1964, and some of your drawings from the 1980s like the *Psychomachia* and *Firestorms* series evoke his water drawings. What is your relation to his work and his figure?

RM What artist has not been impressed with Leonardo? For over 50 years I have kept notebooks. No doubt these documents of thoughts and projects for works were inspired by Leonardo's example (except mine are not written in reverse as were his).

Labyrinth

KS The corridor narrowing to a dead end in *Passageway*, the passages and gate conjured in *Arizona*, the twine of *Waterman*

Switch are all images from the labyrinth. All three works revolve around themes of physical engagement and tightly controlled movement. Were you redeploying the same research in the *Blind Time I* and the *Labyrinth* series in 1973?

RM From the 1960s to the present I have constructed various labyrinths in plywood, marble, granite, fencing, and glass. These have been made in different formats—triangular, round, oval, etc. Some of these, taking off from the 1961 *Passageway*, were constricting and claustrophobic. All labyrinths present the whole or gestalt of the form when seen from the outside and slightly above. This contrasts with the experience of disorientation when traversing the passageways from within. I don't think that the *Blind Time Drawings* works were motivated by the *Labyrinths*. Although a kind of "blindness" may characterize the experience of walking the *Labyrinth*, it is quite a stretch to say that the one motivated the other. Drawing is its own world; dance and labyrinths are two other worlds. The body may be involved in all of these, but to assert that some common experience prevails in all is to misread these works.

KS From your answers you do not seem to subscribe to intermedia, but I believe you do not assert the specificity of a medium. So where do you position yourself? I assume there is still a certain degree of coexistence or friction between the two art forms that are dance and drawing, of which the theater of alter-egos that you set in your text "Robert Morris Replies to Roger Denson (Or Is That a Mouse in My Paragon?)"[18] could be an example.

RM Again, why run the concerns of drawing into those of dance? The two may have something in common but these are two different worlds with two different sets of concerns. Dick Higgins was not a theorist I was much interested in. Intermedia meant nothing to me. I worked at sculpture, at drawing, and briefly at dance. I made no effort to mix the one with the other.

[1] Editor's note: see the essay by Sarah Burkhalter in the present volume, p. 112–129.

[2] Robert Morris, "A Method for Sorting Cows" (1961), *Art and Literature*, no. 2, Winter 1967, p. 180–181.

[3] Robert Morris, "Notes on Dance," in *The Tulane Drama Review*, vol. 10, no. 2, Winter 1965, p. 179–186.

[4] Robert Morris, "Dance," in *Village Voice*, February 3, 1966, p. 8, 24–25.

[5] Robert Morris, "Dance, Part 2," in *Village Voice*, February 10, 1966, p. 15.

[6] Robert Morris, *Continuous Project–Altered Daily: The Writings of Robert Morris*, October Books series, The MIT Press/Solomon R. Guggenheim Museum, Cambridge (MA) and London/New York 1993.

[7] Robert Morris, "Notes on Dance," p. 179.

[8] Liza Bear and Willoughby Sharp, "The Performer as Persona: An Interview with Yvonne Rainer," in *Avalanche*, no. 5, Summer 1972, p. 50.

[9] Robert Morris, "Notes on Dance," p. 179.

[10] Editor's note: the first series of drawings thus entitled date from 1973. Other series were to follow, produced according to different modalities, in 1976, 1985, 1991, 1999, and 2000.

[11] Robert Morris, "Three Folds in the Fabric and Four Autobiographical Asides as Allegories (or Interruptions)," in *Art in America*, vol. 77, no. 9, November 1989, p. 142–151.

[12] Yvonne Rainer, "Some Retrospective Notes on a Dance for 10 People and 12 Mattresses Called *Parts of Some Sextets*, in *The Tulane Drama Review*, vol. 10, no. 2, Winter 1965, p. 178.

[13] Yvonne Rainer, *Feelings Are Facts: A Life*, The MIT Press, Cambridge (MA) and London 2006, p. 397.

[14] See Simon Grant in "Simon Grant interviews Robert Morris" (September 1, 2008), in *Tate Etc.*, no. 14, Autumn 2008, available at http://www.tate.org.uk/context-comment/articles/simon-grant-interviews-robert-morris.

[15] Robert Morris, "Indiana Street," in Nena Tsouti-Schillinger (ed.), *Have I Reasons: Work and Writings, 1993–2007*, Duke University Press, Durham (NC) and London 2008, p. 17–40.

[16] Ibid., p. 37 and 38.

[17] Robert Morris, "Notes on Dance," p. 180.

[18] Robert Morris, "Robert Morris Replies to Roger Denson (Or Is That a Mouse in My Paragon?)," in Robert Morris, *Continuous Project*, p. 287–315.

WRITING

The Figurative Scripts of Dance: Between Notation, Diagram, and Ornament

Gabriele Brandstetter

This essay was originally published in German as "Schriftbilder des Tanzes. Zwischen Notation, Diagramm und Ornament," in Sybille Krämer, Eva Cancik-Kirschbaum, and Rainer Totzke (eds.), *Schriftbildlichkeit. Wahrnehmbarkeit, Materialität und Operativität von Notationen*, Akademie Verlag, Berlin 2012, p. 61–77. For a complete iconography, we refer the reader to the original volume.

The evolution of the term "choreography"—from meaning the recording [*(Auf-)Zeichnung*] of steps in the 16th and 17th centuries, to the modern term "choreographer," creator of dance (art)works—is reflected in the historical development of dance scripts.

The figurative notational scripts [*Schriftbilder*] serve to safeguard and unfold movements: the movement of the hand that draws or writes, the embodiment of dance or music, or the technical movement of a camera. At the same time, notation maintains a captivating connection to the temporality, dynamics, embodiment, and materiality of the movements, qualities that remain elusive even once they are transposed.

The normative understanding of notation as suggested by Nelson Goodman[1] does not offer much insight here. Indeed, the ways in which structure is given to processes of artistic shaping, of visual representation, of modes of documentation and visualization in the graphic media are articulated in and as "notations." The following reflections will thus dwell on the different notational aspects of dance. What is the status of notation as document, as score, as prescript of "pre-scribed" practices, or as autonomous visual form? What are the dynamics that unfold from the tension between notation and performative practice? What are the topographies of temporality that can be deciphered in typographies, notations, or diagrams? And what are the specific forms of spatiality that open up in them? How do notations refer, from within their "operative space" (Sybille Krämer),[2] to transcripts of movement?

A look at an example of notation drawn from the history of dance allows us to sketch out the main interesting perspectives and questions. It is an 18th-century dance notation known as the "Ferrère manuscript" (1782). According to Marian Hannah Winter,[3] this notation represents the oldest attempt to render a "ballet in action" using Feuillet notation. The choreographer Auguste Ferrère relied on this method to describe several ballets he staged in Valenciennes. The pages reproduced here come from his choreography *Le Peintre Amoureux de Son Modelle* (1782), a variation on the theme of Pygmalion, a favorite subject in the 18th century, especially in dance.[4] Ferrère penned this notation under two terms: "partition" (score) and "chorographie" (choreography). He thus distinguishes between musical notation—the score—and the setting down in writing of dance [*Aufschreiben von Tanz*]: according to Raoul-Auger Feuillet, in the 17th and 18th centuries the concept of "chorégraphie" (named here "choro-graphie," in a still clearer reference to "choros," the space of movement) meant the "writing" (setting down in writing) [*"Schreiben" (Aufschreiben)*] of dance figures. The conceptual hybrid of disparate terms of notation, score, and choreography also refers to the visually hybrid character of this figurative script [*Schrift-bild*]. Within its remarkable pastiche-like topography, this very structure—which points to a "picture scene" (Jan Assmann)[5]—opens up perspectives on the topic of notation and movement.

From the very outset the drawing calls forth the question of *perception*: a contemplation that alternates between seeing/

looking and reading. The legibility of this "notation" is thereby determined at the same time by the different graphic systems contained within it: the decipherability of the *writing*, of the *notes of music*, and finally, of the visual *ordering* of choreographic and pictorial elements on the sheet.

The combinatorics of these different alphabetic, (music- and dance-) notational, and iconic forms constitutes a sort of a hybrid score: the musical notation provides information about the temporality and soundscape of this "ballet in action"; it marks the tempo and dynamics, the rhythmic relations, and the form of temporal structure in the repetitive phrases and shorter or longer elements. The choreographic notation described in Feuillet's writing,[6] the vocabulary of the steps, the configuration of the dancers (in symmetrical organigrams), as well as, in part, the paths through space. This script of movement of bodies in space—a literal choreo-graphy [*Raumwege*]—acts as a constellation, in that it transposes spatial positions cartographically, as it were, onto the surface of the figurative script. A sequence of individual vignettes containing stick figures represents the dimension of body movement that cannot be captured in Feuillet's script: that is, the movement and the expression of the torso and head. It is precisely in the meaning ascribed to the expressive body of the dancers that the innovation of the *ballet d'action* resides, defining as it does the dramatic dance theater in the 18th century. That is precisely why no dance notation had been developed until then. The hybrid form of the Ferrère manuscript is presumably, from a historical standpoint, indebted to this new aesthetics of representation that came with the challenge of developing a graphic model for writing down the body's expressive dimension. Since the figure drawings too are only introduced schematically, Ferrère calls on another system of movement notation: writing. With written instructions, comments, abbreviations, and titles, the images, symbols, and signs are provided with reading instructions and translation rules. Furthermore, the script, setting, and text elements embedded in the notation signs and picture graphics somewhat recall a fragmentary libretto. They offer indications about dramaturgical structures, about elements of action, and about the interpretation of the drawn body gestures. The writing further serves to tie together the individual notational elements. It gives the figurative script its format, "prescribes" a genre to the individual parts (e.g. "overture"), and, finally, assigns authorship to this "choreo-score" with the choreographer's signature.

A "notation" of this kind exemplifies how and to what extent notations operate differently from (alphabetic) scripts, not only in primarily "oral" cultures,[7] but also—and especially—in the arts and media of "secondary orality."[8] "What does this Other consist of?" Peter Stein has asked, insisting that "the central difference with linear writing should be that non-linear text is multidimensional: it unfolds in the simultaneity of different impulses; instead of focusing on an explicit sensorial center, it is structured along radiating lines."[9]

In many respects, the structure of the Ferrère manuscript raises questions and offers perspectives about the transfer —its form and its possibilities—of movement in and through notation. With the reflection already initiated about legibility, the question of the *composition* of this "choreo-score" therefore arises. How does the ordering of the various writing/sign/picture elements differentiated above relate to the act of reading? Is there a predetermined reading direction as, for instance, in linear writing or in a musical score? In what way does reading call for breaks, jumps, gaps, forward and backward movements? Or even crossing over the page diagonally, in circles, in varying patterns that are in turn choreographic themselves? What is the temporality suitable for viewing, for reading, and for deciphering? And how does this temporality relate to body movement in the *ballet d'action*? Can we even take it for granted that this drawing, beyond documentation, serves as notation, as a pre-script for a musical-dancing (re-)performance? And which elements of the notation (e.g. the music) lend themselves to being transferred into a performative praxis, and which tend not to (such as a coherent corporeal-dramatic representation of the action in *Le Peintre Amoureux de Son Modelle*)? If, on the other hand, we consider the choreographic drawings of the steps and the figures of the floor paths, these also elicit a *cartographic* reading: as *mappings* of the *compartimento di terreno* essential to dance, of spatial partitioning [*Raum-auf-teilung*] and of path itineraries. Viewed in this way, the notation sheet and the tracing of spatial gesture would be the simultaneous condensation of the temporal succession of dance figures that "divide" the ground. As on a land map, the gaze alights from "above" on the surface made of lines that delineate space and path measurements. This bird's eye view of paths and strides [*Wege und Gänge*][10] displaces them from temporal sequentiality into a simultaneous placement, and enables an overview that the dance—the practice of movement in space—never affords: a synopsis of the ephemeral topographies, segmented in the bodily performance of movement. As inscribed surface, the notation—read as a "map"—not only shows us a picture of a spatiotemporal structure; it also marks the modality of the change from "graph" to performative praxis. The layered visual "writing/picture" systems do not contain any clear reading instruction. Rather, they offer a graphic composition that illustrates the positioning of body, as well as time and space factors. The ordering is therefore correlative and not depictive. This is precisely what constitutes the ideographic space of the figurative script [*Schrift-Bildraum*] in these hybrid notations. Their structure thus also contains the ordering and referential factors of a *diagram*, without, however, representing a single, complete diagrammatic concept.

Indeed, in the Ferrère manuscript the "connection between writing and drawing,"[11] in a "formative" space marked by a frame, presents the characteristics of a "diagram" in which connecting lines, ordering schemes, and an "oriented"[12] visualization of sequences aim at information. To this extent, this notation describes and shows the diagrammatic references of the various time-body-space components of this *ballet d'action*. "In the diagram, 'telling' and 'showing' interact, arbitrariness and similarity do each other's groundwork in order to together allow movement to proceed."[13] The Ferrère notation "tells" and "shows" in the pointed sense Sybille Krämer gives to diagrammatic order. Furthermore, this notation also refers to itself—and to the gesture of showing. It signals the decisions that must be made throughout the processes of reading, writing, or transposing. It is at this point that the diagrammatic ordering and its information structure offer new directions. The Ferrère manuscript presents a compilation—a "pastiche"—in which the coded and improvised elements of typography come

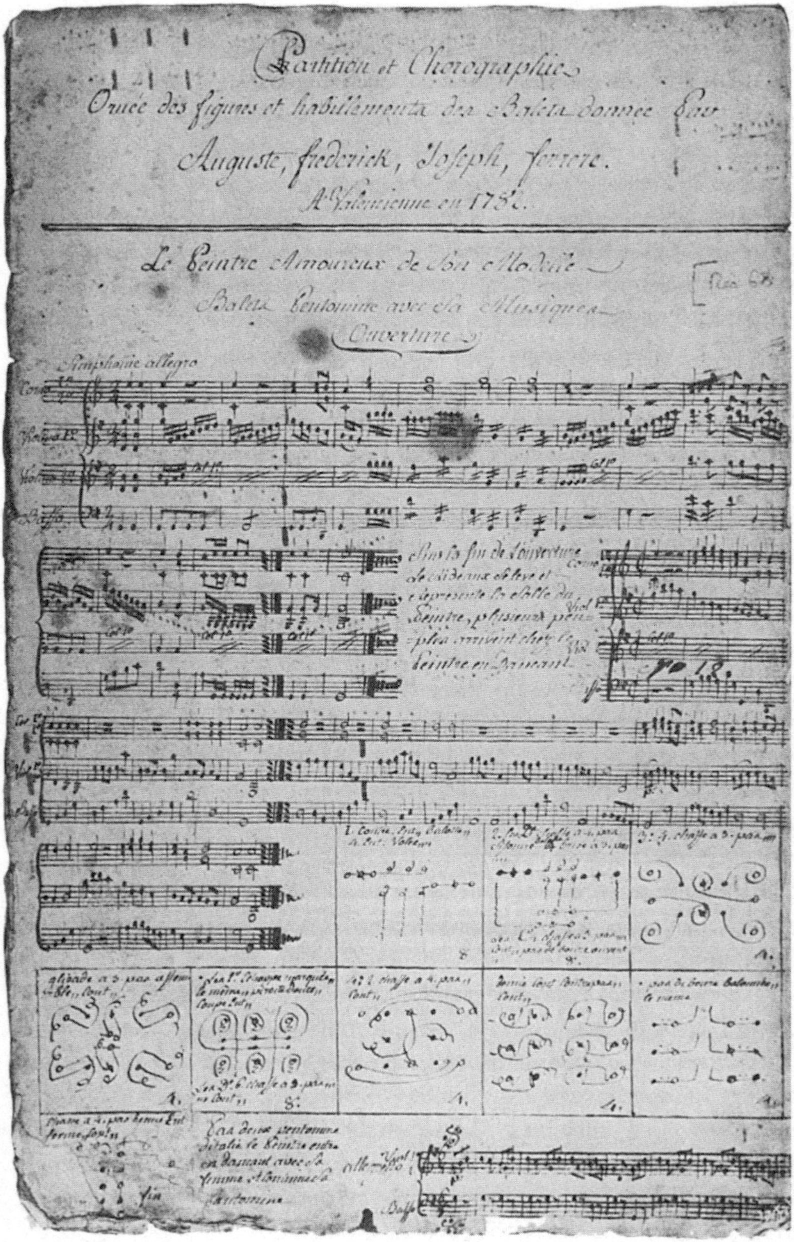

Auguste Frédéric Joseph Ferrère
Partition et Chorographie/Ornée des figures et habillements des Balets donnée Par/Auguste, Frederick, Joseph, Ferrere./A Valencienne en 1782, 1782
Pages 1 and 3: "Le Peintre Amoureux de Son Modelle / Balets Pentomine avec Sa Musique"
Each page: 31.7 × 20.5 cm
Bibliothèque nationale de France, département Bibliothèque-musée de l'opéra, Paris

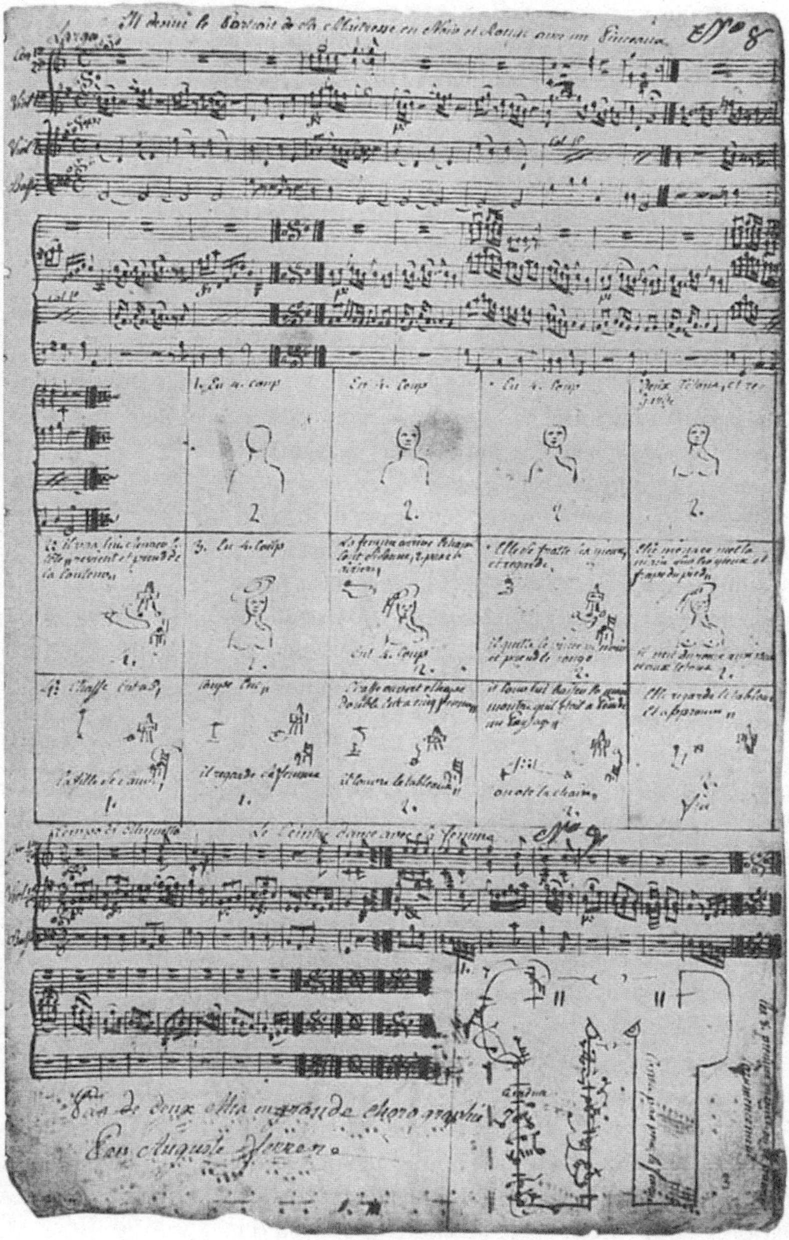

to interfere. In this way, a hybrid, or better yet, a "wild" diagrammatics (riddled with written words, notes, and "tossed" drawings, sketches) leads the way to a self-reflective dimension of its notational composition: the active, creative, and analytical side of notation adds to its "recording" [*Auf-Zeichnung*] purpose. Insofar as this score oscillates between record (as documentation) and conception (as outline),[14] it self-reflectively marks its relational position between work and performance, between image/text and body/movement. It is just here that the "space of operation," as defined by Krämer, appears:

> The perceptibility and thingness of writings discloses a space of visibility and of operativity in which notation not only functions as representational medium and sign system, but opens up an interplay of the eyes, hands, and machines that is characterized to some extent precisely by the disregard for sense and meaning, through the 'loosening' of semantics and representationality. Seeing and understanding, manipulating and grasping can come apart in the figurative script.[15]

Aside from "reading" in the sense of deciphering a notation, there also arises another, *aesthetic perception* of the figurative script. In a certain sense, the Ferrère manuscript can thus be seen as *ornamental drawing*: neither as legible "writing," nor as purely iconic, "depictive" graphics, but as a composition of patterns on the border of notational iconicity.[16] The ordering of elements in this choreo-score, the combinatorics of the figurative script [*Schrift-Bild-Kombinatorik*], the arrangement of surfaces, its interspatiality and graphic rhythm, all point to the possibility of perceiving it as ornament. Alois Riegl, who in his treatise *Stilfragen. Grundlagen zu einer Geschichte der Ornamentik* (1893)[17] defined ornament as "motif on ground" and thus stressed the "figure-ground" constellation as difference become form, emphasized the repetitive traits deployed by rhythm, variation, and movement. What is decisive here for the perception of ornament is the distribution of the figures of writing on the surface, their compositionality, and the intervals of in-between spaces. Walter Benjamin's concept of ornament makes it possible to read a notation such as the Ferrère manuscript as a "constellation." Constellation means a configuration on the surface, like a "constellation of stars"; Benjamin proceeds on the assumption that *constellations of stars* had a part in the origin of ornaments, and that ornament captures *the view of the stars*.[18] In his discourse "Doctrine of the Similar" (1974),[19] Benjamin notes that this image of the "constellation of stars" does not however mean a fixed model, but is characterized rather by its similarity to dance: the ornament appears as a pre- and postscript of the dance's movement. This does not only mean a graphic, rhythmic configuration of the "graphed" surface, but at the same time an aesthetic mode of perceiving the topography of the fleeting: "In the model of the constellation of stars and characters," Bettine Menke underlines, "the figurality of reading as (ornamental) ordering on the surface is related to the background, and it is only through that relation that it determines itself, thus by what it is not, by what is not 'there,' by what is not legible."[20]

To read the Ferrère manuscript as ornament means suspending all decisions about legibility—and about consolidation through transcription—and favoring the polysemy of aesthetic perception; "ornament," in this case, is understood in the meaning given by Benjamin:

> There is no ornament that cannot be looked at from at least two different sides: namely as surface pattern or as linear configuration. For the most part, however, the individual shapes—that can constitute very different groups—enable multiple interpretations. This experience alone already points to one of the innermost peculiarities of the 'crock notes': namely its steadfast readiness to extract from a single and same situation—e.g. a decor or a landscape—a plurality of perspectives, contents, relations.[22]

How does a notation express its potential as room for action and for play? How is the temporal latency of movements expressed in "choreo-graphics" considered as notations? Does the reading gaze as aesthetic experience not give life to the written figure [*Schrift-Figur*]? In his essay "Aussicht ins Kinderbuch,"[22] Benjamin traced the processes of *imagination* and *animation* that can be activated by looking at the figurative scripts of a children's book. Taking as his point of departure a fairy tale by Hans-Christian Andersen that comes alive in a picture book, Benjamin addresses the reverse experience of writing understood as picture scene [*Bild-Szene*]:

> It is not the things that jump off the pages toward the child leafing through the pictures—it is the child who, in looking, steps into them, like a cloud that soaks up the bright colors of the picture world. Before his or her painted book, the child makes the art of Taoist perfection true: he or she masters the false wall of the surface, and between colored fabrics and motley nooks, steps onto the stage where the fairy tale is alive.[23]

The opening and gradual transparency of this "false wall of the surface" on which the signs and lines of pictorial scripts are distributed, represents the basic imaginative operation in the dynamics of notation that transcribes itself in movement, body, space, and time: the self-reference of the figurative script; the switching of figure and ground, line and space; and the development of an image sequence, of a narrative. In this context, Benjamin turns his gaze to alphabet books in which words and pictures are so intertwined that the script's iconicity is preserved: sheets that "brought forward the letters themselves in disguise—if one may put it this way. F appears in the disguise of a Franciscan, C as a clerk, P as a porter."[24]

It would be worth devoting more reflection to the rebus character of notations such as the Ferrère manuscript shown above. The jump in the gaze spurred by the simultaneous orderings of images, letters, and drawings on the surface always recalls picture puzzles and books and spells. The "intuition of fantasy"[25] transforms the notational: it sets free that which, in its topography, is always fleeting and present-absent: movement, dance. "Indeed to every form," as Benjamin underlines, "to every outline perceived by the human being, the latter responds in person in the power of producing it. The body itself in dance, the hand in drawing replicate it and appropriate it."[26]

What does a choreographed dance step look like on the edge between the stabilizing moment of notation and the moving body? What are the forms of figurative scripts that have developed in the history of (European) dance? And how do these "notations" go back and forth between the functional dimension of documentation, the standardizing function of a normative script (and its execution), and the aesthetic freedom of images?

A historical and systematic look at dance notations immediately sheds light on the special status of figurative dance scripts [*Tanz-Schrift-Bilder*] in comparison to various forms of writing or Western musical notation.[27] For unlike various scripts in different cultures, dance notations have not developed a fixed notation system that has been historically recognized, conventionalized, and transmitted over generations with the purpose of conserving "works" for posterity.[28] From this point of view, dance notations, even when they proceed in a certain mode of systematic recollecting and transposing, can very seldom be characterized as scores in the strict sense, that is, as notations of dance *works* that document the latter and enable them to be staged again in the future.[29] If we use the concept of "notation" in dance, we will have to operate with a wide and open "concept" of notation. Goodman's concept of notation, which refers to script, score, and diagram, presupposes allographic forms of recording [*(Auf-)Zeichnungen*] that are characterized by disjunction (each mark belongs to a single sign and not to several), and finite differentiation (a gap exists between two neighboring signs). However, in the history of dance "notations," autograph recordings predominate: they do not present the said structural features, or do so only partially. This does not mean that the very different and multifarious dance notations developed in European culture since the Renaissance do not, nonetheless, possess a dimension of recording. Yet they are hardly ever "documentation" in the sense of a complete record or script [*vollständigen Aufzeichnung beziehungsweise Schrift*] of the performance and the movement. Dance scripts or dance notations actually pertain to a moment of preservation and analysis rather than a prescriptive one: even if one can extract dance phrases from them, notations serve as reference for future performances only when one considers the corresponding contexts. Dance notations—in their highly diverse manifestations—visualize dance as choreo-graphy: as a system of orderings. In their "notational" iconicity [*"Schrift"-Bildlichkeit*], they do not transcribe the act of dancing (in the same way that alphabetical scripts do not fix the performative dimension of speech). Dance notation—as designated space for figurative script [*Schrift-Bild-Raum*], as inscribed surface—rather offers the incentive to reflect and theorize the given (historical) concept of dance: there remains an analytical factor in dance notations, even when they are but fragmentary sketches. Yet conversely, this quality precisely makes it possible to "read" the operational and performative aspects of a transcript in motion, and to materialize them as practice.[30]

Dance notations that are used for reconstructing dances—for instance baroque dances or ballet performances—rely strongly on conjecture, far more than most Western musical notations. Yet these operative aspects of dance scripts[31] leave a wide scope for the performative transfer, as dance, to play out: such scope for free play can only be fulfilled and put into practice if the conventions, traditions, and performative rules relating to the various historical and cultural contexts of the dance productions are integrated, drawn from dance treaties and resources on body images, body positions, and social contexts that apply to the performances in question. The examples of dance notations discussed here convey a sense of the historical variety in the concepts of notational iconicity [*Konzepte von Schriftbildlichkeit*] of choreographies. What is striking about them is the hybrid recording process: the combination of (alphabetical) script, (musical) score, numbers, figure drawings, and conventionalized signs (e.g. the steps of the Feuillet notation) creates a specific notational iconicity [*notationelle Ikonizität*], often akin to an *ars combinatoria* geared toward movement and permutation. If closer attention is given to how the figurative script is constructed in these notations, one is mostly faced with their form as "picture-scene."[32] In the fusion of iconic and arbitrary signs, in their interference and competition, there arises a tension between (legible) script and autonomous figural and ornamental formations. It is precisely these frictions that distinguish "dance notation" as "dance script" and convey its openness: its oscillation between legibility and (pictorial) imagination, its "materiality" as reference to the movement and physicality of the dance-writing act.[33]

Let us take a first look at a notation by Fabritio Caroso from *Il Ballarino* (1581). Because it does not represent a definitive notation of a performance, this example reveals a strong ornamental side: just a few notes indicate the music and the constellation of three pairs (in this case, ladies and gentlemen are identified by letters C and D—*cavaliero* and *domina*) as evidence of its transposition into dance movement. Reference is also made to a rhetorical tradition of choreographic coordination, insofar as the dance rhythm is marked on the circular path by note heads and ancient verse feet (*spondeo* and *dattile*).[34]

Laurence Louppe points out that dance notations do not operate as a fixed vocabulary, but rather that "the miracle of dance is to transcend the gestural glossary."[35] In an emphatic sense of performativity and ephemerality, dance, also in its notations, is "less the sign than the very process of signification that dissolves […] it is a trajectory between the real and the sign. This trajectory is perturbed by the presence of a living body, intervening as such."[36] The concept of choreography has only recently applied to the production of dance works. In the 16th and 17th centuries, it meant—for Thoineau Arbeau and Raoul-Auger Feuillet, for instance—writing dances, setting down their spatial paths in writing, thereby spelling out the steps in the sense of a *compartimento di terreno*, i.e. the distribution of floor paths and the "relationality" of space-creating movements: to constitute dance as *graph*.

Floor lines are very often the basis of dance notations: this means describing space as a "script" and therefore drawing a hybrid between *temporal* division (written in musical notation) and body movement. Masculine and feminine figures are very often drawn into the notation, with steps structuring the floor paths and establishing spatial paths. These three elements—musical notation, signs for steps, and floor paths, as well as drawn (body or stick) figures—characterize the system of dance notations since Feuillet. Scholarly works on dance notations, such as the studies by Ann Hutchinson Guest and Claudia Jeschke, demonstrate that every dance script has to deal with the gap between notation and performance, with what remains unwritten between the record and the recital. The beauty of the graphic line develops—from itself and for itself—a movement of writing: the calligraphic tracing, a tracing that, however, does *not* preserve the entire movement of the dance, for no alphabet of written signs has been defined to denote the performance of bodies. The reading and the deciphering of such dance scripts as *graphs* therefore means following that tracing that leads into the open: it only points to what the letter does *not* say. A story or a narrative of dance scripts is to that extent ever reopened by *blind spots*, by blank spaces—relating to body movement, movement of the limbs, breath, to the entire oscillation between *graph* and body.

Rudolf von Laban, who founded his own system of Kinetography in 1926—later passed on and further developed under the name of Labanotation—was particularly interested in Feuillet's dance notation system because, as he saw it, the weight of each step is visualized, an indication of the diverse kinetics of the steps.[37] Beyond a notational encryption of steps and paths in space, von Laban also sought to capture in his Kinetography the movement of limbs and torso, the interplay of energy and temporality, of dynamics and rhythm.

Since there is no coherent tradition of dance notations—even though Laban's Kinetography has been used diversely under the heading of Labanotation, to record not only dance forms but also everyday movements—a variety of dance scripts has arisen. Whether they are individual sketches, choreographic constellations, storyboards, notes from memory, or even fully elaborated choreographic scores, these dance scripts attest to their diversity in design and concept. Strikingly, however, there are individual, iconic forms of recording that reflect the movement, time frame, and above all the style and individuality of each choreographer in the shape of the drawing, the actions of erasure and of writing. The following examples will make this process clear.

A choreographic drawing by Mary Wigman for *Le Sacre du Printemps* (1957) clearly demonstrates the extent to which dance scripts are shaped by the act of writing itself and the accent of gesture, rather than by script in the narrow sense of the word: the movement drawing contains vectors of direction. These register spatial motifs, circular and rotating forms that organize the relationship between group and soloist. They ultimately transpose by way of the scriptural *style* [*Duktus der Schrift*] something of the dancers' gestures, the dynamics of the performative energy of the dance, and the weight of the body into this "figurative script" [*Schrift-Bild*].

Diametrically opposed is the dance script as figurative script of Childs' *Melody Excerpts* (1977), a graphic transcription of movement that makes visible—in calligraphically precise and ornamental fashion—the repetitive patterns, the structure of the ground patterns, the changes in direction (through small direction vectors), as well as the isolation of individual segments, their coordination and composition. Childs' minimalist working method asserts itself in the calligraphic recording [*Auf-Zeichnung*]. Thus it is also exciting to follow the musically and rhythmically minimalist shifts, whereby this dance script imposes no reading direction, omitting to mark, or define, the entry cue and starting point. The question arises as to whether we can actually speak here of a "figurative script," of a dance script: the drawing rather tends to follow the principle of a regular and rhythmic abstract image composition, in which the body remains left out. But it also becomes clear that notations carry complex decisions, that their script depicts [*im Schriftbild niederlegen*] in many cases the *concept* of the art of dance, rather than *recording* [*als Aufzeichnungen*] the dancers' movements.

A similar statement can be made about Trisha Brown: *Untitled* (1980), a manuscript that records movement instructions in linear writing (from left to right), is covered in drawings and scribbles. The hand's movement, the direction of space, the orientation of surfaces, i.e. the surface of the figurative script itself, are explored. Spatial projection as in-depth body movement [*Tiefen-Bewegung des Körpers*] is eclipsed, and the hand's movement is foregrounded as *graph*, as dance script.[38] The obliteration of the script itself thus corresponds to the act of writing in the thickness of movement: a *de-writing*, a deletion in the act of drawing. It is indeed precisely the negation of legibility (of the script as well as of the dance movement) that (re-)produces a topography of the ephemeral nature of the graphic form.

This series of very different expressions of dance scripts ends with an image at the boundary between diagram and notation: Andy Warhol's *Dance Diagrams: Tango* (1962). Here step patterns are copied from drawings in 1920s dance manuals: a diagram that sets down in writing the footwork, the constellation of dancers, and the movements in space. The steps notated here are coordinated within the simultaneity of the image. The sequence of movements must be reconstituted in the act of reading or dancing, through music and previously known steps or phrases. This diagram indeed contains a prescriptive moment that can serve as matrix and step sequence (following the pedagogical intentions of the manuals on which this work is based). The diagrammatic constellation is thus tied here with the notational. At the same time though, in Warhol's Pop aesthetic this image as dance script plays with the notion of reproducibility of movement as well as of the ephemeral act of dance and performance: the reproduction of this dance script, taken from a tango lesson in the manual, is incorporated into the image as a readymade, and raises the question of copy art, of the possibility of telling apart the original, and its reproducibility.

At this point, it is worth returning to the question initially raised about dance scripts as transformation in the field of notation, of the act of writing, of "practice" and transcription. What does it mean to copy, to practice writing as the repetition of a system of patterns and rules? What is suggested when the ultimate step is to copy the prescription itself (as proposed here by Warhol), to make a law of it, and then to relativize its function, or even to override it? Is this movement of transcription inherent to the act of writing not inevitably riddled with mistakes, *mis-readings*, *mis-writings*, and with supplementary acts of compensation and covering up of errors? Since the history of dance is not based on a primordial script—nor on an *archeo-scriptio* nor on an *archeo-choreographia*—but always already conveyed in the plural, as *choreo-graphies*,[39] the question arises yet again: do the blank spaces in the history of dance scripts, that is, the *lack* of notationality and the absence of an established notation system, not offer the *opportunity* for many contemporary dance works to call into question the "diktat" of writing, its normative function, its prescriptive character, and its order?

[1] Nelson Goodman, *Languages of Art. An Approach to a Theory of Symbols*, Bobbs-Merrill, Indianapolis 1968.
[2] Sybille Krämer, "'Operationsraum Schrift'. Über einen Perspektivenwechsel in der Betrachtung der Schrift," in Sybille Krämer, Gernot Grube and Werner Kogge (eds.), *Schrift – Kulturtechnik zwischen Auge, Hand und Maschine*, Wilhem Fink, Munich 2005, p. 343–356.
[3] See (also list of ill.): Marian Hannah Winter, *The Pre-Romantic Ballet*, Pitman and Sons, London 1974, p. 182ff.
[4] Gabriele Brandstetter: "Der Tanz der Statue. Zur Repräsentation von Bewegung im Theater des 18. Jahrhunderts," in Mathias Mayer and Gerhard Neumann (eds.), *Pygmalion. Die Geschichte des Mythos in der abendländischen Kultur*, Rombach, Freiburg i. Br. 1997, p. 393–423.
[5] Jan Assmann, "Zur Ästhetik des Geheimnisses. Kryptographie als Kalligraphie im alten Ägypten," in Susanne Kotzinger and Gabriele Rippl (eds.), *Zeichen zwischen Klartext und Arabeske*, Rodopi, Amsterdam and Atlanta, 1994, p. 181.
[6] On Feuillet notation, see the explanations about the illustration text in the second part of this paper.
[7] Peter Stein, *Schriftkultur. Eine Geschichte des Schreibens und des Lesens*, Primus, Darmstadt 2006, p. 29ff.
[8] Waltraud Wiethölter, Hans-Georg Pott and Alfred Messerli (eds.), *Stimme und Schrift. Zur Geschichte und Systematik sekundärer Oralität*, Wilhelm Fink, Munich 2008, especially Waltraud Wiethölter, "Stimme und Schrift: Szenen einer Beziehungsgeschichte," p. 17ff.
[9] Peter Stein, *Schriftkultur*, p. 29ff.
[10] Michel de Certeau, *The Practice of Everyday Life*, trans. Steven Rendall, University of California Press, Berkeley and Los Angeles 1988, especially Part III: "Spatial Practices," chapter 7: "Walking in the City," p. 91–110.
[11] Sybille Krämer, Gernot Grube and Werner Kogge (eds.), *Schrift*, p. 38.
[12] Ibid., p. 39.
[13] Ibid.
[14] On the creative and "critical" role of notation, see John Rajchman, "Die Kunst der Notation," in Hubertus von Amelunxen, Dieter Appelt and Peter Weibel (eds., in collaboration with Angela Lammert), *Notation: Form und Kalkül in den Künsten*, Akademie der Künste/ZKM, Berlin/Karlsruhe 2008, p. 68–77.
[15] Sybille Krämer, "'Operationsraum Schrift,'" p. 52.
[16] About the relationship between line and ornament as "poetological graphs," Sabine Mainberger, *Experiment Linie. Künste und ihre Wissenschaften um 1900*, Kulturverlag Kadmos, Berlin 2010, especially p. 147ff.
[17] Alois Riegl, *Stilfragen. Grundlagen zu einer Geschichte der Ornamentik*, Berlin 1893; on the ornament, see Markus Brüderlin (ed.), *Ornament und Abstraktion. Kunst der Kulturen, Moderne und Gegenwart im Dialog*, exh. cat., Fondation Beyeler/DuMont, Riehen/Cologne 2001.
[18] Walter Benjamin, *Schriften*, vol. II, Rolf Tiedemann and Hermann Schweppenhäuser (eds.), Suhrkamp Verlag, Frankfurt 1974, p. 858; on the theme of the ornament in Walter Benjamin, see the excellent essay by Bettine Menke, "Ornament, Konstellation, Gestöber," in Susanne Kotzinger and Gabriele Rippl (eds.), *Zeichen zwischen Klartext und Arabeske*, p. 307–327.
[19] Walter Benjamin, "Lehre vom Ähnlichen," in *Gesammelte Schriften*, vol. II, p. 204–210.
[20] Bettine Menke, "Ornament, Konstellation, Gestöber," p. 314ff.
[21] Walter Benjamin, *Über Haschisch*, Suhrkamp, Frankfurt 1972, p. 57. Trans. Christian Roy and the editors.
[22] Walter Benjamin, "Aussicht ins Kinderbuch," *Angelus Novus, Ausgewählte Schriften 2*, Suhrkamp, Frankfurt 1966.
[23] Ibid., p. 151. Trans. Christian Roy and the editors.
[24] Ibid., p. 153.
[25] Ibid., p. 156.
[26] Ibid.
[27] Claudia Jeschke, *Tanzschriften. Ihre Geschichte und ihre Methode. Die illustrierte Darstellung eines Phänomens von den Anfängen bis zur Gegenwart*, Comes Verlag, Bad Reichenhall 1983, as well as Claudia Jeschke, "Tanznotation," in Sibylle Dahms (ed.), *Tanz*, Bärenreiter Verlag, Kassel/Basel 2001, p. 15–24; Laurence Louppe (ed.), *Traces of Dance: Drawings and Notations of Choreographers*, Dis Voir, Paris 1994.
[28] Nelson Goodman's concept of notation, *Sprachen der Kunst. Entwurf einer Symboltheorie*, Frankfurt 1998, chapters IV and V, p. 125–204 [1st ed.: Indianapolis 1968].
[29] Ibid., p. 125 and p. 198ff.
[30] The questions of the possibilities of a digital processing of notations are discussed by Henner Drewses in his investigation *Transformationen. Bewegung in Notation und digitaler Verarbeitung*, Josef Fellsches (ed.), vol. 18, Folkwang-Texte, Essen 2003. Drewes analyzes in particular the most used notation systems, the Eshkol-Wachmann Movement Notation and Laban's Kinetography/Labanotation with respect to their documentary, analytical, and creative potential, with a view on digital programming and the use of these systems.
[31] In what follows, I will be using the term "dance scripts" rather than "notation" because it emphasizes the scriptural—and so, at the same time, the open—character of these typographies, rather than their character as score and notation/writing down as their script modality. On the operationality of script, see Sybille Krämer, "Operationsraum Schrift," here, p. 23–61.
[32] I am borrowing Jan Assmann's concept of the figural composition of hieroglyphs; see Jan Assmann, "Zur Ästhetik des Geheimnisses," p. 175–187, here p. 181.
[33] Claudia Jeschke, *Tanzschriften*, p. 190ff.
[34] Ibid., p. 191.
[35] Laurence Louppe, *Traces of Dance*, p. 9.
[36] Ibid., p. 10ff.
[37] See among others: Rudolf von Laban, *Choreographie*, Diederichs, Jena 1926, p. 60ff. See also Rudolf von Laban, *Principles of Dance and Movement*, Macdonald & Evans, London 1956; Albrecht Knust, *Abriß der Kinetographie Labans*, Hofmeister, Leipzig 1957.
[38] See Angela Lammert, "Trisha Brown. Tänze auf Papier und Zeichnungen in der Luft," in Armen Avanessian and Franck Hofmann (eds.), *Raum in den Künsten. Konstruktion – Bewegung – Politik*, Fink Verlag, Munich 2010, p. 147–158; also on this topic, *Trisha Brown. Danse, précis de liberté*, exh. cat., Musées de Marseille, Réunion des musées nationaux, Marseille 1998.
[39] Christie V. McDonald, "Choreographies: An Interview with Jacques Derrida," in Peggy Kamuf (ed.), *A Derrida Reader: Between the Blinds*, Columbia University Press, New York 1991, p. 441–456. From *Diacritics*, vol. 12, no. 2, "Cherchez la Femme Feminist Critique/Feminine Text," Summer 1982, p. 66–76.

Scarlet Letters on the Roof: Figuration and De-Figuration in Trisha Brown's *Roof and Fire Piece* (1973)

Alexander Schwan

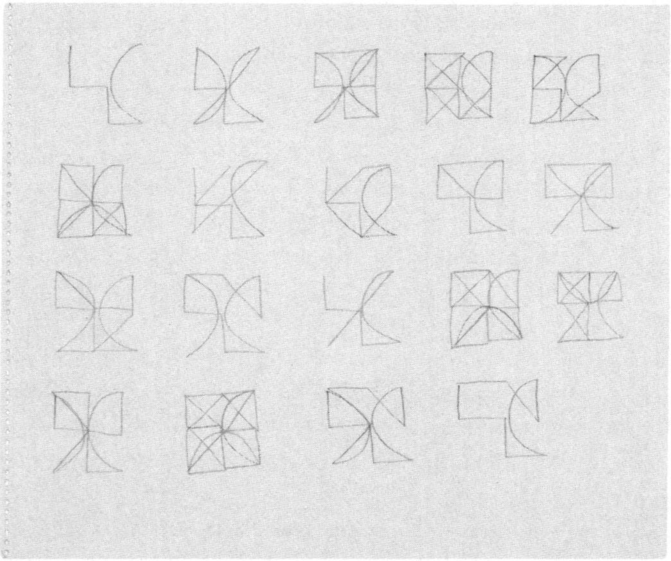

Trisha Brown
Untitled, 1973
Graphite on paper, 35.9 × 43.2 cm

Picking

A *trillium*, a three-petaled flower from the Melanthiaceae family, also called *tri flower*, *birthroot*, or *wake-robin*, inspired Trisha Brown's New York debut as a choreographer. Firstly, she named her 1962 three-minute-long solo dance *Trillium*,[1] and referred to the three-petaled shape of the flower by using "three elemental actions—stand, sit, and lie down—performed in indeterminate, improvised relationship to one another, without transitions."[2] Secondly, Brown's entire concept of movement was connected to her particular experience with the small flower growing in the woods of the Pacific Northwest where she spent her childhood. Jill Johnston, one of the witnesses of Brown's early dance piece, referred to its concept rather metaphorically, saying that the "short dance grows, flowers of its own natural accord from its first physical impulse of simply getting up and lying down."[3]

However, even Steve Paxton explicitly explained the flower-dance analogy in Brown's early work: "Trisha told me that a trillium was a flower that she had found in the woods [...] She said that she used to pick them in the woods, but the time she got home they would be wilted and faded. And that's what she thought about movement. It was wild; it was something that lived in the air."[4]

Comparing the evanescence of a trillium flower with the ephemerality of movement, Brown began to deal with the transience of dance and the problem of how to capture something that is always already lost in the moment of its production. Her subsequent choreographic attempts to embody this dilemma seemed to distinguish the execution of a choreographed movement from the choreographic structure, attributing to the latter a durable character that the first inevitably fails to obtain. Thus, "Brown reacted against critics' perception of *Trillium* as impromptu and overly subjective, using different tactics to make *visible* her choreography's structure as that which remains,"[5] and opening up a remarkable gap between her idea of meticulously scored and reproducible dances and the allegedly free but nonetheless technically and agreement-regulated movement improvisation. Differently from *Trillium*, where the spontaneity and flower-like evanescence of movement still hid the concept beneath it, Brown's works in the following decade—pieces like *Rulegame 5* (1964), *Homemade* (1966), and particularly the different versions of *Accumulation* (1971ff)—focused on indeterminate structure, and characterized the choreographic as distinct from the danced and marked by a "relatively unchanging logic."[6]

In spite of emphasizing the concept of repeatable movements rather than embracing the unavoidable inexactness and individuality of each repetition, Brown's choreography was paradoxically still dependent on the absence of durability in the actual performance. Her idea of how the act of dancing should be executed is therefore comparable to a writing system seeking the permanence and rereadability of a written text, but at the same time inevitably depending on the performance of the act of writing. With the particular exception of *Trillium*, the concepts of Brown's early choreographic work *prescribed* the actual movement in the performance by giving tasks and rules to herself and to her dancers for almost a decade. Brown's pieces encircled the idea of choreography's durability, and, despite being visible only as highly ephemeral acts, they apparently tended to neglect the evanescence of dance as an act of instantly vanishing bodily writing.[7]

Only at the beginning of the early 1970s, and after having experimented with unusual movements supported by technical equipment—like walking on walls (*Planes*, 1968), moving through suspended pieces of cloth (*Floor of the Forest*, 1970) or, most famously, walking on exterior house walls (*Man Walking Down the Side of a Building*, 1970), did Brown reinforce both the notion of ephemerality in her work and the analogy of dancing and writing. Several of her pieces in the 1970s deliberately organized movement as a process of writing by following a prescribed choreographic text, which was then intentionally altered and deformed in the process of performance. Brown's tendency to an explicitly graphic understanding of choreography cumulating in *Locus* (1975) thus referred to the long tradition of comparing dancing and writing dating back not only to Stéphane Mallarmé and his use of the term "écriture corporelle,"[8] but also to the meaning of the Greek words *chorós* and *gráphein*, which literally mean dance or place for dancing and writing, so that choreography can refer to both spatial and temporal inscriptions.[9] The latter word, *gráphein*, is hereby of particular importance since it includes within its range of meanings also *scratching, carving, cutting*, and, not completely unsurprisingly, *drawing*.[10]

In what follows, I will look more closely at the analogy between dancing and writing with regard to *Roof and Fire Piece* from 1973,[11] a later version of Brown's *Roof Piece* from 1971.[12] For not only were these pieces accompanied by a series of untitled drawings by Brown, making the analogy of dancing and writing even more visible, but in addition the system of *Roof Piece* refers back to Brown's New York debut and its reflection on processes of fading and defiguration.[13] Both *Trillium* and *Roof Piece* deal with moments of picking and their congruence with processes of wilting and dying. While *Trillium* reflects metaphorically on the inability to pick a flower in the forest and carry it home alive, *Roof Piece* makes a more literal use of picking. Here the dancers pick a movement sequence they see performed by their partners and try to repeat it; yet, by imitating it, they involuntarily change the movement sequence, so that in this particular dancing, picking and fading converge as if in a flower.

Waving

The scarlet letters on the rooftops move. Waving their arms, stretching their legs, bowing, and turning, the 16 dancers —dressed in red costumes and positioned on rooftops in SoHo—constantly transform the shapes of their bodies as if they were signs of an undecipherable inscription, at once written and incorporated by the dancers themselves. An ephemeral dance-inscription is sent from rooftop to rooftop as each dancer copies the movement they see on the rooftop in front of them, and is then in turn copied by the dancer behind them. This transmits a sequence of signalling movements across the urban topography of Downtown Manhattan, beginning on a rooftop at West Broadway and Houston, crossing seven blocks on the north-south axis and three blocks on the east-west axis, and finally ending on a rooftop at White and Church Street.[14]

Brown is positioned on the northernmost rooftop with her body oriented toward the south, and dancing with improvised but not completely unpredictable movements. These are then copied by all the dancers, stretched south of her, facing northward and waiting to pick up each movement like a semaphore signal. When, after approximately 15 minutes, the last dancer in the line, Carmen Beuchat, has completed the final movement of the transmitted sequence, the whole system reverses: the dancers turn southward and begin transmitting, for another 15 minutes, the movements sent by Beuchat, until they have all returned to Brown.[15] The piece is called *Roof and Fire Piece* in reference to the red costumes of the 16 dancers. It split its audience up into two groups positioned on rooftops, with each group only able to see some of the dancers, while the predating *Roof Piece* from 1971 had no audience except the dancers themselves and probably some invited friends.

Roof and Fire Piece can be compared with historical systems of optical telegraphy that once transmitted messages over long distances by using encoded configurations of visual elements—much as Brown's dancers do by sending movements and poses from one rooftop to another. After earlier attempts to communicate over long distances by using visual signalling, the first successfully operating system of optical telegraphy was invented in 1791 by the French engineer Claude Chappe and his brothers Abraham and Ignace.[16] Their *tachygraph* (literally meaning *fast writer* and only later called *telegraph, far writer*) consisted of a pole or semaphore with movable wooden arms, whose positions were encoded with distinctive meanings.

The arms of the tachygraph were manipulated by a single person at each station, while a second person watched the transformation of the semaphore arms from the next station. A code-book for decoding the configuration of the semaphore arms, referring to letters, words, and even entire sentences, was only available at the first and last stations, thus providing the possibility of transmitting a message secretly. For reasons of greater visibility, such optical telegraphs were positioned on towers, hills, and rooftops. They covered France with a network of more than 500 stations stretching a total distance of nearly 5,000 kilometers, and were used for military and national communications. Systems of optical telegraphy such as the Chappe system, with its 196 signs, as well as other highly developed systems existed in several European countries and the US and were in use until the 1850s, when they were replaced by electric telegraphy.[17]

The similarity between the system of optical telegraphy and Brown's choreography in *Roof and Fire Piece* is evident. Both of them work on exposed and elevated geographical points and both transmit sequences of movement and poses over a long distance by using the possibilities of different configurations of bodily shapes, namely of arms in relation to a vertical, erected body. We know from Brown that she herself—like some contemporary critics of the performance—was aware of the visual similarity between *Roof and Fire Piece* and the semaphore movements, although a mimetic approach toward optical telegraphy may not have been primarily intended.[18]

The similarity between both systems of movement transmission becomes more evident when the set of possible configurations in the Chappe system is compared with drawings made by Brown around the same time as the *Roof Piece* dances. The drawings were not strictly related to the choreography as a notational system but, like the set of configurations in the Chappe system, they play with a set of possible and taxonomically systematized allocations of lines and angles as if they were studies for an alphabet of dance movements.[19]

Scribbling

However, despite the visual similarity between the two, both choreography and telegraphy are strongly distinguished from one another in at least two aspects that are of particular importance for the analogy of dancing and writing in general. First, in contrast to telegraphy, the *Roof Piece* sequence is not encoded with an alphabet. The dance itself is meaningless, not only unreadable due to a missing decryption code, but rather undecipherable in general. In addition, even if the dance movements were encoded with an alphabet—as in Brown's *Locus*—the decoding would not necessarily be readable because, unlike optical telegraphy, a dance piece always shows far less exactitude in the transmission of sequential movements and poses. During the course of the repetitions, and due to the bodily individuality of the dancers, their movements involuntarily change, either in terms of dynamics and rhythm or in the vocabulary of movement itself.

Secondly, optical telegraphy, even if also prone to mistakes, is systematically dependent on the exactness with which the configurations of the semaphore arms are transmitted, an exactness that is familiar to the iterability of writing systems, where each sign has to be able to be repeated in an unaltered way. In contrast, and particularly in the case of *Roof and Fire Piece,* where the dancing bodies have to repeat originally improvised movements from the rooftops in front of them that they are barely able to see, dancing is always already affected by the non-iterability of movements. This results in singularity in each dance due to the fact that each dancer dances in a slightly different way and is not able to repeat even a single dance movement without variation. Each copied movement in *Roof and Fire Piece* will always be slightly longer or shorter than the one before, and physical constitutions and emotional and cognitive processes will always influence and change the way a pose is struck, a leap is set, or a figure is enacted.

In terms of the analogy of dancing and writing, dancing can only be seen as a highly imprecise inscription with a tendency to become a mere scribble, thus oscillating indistinguishably between writing and drawing, between figuration and defiguration.[20] Like the telephone game, where a sequence of spoken information is exposed to a process of transformation and erosion during its transmission, *Roof and Fire Piece* is qualified by "an incremental, successive subtraction, which, if performed ad infinitum, would bring gesture to the point of almost completely shedding itself."[21] The piece thus problematizes the simple equation of perfor-mance with inevitable self-annihilation, and conceptualizes the self-erasure itself. This leads to the paradoxical effect that Brown's choreographic concept can survive as an absence made present through highly expedited erosion of movement.[22]

In addition, particular tribute has to be paid to the role of perception in *Roof and Fire Piece*, since no one in the audience, which was positioned on two rooftops, could see the entire chain of signalling movements while, from street level, the dancers and the choreography were invisible. Thus, the phantasmagorical character of the perceived dance piece is even more emphasized: not only did the copied movements slightly vary from dancer to dancer, and were therefore highly individual in themselves, the difficulty in the perception process due to the positions of the dancers led to a fragmentation of spectatorship. The perceived movements co-creatively written by dancers and audience differed from each single perspective, so that in this particular case the "écriture corporelle" of dance was not only highly ephemeral but also entirely fragmented in multiple singularities.[23]

Marking

Roof and Fire Piece was a part of Brown's early choreographic work that dealt intrinsically with the relationship between dance and urban space. Performed on rooftops, park benches, or exterior house walls, some of her most famous pieces of postmodern dance profoundly examined how choreography can interact with the topography of a city. Dance here did not merely react to the city as a stage, but rather created and transformed its own surrounding space by leaving ephemeral inscriptions within the network of urban structures. In spite of its elusiveness and fragmentation, *Roof and Fire Piece* had a strong impact on the urban topography of Downtown Manhattan. It marked the city with an inscription that, although ephemeral, was deeply involved in the architectural and social situation of SoHo in the early 1970s, a time when SoHo was not yet the gentrified neighbourhood it became in the following decades, and art in public space was not yet part of a mainstream culture.[24]

The inscription of *Roof and Fire Piece* marked the surrounding city space in at least two ways. Firstly, as a form of body-calligraphy with all its aspects of ephemerality, it contrasted with the more static inscriptions of architectural forms and enabled the viewer to read the city architecture around the performance. By dancing on the rooftops and asking viewers to see the city from an unusual angle, architectural elements that were normally overlooked from street level became visible. The unstructured *topos* in which the dancing took place became a space by being moved in and by being perceived from the perspective of an always-changing body.[25] In the particular case of *Roof and Fire Piece,* dancing as writing in the city had therefore both critical and poetic potential to change and recreate its own surroundings.[26]

However, the inscription-like character of dancing also involved the connotation of appropriation: the city was marked by being danced in and was thus taken possession of. It would not be an exaggeration to say that *Roof and Fire Piece,* as one of the most iconic performances of the early 1970s, was complicit in the long process of SoHo's gentrification from former industrial use to expensive private housing. This process itself is a resculpting of urban space and of the social structures of the people who live and work there —or those who used to work and live there but can no longer afford it. The piece thus indicates the changes in SoHo's social structure that had already begun in 1964, when artists were first permitted to legally inhabit two floors of the industrial loft buildings of SoHo, and to designate their homes with the initials A.I.R., for artists in residence.[27] Funded by the National Endowment for the Arts in 1973[28] probably also with the purpose of further establishing SoHo's gentrification process via artistic intervention, Brown's work not only reflected this process, but also took an active part in it.

It is not a coincidence that the major exhibition and performance program *New York—Downtown Manhattan: SoHo. Exhibitions, Theatre, Music, Performance, Video, Film* presented at the *Akademie der Künste Berlin* in 1976 on the occasion of the Bicentennial of the United States of America, and exploring the entanglement of art and social structure in SoHo, used Babette Mangolte's famous photograph of Brown's *Roof and Fire Piece* as its poster.[29] The dance was so emblematic of SoHo's transformation, not just in terms of SoHo's galleries, but also in terms of Brown's interaction with this particular urban landscape. The exhibition catalogue indeed phrases the involvement of art in a successful urban development as follows: "What we have in SoHo is an artists' quarter. The settlement of the area by artists was a predisposing condition, but it is not the sole reason for the area's continuing success. This has been ensured by the establishment of art galleries and their attendant services aimed not only at the residents but at the visitors (the consumers) […] SoHo is a Bohemia very concerned with marketing of course."[30] In the light of this entanglement of art and urban development, and in spite of its subversive character in questioning the traditional use of a city landscape by dancing on the rooftops of industrial loft buildings, one may even say that *Roof and Fire Piece* served as a catalyst for SoHo's gentrification. Simply by dancing in the urban landscape, the piece helped to turn a former cheap living area into a more attractive one with rising rents and real estate prices.

The impact of *Roof and Fire Piece* in appropriating space and as a spatial inscription becomes even more visible through its reenactment (simply called *Roof Piece*) along the southern end of the High Line in Chelsea, New York City, in 2011. This manifestation had almost completely lost the critical and ironic potential the choreography had once had in early 1970s in SoHo.[31] According to the critic of the *New York Times*, *Roof Piece* "at the High Line still preserved the work's integrity, but the setting edged it precariously close to a gimmick."[32] In contrast to being hardly visible in 1973 (and bearing in mind the entirely private performance of the predating *Roof Piece* from 1971 which had almost no audience at all), the choreography could be studied much more easily in 2011, when the audience was invited to literally follow the changing of the signals by moving from one dancer to the next.[33] The movements of just nine dancers in 2011 were more refined and their costumes more stylish than in 1973, and in addition the entire surroundings of the choreography had changed.

1973 saw dark and half-rotten rooftop architecture whose almost sublime character was emphasized by the spatial inscription of the dancers "revealing the majesty and privacy of downtown roofs and the sculptural effect of its water towers."[34] Yet the urban landscape along the High Line in 2011 presented itself as a symbol of gentrification, combining new or recently rebuilt architecture with decoratively redesigned traffic and industrial elements. This ultimately shows that the urban background of *Roof and Fire Piece* is itself part of the ever-changing choreographic process, which generates a different dance each time the piece is performed. Whether further reenacted by the Trisha Brown Company as in the Getty Center, Los Angeles, California in 2013,[35] or artistically appropriated and alienated by other artists, as in Christian Jankowski's *Rooftop Routine* (2007) with a hula-hoop choreography transmitted on the rooftops of New York's Chinatown[36] and in Anahita Razmi's version *Roof Piece Teheran* (2011),[37] different urban topographies always change the corporeal calligraphy and are in return made visible as changing in themselves.

Since the ephemeral character of dance as a spatial inscription remains in each performance, *Roof and Fire Piece* could be seen as just another form of architecture, less persistent and much more fluid and ephemeral than the one in which it is set. The ephemerality of moving body architecture, much like the elusiveness of an "écriture corporelle," emphasizes the transitory character of urban topography and its architecture.[38] Both the city-space and the dance are variable and unstable, having as their destiny to finally vanish, either fast or slowly. As in the Greek word *gráphein*, all forms of marking converge. Drawing becomes writing becomes architecture becomes dance, and all these inscriptions will end, sooner or later, in the interweaving of figuration and defiguration, through which dance, as the most urgent form of inscription, is always already affected.

[1] Premiere: Maidman Playhouse, New York, March 24, 1962. Choreography and Dance: Trisha Brown; Music: Simone Forti, performed by herself.

[2] Susan Rosenberg, "Trisha Brown: Choreography as Visual Art," in *October*, vol. 140, Spring 2012, p. 23–25.

[3] Jill Johnston, "Boiler Room," in *Village Voice*, March 29, 1962, p. 14, quoted from Sally Banes, *Democracy's Body. Judson Dance Theater, 1962–1964*, Duke University Press, Durham (NC) 1993, p. 121.

[4] Quoted from an interview with Steve Paxton by Sally Banes, Bennington (VT), April 1980, in Sally Banes, *Democracy's Body*, p. 121.

[5] Susan Rosenberg, "Trisha Brown: Choreography as Visual Art," p. 25.

[6] Ibid., p. 28.

[7] Ibid., p. 29.

[8] Stéphane Mallarmé, "Ballets," in Stéphane Mallarmé, *Divagations*, Bibliothèque-Charpentier, Paris 1897, p. 173.

[9] Henry George Liddell and Robert Scott, "grápho," in *A Greek-English Lexicon*, Oxford University Press, Oxford 1996 [9th ed.], p. 360; Gabriele Brandstetter, "Graph. Den Körper schreiben," in *Ballett international/Tanz aktuell*, vol. 3, 1999, p. 28–29.

[10] Alexander Schwan, "Body-Calligraphies: Dance as an Embodied Fantasy of Writing," in Suzanne Anker and Sabine Flach (eds.), *Embodied Fantasies: From Awe to Artifice*, Art/Knowledge/Theory, vol. 1, Peter Lang, Bern 2013, p. 217–227.

[11] Premiere: 420 West Broadway to 35 White Street, New York, June 24, 1973. Choreography: Trisha Brown; Dancers: Carmen Beuchat, Trisha Brown, Douglas Dunn, Tina Girouard, Caroline Goodden, David Gordon, Nancy Green, Susan Harris, Elsi Miranda, Emmett Murray, Sylvia Palacios, Eve Poling, Sarah Rudner, Nanette Seivert, Valda Setterfield and Liz Thompson. Hendel Teicher, "Chronology of Dances, 1961–1979," in Hendel Teicher (ed.), *Trisha Brown: Dance and Art in Dialogue, 1961–2001*, The MIT Press, Cambridge (MA) and London 2002, p. 299–318.

[12] Premiere: 53 Wooster Street (Trisha Brown's residence) to 381 Lafayette Street (Robert Rauschenberg's studio), New York, NY, May 11, 1971, Choreography: Trisha Brown; Dancers: Trisha Brown and up to 11 other dancers, names and exact number unknown. Hendel Teicher, "Chronology of Dances, 1961–1979." According to Trisha Brown's own essay "Three Pieces" from 1975, the performance of *Roof Piece* took place in November 1971 while the summer performances in New York City in 1973 were followed by other versions of the piece performed at Mills College, Oakland (CA), on July 17, 1973, with "instructions interpreted and directed by Rebecca Fuller. Circular format rendering the sender and receiver of the movement simultaneously visible to the audience. Indoor and outdoor versions. Public performances." Trisha Brown, "Three Pieces," in *TDR–The Drama Review*, vol. 19, no. 1, 1975, p. 26.

[13] Erich Auerbach, "Figura," in *Archivum Romanicum*, vol. 22, 1938, p. 436–489; Gabriele Brandstetter, "Defigurative Choreography: From Duchamp to William Forsythe," in *TDR–The Drama Review*, vol. 42, no. 4, 1998, p. 37–55.

[14] See the shooting of *Roof and Fire Piece*'s original performance in *Trisha Brown. Early Works 1966–1979*, DVD 1/2, San Francisco, ArtPix, 2005.

[15] Amanda Jane Graham, "Out of Site: Trisha Brown's *Roof Piece*," in *Dance Chronicle*, vol. 36, no. 1, 2013, p. 59–76.

[16] Fédération Nationale des Associations de Personnel des Postes et Télécommunications pour la Recherche Historique (FNARH), *La télégraphie Chappe*, Jarville-La Malgrange, Éditions de l'Est, 1993; Kenneth George Beauchamp, *A History of Telegraphy: Its Technology and Application*, IEE History of Technology Series, no. 26, London, Institution of Electrical Engineers, 2001, p. 6–19.

[17] Roland Wenzlhuemer, *Connecting the Nineteenth-Century World: The Telegraph and Globalization*, Cambridge University Press, Cambridge and New York 2013, p. 63–64.

[18] Trisha Brown, "Three Pieces," p. 26.

[19] *Trisha Brown. Danse, précis de liberté*, exh. cat., Musées de Marseille/Réunion des musées nationaux, Marseille/Paris 1998, p. 40–41; Peter Eleey (ed.), *Trisha Brown: So That the Audience Does Not Know Whether I Have Stopped Dancing*, exh. cat., Walker Art Center, Minneapolis 2008, p. 47–54. On the relationship between drawing and dancing in general and with a particular regard to Trisha Brown's later graphic work, see Helen Molesworth (ed.), *Dance/Draw*, exh. cat., Hatje Cantz/The Institute of Contemporary Art, Ostfildern/Boston 2011.

[20] Alexander Schwan, "'Dancing is like scribbling, you know': Schriftbildlichkeit in Trisha Browns Choreographie *Locus*," in *Sprache und Literatur*, vol. 107, 2011, p. 58–70.

[21] Susan Rosenberg, "Trisha Brown: Choreography as Visual Art," p. 37.

[22] Ibid.

[23] Regarding the inevitable fragmentation of choreography in a plurality of spatial inscriptions, see "Interview: Choreographies: Jacques Derrida and Christie V. McDonald," *Diacritics*, vol. 12, no. 2, "Cherchez la Femme Feminist Critique/Feminine Text," Summer 1982, p. 66–76.

[24] Lydia Yee, "When the Sky Was the Limit," in Lydia Yee (ed.), *Laurie Anderson, Trisha Brown, Gordon Matta-Clark: Pioneers of the Downtown Scene, New York 1970s*, Prestel, Munich, London and New York 2011, p. 17.

[25] Michel de Certeau, *The Practice of Everyday Life*, trans. Steven Rendall, University of California Press, Berkeley, Los Angeles, and London 1984, p. 117.

[26] Ramsay Burt, "Against Expectations: Trisha Brown and the Avant-Garde," *Dance Research Journal*, vol. 37, no. 1, 2005, p. 25.

[27] Lawrence Alloway, "SoHo as Bohemia," in René Block (ed.), *New York—Downtown Manhattan: SoHo*, Akademie der Künste Berlin/Berliner Festwochen, Berlin 1976, p. 143.

[28] In 1973, Trisha Brown was funded by the National Endowment for the Arts to the tune of $7,360.00. Babette Mangolte's famous picture of *Roof and Fire Piece* even decorated the Annual Report of the same year. See the National Endowment for the Arts/National Council on the Arts' *Annual Report Fiscal Year 1973*, Washington, D.C., n. publ., no. 45, 1973, p. 56: http://arts.gov/publications/1973-annual-report.

[29] September 5–October 17, 1976.

[30] Lawrence Alloway, "SoHo as Bohemia," p. 145.

[31] Performed on rooftops surrounding the High Line, Manhattan, New York, June 9–11, 2011: http://www.trishabrowncompany.org/index.php?page=view&nr=483.

[32] Gia Kourlas, "Red Chain Reactions Against the Sky," in *The New York Times*, June 12, 2011: http://www.nytimes.com/2011/06/13/arts/dance/trisha-brown-dance-company-at-the-high-line-review.html.

[33] Amanda Jane Graham, "Out of Site," p. 73.

[34] Babette Mangolte, "About Roof Piece," 2007, published online: http://www.babettemangolte.com/maps.html.

[35] The context of the reenactment of *Roof and Fire Piece* in the Getty Center, Los Angeles on April 6, 2013, was even more unlike SoHo in the early 1970s. Set against a blue Californian sky and with dancers wearing sunglasses, this version had its visitors spontaneously mimicking the dancers, thus adding further alterations to the changing movement sequence. See Laura Bleiberg's review: "From Rooftops to Subways, Dancing Makes Los Angeles the Stage," in *The Los Angeles Times*, April 7, 2013: http://articles.latimes.com/2013/apr/07/entertainment/la-et-cm-trisha-brown-stephan-koplowitz-review-20130407. Another museum version of *Roof Piece* named *Roof Piece Re-Layed* was

performed by The Trisha Brown Company in The Museum of Modern Art, New York City on January 12, 15, and 16, 2011: http://www.moma.org/visit/calendar/exhibitions/1127.

[36] Christian Jankowski, "Rooftop Routine," in RoseLee Goldberg (ed.), *Everywhere and All at Once: An Anthology of Writings on Performa 07*, JRP|Ringier, Zurich 2009, p. 48–51.

[37] Videoinstallation, 12 videoloops, 18'11" each, 2011. See: http://www.anahitarazmi.de/Roof-Piece-Tehran.

[38] Bruno Latour and Albena Yaneva, "'Give Me a Gun and I Will Make a Buildings Move': an Ant's View of Architecture," in Reto Geiser (ed.), *Explorations in Architecture: Teaching, Design, Research*, Birkhäuser, Basel 2008, p. 80–89.

Diagram, Dance, Diagram: Trisha Brown's *Locus* (1975)

Susan Rosenberg

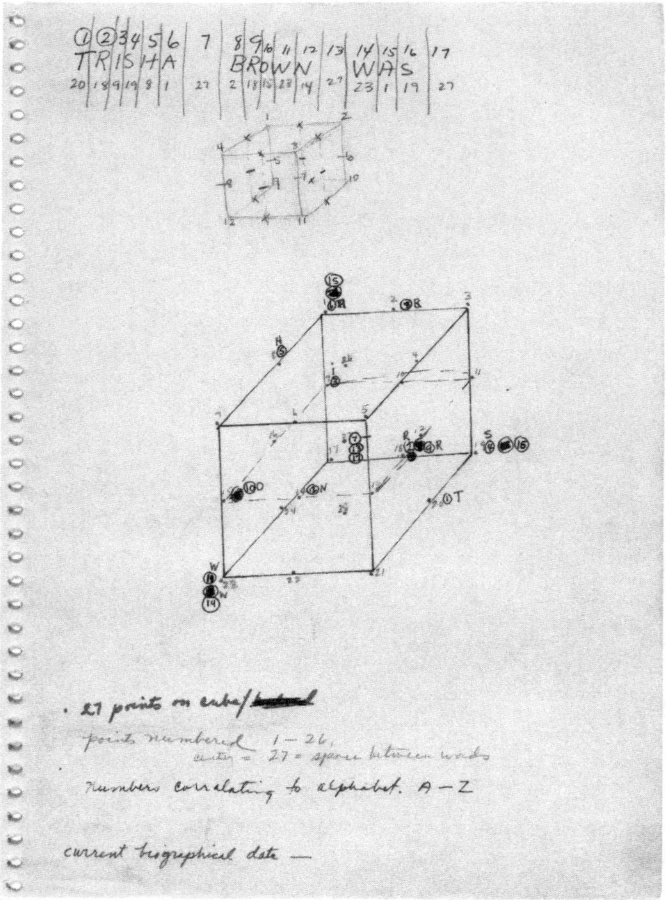

Trisha Brown
Untitled (Locus), 1975
Felt-tip pen, colored ink, and pencil on notebook paper, 30.5 × 22.9 cm
The Museum of Modern Art, New York

The story of *Locus* (1975) begins with a postcard Trisha Brown mailed to Carol Goodden on February 24, 1974, addressed to the New York office of Art Services, the Paris-based non-profit organization established to oversee international bookings of downtown New York theater and performance.[1] Brown was en route to a Grand Union performance when she wrote Goodden: “Time to board the Aeroplane. Have a new piece in mind, do you suppose that has any relation to the fact that I found a List Lost Loft yesterday?”[2]

The first inklings of Brown’s idea for *Locus* connect a dance idea to a biographical event and a site: the discovery of a fifth floor loft at 541 Broadway, purchased in a March transaction initiated by Fluxus founder and SoHo real estate impresario, George Maciunas, but closed with the building’s owner.[3] A former sweatshop with sewing machines bolted to the floor[4] but no interior columns, its 37 × 50 ft front room was transformed by Brown into a studio—the place where she made *Locus*, and showed it as a work-in-progress in June 1975.

Locus' January 1976 public premiere at the Brooklyn Academy of Music's recently opened Leperq Space marked the first time in Brown's career when she revealed drawing's role in her imaginative process. In *The New York Times*, Anna Kisselgoff reported on Brown's "opening up a notebook to show the 'score' of the dance […] displaying a diagram of a cube with 27 numbered points on it."[5] From Kisselgoff's description, it appears that Brown shared *Locus*' first sheet, which contains the image of a cube and rules for generating, ordering, and spatializing movement: "27 points on cube"; "points numbered 1–26 with 27 a space between words"; "numbers correlating to alphabet A–Z"; and "current biographical data." Through correlating letters to numbers, and then spelling out a sentence that begins "TRISHA BROWN WAS," Brown arrived at instructions for touching each of the cube's numbered points with a bodily action. Disclosing her scores, Brown announced her works' relationship to visual art: *New York Times* critics deemed her a "minimal and conceptual choreographer."[6]

Locus' significance to Brown's artistic development as a choreographer deserves attention equal to that given to the dance's visual representation in drawings. Working back and forth between graphic and kinesthetic exploration, Brown produced a series of drawn scores that inculcated the movements' expansion into fully three-dimensional space, as Kisselgoff's titled review acknowledged: "Wall Dancer Adds a New Dimension."[7] The scores enabled Brown's extension of a gestural vocabulary, originated in her *Accumulations* (1971–1973), into a movement vocabulary conforming to Ferdinand de Saussure's structuralist definition of language, as a system of differences and substitutions. This was achieved through procedures of encoding autobiographical information onto a structure of personal import, the "white cube" of her loft-studio, a literal instance of structuralist activity, as discussed in Rosalind Krauss's 1978 essay on the grid's role in modernism's history: its spatialization and suppression of narrative through abstract form.[8] Furthermore, Claude Lévi-Strauss' structural analysis of cultures' founding myths serves to contextualize *Locus* in terms of the white cube's institutional and aesthetic functions in visual art: this was the subject of essays by Brian O'Doherty published in *Artforum* the same year as *Locus*' debut[9] and compiled in the book *Inside the White Cube: The Ideology of Gallery Space.*[10]

Arguing that the "white cube" reflects the art world's hermeticism, O'Doherty attacks its "mythic" neutrality: its enabling the fiction of art's autonomy from life and commerce; its prejudicial emphasis on art's opticality; and its use in artistic acts referring to the art frame itself, what he called "whole gallery gestures."[11] This insight is relevant to *Locus*, as O'Doherty observes that in contemporary art's "curiosity about how consciousness is constructed […] Location is a key word […] [telescoping] concerns about where (space) and how (perception)."[12] In Brown's score and dance, the cube mediates between the *how* of visual experience (drawing) and the *where* of space (dancing). Analogizing an empty gallery to "an elastic space we can identify with Mind, modernism's greatest invention,"[13] O'Doherty gives resonance to *Locus*' intellectual construct, the result of interacting, self-contained, and self-generative conceptual, graphic, and kinesthetic processes condensed within its title's definition: "a place where something is situated or occurs" and "the set of points or whose location is determined by one or more specific conditions."[14]

Locus' eight separate pages record permutational principles that create directives for the choreographic scores' realization in movement.[15] Brown's professional biography is elaborated across five sheets,[16] correlated on the cube; some sheets show it elaborately marked with numbered points; one is naked but for numbers 1 to 27 indicated on the cube with an informational sentence written below. Three sheets contain a partial record of the second of the work's four solos, realized in a textual-visual shorthand augmented with stick figures.[17] Recently, eleven sheets notating *Locus*' other solos—numbers 1, 3, and 4—came to light, completing our knowledge of the dance's notation. One page merely contains a rendering of the cube and its internal divisions; two others include small-scale images of the cube together with the same verbal-visual and stick figures that Brown used to notate solo number two. This graphic method continues on the remaining sheets, as Brown applied the same personal style of documentation used in the second solo—until now considered the only extant record of *Locus'* movement.

Brown's indeterminate system is comparable to John Cage's graphic scoring in *Variations I* (1958), whose musical outcome results from overlaying sheets of variable linear configurations on pages marked with 27 points. It leaves open-ended the instruments, their number, and how points and lines translate to sounds and duration.[18] Similarly, Brown's scores do not indicate movement's substance. "The scores," she has said, were "always a reminder for the work, they were not a *representation*," and "tell nothing about the flesh of the piece."[19]

Locus brings the seriality of conceptual art[20] into the scores and choreography. The interrelation of drawing to dance emulates the format of conceptual art as graphic, textual, and numerical instructions—or as documents and certifications of artworks that may or may not be actualized. All-pervasive in sculpture, and in artworks that incorporate the space of art's making and presentation, the cube (and subsidiary notations), recall fabrication drawings by Donald Judd and Dan Flavin, which act as blueprints for realizing three-dimensional objects or installations.

Treated as drawings, separate from the choreography and the dance that they were conceived to *cause*, the scores' visual effect manifests a rejection of drawing's role in showcasing the virtuosity of the artist's hand. Instead the scores reflect an embrace of drawing as a tool for, and record of, systematic thought. The score's appearance and its circulation in publications and exhibitions epitomize the insinuation of visual art into Brown's choreography—and her work's contestation of the dance and drawing binary.

After *Locus'* BAM performance, three sheets of the scores and a photograph by Babette Mangolte illustrated RoseLee Goldberg's 1976 essay "Performance: The Art of Notation" in the art magazine *Studio International*. Noting parallels between art world interest in the "dematerialization of the object" and the ephemeral art of dancing, Goldberg stopped short of comparing *Locus* to conceptual art. Rather, she said that as ephemera produced in the course of realizing ephemeral works (dances), choreographic notations "in no way […] pretend to any aesthetic qualification nor are they considered as *art objects* […] [which] may explain why they get so little exposure."[21] Similarly, French dance scholar Laurence Louppe, writing about the problematic history of dance notation, stated: "Dance notations have no precise cultural status […] [They] have never been the object of official interest, and even less of institutional interest."[22]

This view was contradicted when *Locus* was included in the Yale University Art Gallery exhibition, *Numerals, 1924–1977*, organized by curator Rainer Crone. After opening at the Leo Castelli Gallery in New York, it traveled to eight venues.[23] *Locus* was exhibited accompanied by drawings and musical notations by Brown's contemporaries, all using computational principles, works by Mel Bochner, Carl Andre, John Cage, Hanne Darboven, Dan Flavin, Philip Glass, Donald Judd, Sol Lewitt, Steve Reich, and Robert Smithson.[24] One of Brown's exhibited scores (*Pyramid*, 1975) was purchased by a private collector; and at the Yale exhibition her work was exhibited in relation to many of the same artists who were part of the Castelli-Sonnabend stable, with whom she and her company appeared in major European exhibitions of the early 1970s. Furthermore, recognition of Brown's graphic work continued when an example was shown at the American Pavilion of the Venice Biennale in the 1980 exhibition *Drawing: The Pluralist Decade*,[25] organized by Janet Kardon of Philadelphia's Institute of Contemporary Art, to which the show subsequently traveled.

Over the years, in countless lecture-demonstrations —formal and impromptu—Brown has insisted on the indivisibility of the dance and the drawings, simultaneously performing and verbally explicating *Locus* as a single entity. These repeated acts raise the issue of whether the scores deserve priority over the dance, or vice versa. Demonstrating how Brown's processes for generating choreography paradoxically brought her work (drawing and dance) into visual art's matrix, *Locus*—more than any other of her dances—announces Brown's unprecedented situation as an artist working at the crossroads of dance and visual art.

Locus, Brown's most explicit, historically self-aware investigation of writing's originary role in the definition of choreography, began, she said, with "an idea about a kind of distribution and sequencing of dance in my immediate vicinity" for which she subsequently "invented a score to help [her] do it."[26] *Outside* (1966), her first work based on a geometric framework, is an important antecedent for *Locus*, as Brown recognized when in 1978 she retroactively published a drawing of its simple rectangular structure.[27] *Locus'* genesis dates back to 1972, when, riveted by the problem of gesture's invention, Brown was torn between two opposed models, one systematic, the other improvisational, "a free-wheeling, semi-crazed, now you see it, now you don't form."[28] Abandoning the latter approach, she revisited it in 1975, in scores created to regulate her "highly instinctual system of movement"[29] in an architectural enclosure: this way to be "contained and systematized, but free to dance,"[30] coincided with her move to 541 Broadway.

Brown had previously explored individual dance "planes" in her *Equipment Dances* (1968–1971). She sent dancers walking horizontally across the walls of the Whitney Museum of American Art in 1971; she obviously danced on the floor; and with *Skymap* (1969), she created a spoken word dance for a gallery's ceiling. *Locus'* cubic volume integrates six planes in a single work. Whereas Brown's previous dance scores—derived from architecture or sculpture—merely permitted the body's surface travel between two fixed points, *Locus'* 27 points in space extend the dimensionality of movement even beyond the self-imposed restrictions that defined Brown's solo *Accumulation* (1971), which maintains a frontal, relatively unmoving pose that is violated in a single step backward and a brief forward step away from, and returning to, center.[31] In an interview with Deborah Jowitt, Brown explained: "My preoccupation with a given space—a room a stage or my end of town—is now internalized. It's the understructure of the work."[32]

Brown's approach to space in *Locus* contrasts with Merce Cunningham's belief that "There are no fixed points in space."[33] *Locus'* numbered cube undoes any preestablished numerical framework of gestures (*Accumulation*'s foundation), through a system that produces an (expandable) inventory of 250 movements. Until now Brown's focus had been the invention of choreographic machines that result in gesture as the inevitable result of their structures. The aleatoric quality of *Locus*' score, her most complex dance machine, facilitated the inception of her interest in "dance movement."[34]

If *Locus*' planes circumscribe in advance, and impose limits on movement, the travel between its alphanumeric points produces spatial locomotion, whether vertical, horizontal, diagonal, up, or down. The method remained attached to Cage's emphasis on impersonal artistic choices, and structuralist models. Brown described *Locus* as a squaring of the sphere,[35] referring to Rudolf von Laban's round "kinesphere," devised to "formulate a grammar of motion and a system of notation,"[36] in terms of the body's immediate spatial surround. A January 1975 drawing visualizes this idea through right-angled arm gestures related to *Accumulation*. Also rendered are two overlapping figures in profile, one vertical, the other bent forward at the waist. The squared off positions of arms, torso, and legs, relate to Brown's "plac[ing] a grid on [her] body,"[37] to create "a sphere of personal space."[38] Geometry reduced the "free play" of her "unpredictable and elusive"[39] movement inclinations. This drawing delineates a key dynamic in *Locus*: a conceptualization of the cube's center as the point from which bodily extensions emanate and to which they return, suggesting Brown's interest in human proportion. Her description of *Locus* as embodying a "surrogate classicism" is suggested by an inscription on the cover of the *Locus* sketchbook, where she wrote the name of the first book accurately surveying and measuring ancient Greek architecture, James Stuart and Nicholas Revett's *Antiquities of Athens* (1762–1816).

It is not the transparent relationship between the score and its corporeal rendition, nor one-to-one correspondences between gestures and letters that define *Locus*' importance in Brown's evolution. Rather, it is the failure of translation, the discrepancies between the graphic and the kinesthetic which open a productive gap. Brown did not create fabric linking one move to another. "Movements," she said, "should not be tied together with a connecting movement just because they appear sequentially."[40] Performed without choreographed transitions, each movement has equal weight and the tempo remains even, avoiding the drama of climactic moments, just as Brown's conviction about choreography's self-sufficiency as an art form is reflected in her choice of silence (and breath) as *Locus*' musical accompaniment. In performance, this differing of dance and score, the game of moving from "T" to "R" to "I," generates motion, stimulating Brown's most dance-like movement to date. *Locus*' un-choreographed transitions brought volatility, softness, and fluid slippages. Brown categorized these movements—produced through, yet escaping the score's rigorous inscriptive system—as *dancing*.

Plotting the score, first in a March 1975 drawing, Brown wrote three words of a mundane biographical sentence: "TRISHA BROWN WAS" which continued on the second sheet, "BorN in Aberdeen WASh."[41] The words deliver a sequence of letters. As in *Accumulation*'s mathematics, the vehicle of motion in *Locus* is informational: "I didn't choose the Bible or Rimbaud," she said, "I tried to keep it simple and personal."[42] The relation of letters to numbers creates a numerical sequence (i.e. T = point 20; R = point 18) *and* a spatial sequence ordering movements on the cube. Brown's introduction of an additional computation mitigated confusion about the repetition of an individual letter-number in the score—a key decision, since she was committed to inventing unique movements in a differential language, not a literal vocabulary defined by one-to-one connection between letters, gestures, and points.[43]

The score, Brown told David Sears in 1981, gave her "a certain amount of spatial information,"[44] because "after all the score doesn't make beautiful dance at all—it's just a score."[45] Working in the studio with a square taped to the floor, Brown referenced her numbered cube, visualizing different movement tasks with the idea of linking a succession of points to realize physical and rhythmic patterns. She relinquished a hierarchical attitude toward the body's facings, instructing herself to realize the score's requirements as efficiently as possible, using the body part closest to each point without turning in space or hitting multiple points in one go. A seemingly impossible task might produce an unforeseen physical solution. The ordinary, pedestrian movement is of enhanced difficulty compared to earlier works, and *Locus* required trained dancers.

Importantly, movements/letters do not adjacently accumulate, but are simultaneous. A raised leg is combined with a curved torso or one body part touches a point, while another stays in its current location, as indicated in a notation where a hip, ass, knees, and head simultaneously occupy different points on the cube. In an unusual instruction, the head leads, and clustered points indicate micro-sequential rhythms within the whole. Such juxtapositions and transitions brought elasticity to Brown's language based on the body's natural, logical, and sequential functionality in which the torso is a stable core. Despite contrasts of unison and dis-unison, the performers share a relaxed comportment; photographs by Babette Mangolte show each dancer performing her own movement and orientation to the cube: despite different facings—profile, front, or back—unity is maintained through a common geometricized movement style.

Mangolte likewise highlights *Locus*' differential physical vocabulary: in her images, each dancer's unique iteration of the score amplifies the letter-like properties of movement. The photographs celebrate Brown's cultivation of natural variations, an individual body's imprint on her forms. Critics recognized that movement looked different on each dancer's body.[46] Yet from this disparate information they attempted to extract distinguishing features of Brown's dancing, as this was precisely what *Locus* consolidated and exposed: a rejection of the "pulled up" back of ballet and modern dance; unpointed relaxed feet; the head sitting weightlessly in natural alignment with the spine's movement; the weighted, pendular swing of arms and legs; and the use of joints as hinges through which movement is redirected.[47]

Recognizing the fertility of her score's numerical arrangement, Brown created four different movement sequences —a three-part quartet for her all-female company. This compares to Sol LeWitt's *Incomplete Open Cubes* (1974), an exhaustive exposure of the cube's variant compositional possibilities in different mediums. As a row of four simultaneous solos, *Locus'* first section of four gestural sequences give dancers the freedom to shift between the cube's four faces or onto an adjacent cube. This longest part shows audiences the extent of the score's variations, from different perspectives. In section two, each dancer faces front to perform one of the four sequences. Spatially identical, each differs in its movement and timing. As Mona Sulzman observed, indeterminacy defines section three: dancers choose to face, shift, or draw from, and reorganize, the total movement inventory. Duets, trios, and quartets thus arise spontaneously.[48]

The score's use of a platonic, ideal geometric form, echoes with "Notes on Sculpture" (1966) by Robert Morris, who writes: "Characteristic of a gestalt is that once it is established, all the information about it, *qua* gestalt, is exhausted […] Furthermore, once it is established, it does not disintegrate. One is then both free of the shape and bound to it. Free or released because of the exhaustion of information about it, as shape, and bound to it because it remains constant and indivisible."[49] Despite the cubic gestalt's infrastructural presence, *Locus*' structural principles remained indiscernible, though critic Roger Copeland noted *Locus*' importance as the work in which Brown "reincorporated many of the elements [i.e. dance movement] which had been rigorously excised from her earlier pieces."[50]

Brown saw a widening gap between the score and her dance, owing to practiced repetition, the "aging period."[51] "Of course I don't think you can say, 'Oh I get it, there's a cube, 27 points,' but the planes, the corners, the angles of the dance are much more visible. I think of it as a song."[52] In 1990, she said the elaboration of *Locus* "seemed very cerebral, but it passed into the body, like all dance work passes into the body."[53]

Ultimately Brown abandoned a graphical method of dance scoring: in *Water Motor* (1978), *loci* of memory—a personal narrative, a landscape and atmosphere—informed her free-form treatment of space and exploration of the body's idiosyncratic movement possibilities and timing. This was an embrace of subjectivity's "freeplay" that she rejected when she embarked on *Locus*' making.[54] After its 1976–1978 performances, *Locus* remained the DNA for subsequent choreographies, and an exercise learned by generations of Trisha Brown dancers. Refusing codification of her movement language in anything resembling a "technique," Brown considered *Locus* the closest analogue she had to a barre,[55] a method for warming up body and mind.

In programs of "Early Works" of the 1970s, celebrating the Trisha Brown Dance Company's 40th anniversary season, *Locus* was reprised as a solo, performed by veteran Trisha Brown dancer and one of the company's current Associate Artistic Directors, Diane Madden. In January 2011 Madden danced its entire gestural sequence in the square atrium of The Museum of Modern Art in New York, with a square taped on the floor. Then the *Locus* scores entered the museum's permanent collection of drawings.

Locus' foundation, the "white cube" of visual art, was always inevitably its destination. The museum's guaranteed custodianship of her drawings secured *Locus*' potential to endure. In the museum's collection, Brown's choreography has entered traditions and histories of visual art—albeit with dancing as the absence to which the scores always refer. Brown's choreography contradicts, to theorize in itself, Gabriele Brandstetter's idea that choreography "[…] always includes something of a requiem … This space between the material and the immaterial world opens and closes by means of the gesture of turning, by the torsion of the body which 'holds open the door to the grave.'"[56] With the museum as its permanent home, *Locus*' challenges current focus on dance's literal, inevitable death and unalterable inherent vice of immateriality and disappearance—against which *Locus*' artistic and historical exceptionality announces a singular protest.

[1] Founded by Bénédicte Pesle at Iolas Gallery, Paris, in 1972, Art Services' New York office was established by Mimi Johnson and Jane Yockel. Mimi Johnson, interview with the author, January 30, 2013, New York. Today the organization is known as Performing Art Services, Inc.

[2] See Grand Union Records, Folder 132–28, New York Public Library for the Performing Arts, New York. Goodden performed with Brown's company in the early 1970s.

[3] Thomas Kellein, *The Dream of Fluxus: George Maciunas, An Artist's Biography*, Editions Hansjorg Mayer, London and Bangkok 2007, p. 138; this dates Brown's transaction to March 29, 1974.

[4] Joyce Wadler, "Artists In New York, Article III: Trisha Brown," in *The New York Post*, July 19, 1975. Clipping, review files, Trisha Brown Archive, New York.

[5] Anna Kisselgoff, "Wall Dancer Adds New Dimension," in *The New York Times*, January 8, 1976, p. 26.

[6] Anna Kisselgoff, ibid., and Roger Copeland, "The 'Post-Modern' Choreography of Trisha Brown," in *The New York Times*, January 6, 1978.

[7] Anna Kisselgoff, "Wall Dancer Adds New Dimension," 1976, p. 26.

[8] Rosalind Krauss, "Grids," in *October*, vol. 9, Summer 1979, p. 50–64. Reprinted in Rosalind Krauss, *The Originality of the Avant-Garde and Other Modernist Myths*, The MIT Press, Cambridge (MA) and Boston 1985, p. 13.

[9] Brian O'Doherty, "Inside the White Cube: Notes on the Gallery Space," in *Artforum*, vol. 14, no. 7, March 1976, p. 24–30; Brian O'Doherty, "Inside the White Cube, Part II: The Eye and the Spectator," in *Artforum*, vol. 14, no. 8, April 1976, p. 26–34; Brian O'Doherty, "Inside the White Cube, Part III: Context as Content," in *Artforum*, vol. 15, no. 3, November 1976, p. 36–44.

[10] Brian O'Doherty, *Inside the White Cube: The Ideology of the Gallery Space*, University of California Press, Berkeley and Los Angeles, 1997.

[11] Ibid., p. 100.

[12] Ibid., p. 78.

[13] Ibid., p. 87.

[14] http://www.merriam-webster.com/dictionary/locus.

[15] An additional ninth sheet, reproduces almost exactly the second in the group.

[16] The entire sentence reads "1) TRISHA BROWN WAS 2) BorN IN Aberdeen WAsh 3) INGTON IN 1936 SHE RECEIVED HER BA IN 4) DANCE from MILLS COLLEGE and after taught there 5) At Reed College in Portland Oregon and then as adjunct assistant professor at New YORK UNiVERSity 1967."

[17] These drawings are in the collection of The Museum of Modern Art, New York, while the recently recovered eleven sheets of movement notations for solos 1, 3, and 4 remain in Trisha Brown's personal collection.

[18] David P. Miller, "The Shapes of Indeterminacy in John Cage's *Variations I* and *Variations*," in *FZMw*, vol. 6, 2003, p. 18–48.

[19] Trisha Brown, quoted in RoseLee Goldberg, "Performance: The Art of Notation," in *Studio International*, vol. 192, no. 982, July/August 1976, p. 57.

[20] Mel Bochner, "Serial Art, Systems, Solipsism," in *Arts Magazine*, vol. 41, Summer 1967, p. 39–43. Reprinted in Gregory Battcock (ed.), *Minimal Art: A Critical Anthology*, E.P. Dutton, New York 1968, p. 100: "[…] the idea that the succession of terms (divisions) within a single work, is based on a numerical or otherwise predetermined derivation (progression, permutation, rotation, reversal […])."

[21] RoseLee Goldberg, "Performance: The Art of Notation," p. 58.

[22] Laurence Louppe, "Les imperfections du papier," in Laurence Louppe (ed.), *Traces of Dance: Drawings and Notations of Choreographers*, exh. cat., Dis Voir, Paris 1994, p. 19.

[23] Leo Castelli Gallery, New York, January 7–28, 1978; Yale University Gallery, New Haven/CT, February 14–March 26, 1978; Dartmouth College Museum and Galleries, Hopkins Center, Hanover/NH, April 21–May 21, 1978; University Art Gallery, University of North Dakota, Grand Forks/ND, August 29–September 26, 1978; The Minneapolis College of Art and Design, Minneapolis, October 4–November 1, 1978; Fine Arts Gallery, University of California, Irvine/CA, November 10–December 10, 1978; Art Museum of South Texas, Corpus Christi/TX, January 5–February 4, 1979; Center for the Visual Arts Gallery, Illinois State University, Normal/IL, February 17–March 16, 1979; Center for the Arts, Muhlenberg College, Allentown/PA, March 30–April 28, 1979; The New Gallery of Contemporary Art, Cleveland/OH, May 15–June 15, 1979.

[24] Rainer Crone, *Numerals, 1924–1977*, exh. cat., Yale University Art Gallery, New Haven 1978, n. p.

[25] 39th Venice Biennale, American Pavilion, June 1–September 30, 1980; Institute of Contemporary Art, University of Pennsylvania, Philadelphia, October 4–November 9, 1980; Museum of Contemporary Art, Chicago, May 29–June 26, 1981.

[26] Trisha Brown, lecture-demonstration, undated notes, Trisha Brown Archive, New York.

[27] The score was published in Anne Livet (ed.), "Trisha Brown," *Contemporary Dance. An Anthology of Lectures, Interviews and Essays with Many of the Most Important Contemporary American Choreographers, Scholars and Critics*, Abbeville Press in Association with the Fort Worth Art Museum, New York 1978, p. 45. There, Brown retitled it *Inside* (1966).

[28] Trisha Brown, "Three Pieces," in *TDR–The Drama Review*, vol. 19, no. 1: "The Post-Modern Dance Issue," March 1975, p. 28.

[29] Hendel Teicher and Trisha Brown, "Danse et dessin/Dancing and Drawing," in Corinne Diserens (ed.), *Trisha Brown. Danse, précis de liberté*, exh. cat., Centre de la Vieille Charité/Réunion des musées nationaux, Marseille/Paris, 1998, p. 16.

[30] Trisha Brown, undated typewritten note, Trisha Brown Archive, New York.

[31] See Susan Rosenberg, "Trisha Brown: Choreography as Visual Art," in *October*, vol. 140, Spring 2012, p. 18–44.

[32] Deborah Jowitt, "Reckless Again," in *Village Voice*, May 22, 1978, p. 73.

[33] Quoted in Jacqueline Lesschaeve, *The Dancer and the Dance: Merce Cunningham in Conversation with Jacqueline Lesschaeve*, Marion Boyars, New York and London 1991, p. 18 [1st ed.: 1985].

[34] Lorraine Haacke, "Trisha Brown Dancing Naturally," in *The Dallas Times Herald*, April 11, 1976, n. p.

[35] Hendel Teicher and Trisha Brown, "Danse et dessin/Dancing and Drawing," p. 18.

[36] Katharine Everett Gilbert, "Mind and Medium in the Modern Dance," in *The Journal of Aesthetics and Art Criticism*, vol. 1, no. 1, Spring 1941, p. 110.

[37] Hendel Teicher and Trisha Brown, "Danse et dessin/Dancing and Drawing," p. 16.

[38] Ibid., p. 18.

[39] Ibid.

[40] Trisha Brown, Notebook entry, October 5, 1975, Trisha Brown Archive, New York.

[41] This drawing appears to be "preparatory": a finished version of the same drawing, in a different graphic medium, is part of The Museum of Modern Art collection of the complete *Locus* series. The location of the drawing is unknown today; it had been in the possession of Brown's gallery, Sikkema Jenkins, in New York.

[42] Allen Robertson, "Trisha Brown Dance Company," in *Minnesota*. Unidentified source. Clipping, review files, Trisha Brown Archive, New York.

[43] Rachel Haidu, "I Inhabit the Cube," in Nicholas Baume (ed.), *Sol Lewitt: Structures, 1965–2006*, Yale University Press/ Public Art Fund, New Haven and London/New York 2006, p. 96. Haidu says "Brown is literally substituting movement for letters and thus abstract gesture for communicable content." In fact Brown's system for generating unique gestures ensured that there was *not* a *literal* substitution of movement for letters, but a differential system: each letter's appearance in the overall sentence/numerical sequence results in a new movement.

[44] Trisha Brown interviewed by David Sears, August 29, 1981, New York. Sound cassette. New York Public Library for the Performing Arts, New York.

[45] Anna Kisselgoff, "Dance View: Trisha Brown, Simplicity within Complexity," in *The New York Times*, March 3, 1991. http://www.nytimes.com/1991/03/03/arts/dance-view-trisha-brown-simplicity-within-complexity.html.

[46] Deborah Jowitt, "When I Dance, Who am I?" in *Village Voice*, July 7, 1975, p. 88.

[47] Mindy Aloff, "Review. Performance at Portland Center for Visual Arts (Portland, OR)," 1977, n.p. Unidentified source. Clipping, review files, Trisha Brown Archive, New York.

[48] Mona Sulzman, "Choice/Form: Trisha Brown's *Locus*: A View From Inside the Cube," in *Dance Chronicle*, vol. 2, no. 2, 1978, p. 117–130.

[49] Robert Morris, "Notes on Sculpture," in *Artforum*, vol. 9, no. 6, February 1966, p. 42–44. Reprinted in Gregory Battcock, *Minimal Art*, p. 228.

[50] Roger Copeland, "The 'Post-Modern' Choreography of Trisha Brown," in *The New York Times*, January 4, 1976.

[51] Jean Nuchtern, "Accumulating Trisha Brown," in *SoHo Weekly News*, January 8, 1976. Clipping, review files, Trisha Brown Archive, New York.

[52] Ibid.

[53] Marianne Goldberg, "Du Simple au Complexe," in *Le Bulletin*, no. 5, January 1990, p. 9.

[54] Susan Rosenberg, "Trisha Brown's *Water Motor:* Forever, Now, and Again," in *TDR–The Drama Review*, vol. 56, Spring 2012, p. 150–157.

[55] Trisha Brown, interview with the author, April 17, 2007, New York.

[56] Gabriele Brandstetter, "Choreography as Cenotaph: The Memory of Movement," trans. Andrea Scrima and Rainer Emig, in Gabriele Brandstetter and Hortensia Völckers (eds.), *ReMembering the Body*, Hatje Cantz, Ostfildern-Ruit 2000, p. 104.

Recording the Signs of Life
An Interview with Alan Storey
Katrin Gattinger

This interview took place by email between March and April 2014.

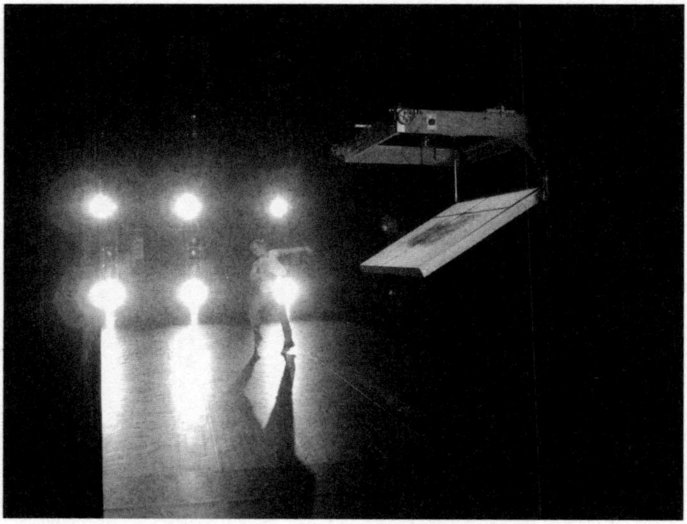

Alan Storey
Device for Drawing The Movements of a Ballerina, 2008
Originally performed by Makaila Wallace at the Queen Elizabeth Theater, Vancouver, 2008

In the work of Alan Storey, inventor of startling mechanical and technological systems, movement is a constant element. Known for his large mobile installations that take over architectural and social space and establish relationships between people and their environment, the artist has developed in parallel a body of "drawing machines," the common feature of which is that they record line movements of very different origins: those tied to variations in climatic conditions (*Climatic Drawing Machine*, 1990), those of the viewers moving to and fro watching the drawings being produced (*Thirteen*, 1991), or even those proper to the machine (*Draw*, 1984; *Handle with Care*, 1991). The following interview focuses mainly on *Device for Drawing the Movements of a Ballerina* (2008), a drawing performance for which Storey has designed a machine capable of transmitting by infrared the motions of a ballerina dancing to *The Four Seasons* by Antonio Vivaldi.

A large drawing of the deployment of the dancer's body through space and time is then produced live above the stage. Storey sees in the drawing a record not just of the dancer's movements, but also of the emotional history of shifting through the four seasons. Here, the artist looks back at the making of this collaborative work and gives his point of view on the affinity between drawing and dance that is at the heart of this experiment.

* * *

KATRIN GATTINGER For the last 30 years you have been producing large-scale, mechanically animated mobile installations as well as drawing-in-progress exhibitions. Why is movement so important in your work?

ALAN STOREY I grew up in a fairly animated world. My father was a physics teacher, but also a builder of things. Half of the house that he built when I was a child was a workshop in which he/we built sailboats, airplanes, and his main extended hobby: early baroque musical instruments such as harpsichords, clavichords, virginals etc. I engaged in the design and building process and very little was ever static. Subsequently in my ongoing practice of making art, movement and mechanical functionality became inherent. Time and spatial perceptions have always interested me. I don't make things to move just to make them more interesting. I make things that move or react to forces and parameters of the given situation, or circumstances of time and space. This entices a broader interaction, exploration, and questioning.

KG Regarding your drawing machines, could you tell us how the drawing relates to their creative process? Is it a recording, a map, a trace, or maybe a digest of the event?

AS The drawings primarily are a digest of the event or circumstances that the drawing machine has been set up in. They become a historical record of the creative process. In creating the device, I am working with a set of parameters and controls based on the contextual situation. Once the device functions with the rules I set, then a large part is ultimately left to chance in the outcome.

KG Why did you choose, for some drawing machines, to delegate the graphic work to a third element, over and above the mechanisms, to set them off, such as the wind and atmospheric variations in *Climatic Drawing Machine*?

AS My interest is in the relation of external forces that are used in parameters that are set for certain circumstances. All of the drawing machines have some inherent context that they are created for, and the curation by me of the forces that work together to cause the drawing itself about itself and its existence. *Climatic Drawing Machine* is based on a hygrothermograph, the device that one finds inside galleries and museums to monitor the climatic conditions inside a building designed for art. My *Climatic Drawing Machine* is built specifically to be in context outside the art gallery/museum. It is partially a comment on that context … and in turn it is set to monitor the conditions that are exterior to the gallery. Our Canadian climate through winter can be quite brutal. I was asked to create a work that would stand outside the art center [the Power Plant, Toronto] throughout the winter season. It seemed entirely appropriate to make the work about monitoring the climate conditions to which it would be subjected, and to create a question about process and climate change. The gallery staff was instructed to change the paper every two weeks, just like the hygrothermograph inside.

Each drawing device varies in its circumstance, but they all utilize external elements or forces that tie them to their given situation.

KG If that means that the *Climatic Drawing Machine*'s drawing is produced by the same climatic variations that are usually considered as a threat to the preservation of artworks, how does this work for your other projects?

AS Other projects such as *Handle with Care* (the drawings are produced by sudden movement during their transport) and *Thirteen* (the drawings are produced by the comings and goings of the spectators who approach them) utilize external forces in a relevant way so as to comment on or point out a questioning process about how and what they are doing. For *Handle with Care*, there was in fact different handling language on the outside of each crate, as one crate had "This Side Up" written on one side with arrows pointing up on the four sides and then "Other Side Up" on the bottom, another crate had "Other Side Up" written on all six sides so that when it was encountered in the loading dock the transport worker would turn the crate over, and then perhaps over again. The response to the handling language was an important external input for the drawing(s).

KG With *Device for Drawing the Movements of a Ballerina*—that you produced with Makaila Wallace from the British Columbia Ballet in 2008 in Vancouver—it is surprising to see in the end that you again gave responsibility for the drawing to human movement! Why did you make this choice and what made you choose dance in particular?

AS *Device for Drawing the Movements of a Ballerina* was made for a specific performance by the British Columbia Ballet of Vivaldi's *The Four Seasons.* It was a large drawing device based on an x-y plotter that had a horizontal drawing surface of approximately 2 × 3 m, basically the proportions of the stage. It was suspended 8 meters above the stage and the front edge of the canvas was visible to the audience as just a white line against the black background. The audience could perceive that something was happening in the device, but could not see what it was. There was also an infrared camera suspended above the stage with the drawing device. It pointed straight down and had the entire stage floor as its scope. The lead dancer had an infrared LED emitter array woven into the bun of her hair that was detectable by the camera. All of her movements were then transposed onto the drawing surface by the pen in the device above. In the last 2 minutes of the performance the drawing device was lowered to 2 meters above the floor and it then opened up to reveal the drawing in the last 30 seconds.

Vivaldi's *The Four Seasons* is a timeline of one's travels through life, as an analogy, through the four seasons of life. The final drawing, revealed at the end of winter, traced a history of the movements of the dancer as she completed her meanderings, and in turn, a metaphor for her emotional progression through the four seasons. This means her journey through life is expressed emotionally, through the line and the music as a metaphor. The drawing becomes a document of this.

I was asked to be the set designer for the project on the premise that there would be some kind of drawing analogy to the tracing of the timeline of life's journey. The piece developed out of the circumstances at hand and what was needed to accomplish the brief.

KG Finally, do you see an analogy between the drawing and what you call "life's journey"?

AS Yes, for the *Device for Drawing the Movements of a Ballerina*, in the context of the work this is a clear representational analogy. Other drawing machine works record their own life or existence. In a sense they are machines with a life of their own, which document in the linear form of ink on paper/wall/surface and as an analogy of the journey of their own life.

KG As a focal point for the drawing, you chose Makaila Wallace's bun—and thus the central axis of her body. This shows that you are more interested in her movement in space than in her gestures: can you explain why?

AS In this particular project it was indeed more about the overall movement through time (life) and space and the analogy to the four seasons, rather than her more intimate gestural detail.

KG Knowing the process the drawings originated from stimulates the imagination. The expressiveness of "scribble" drawing is paralleled by a narrative whose threads can't be disentangled, as we receive it all at once, or rather in the form of a slightly diffuse cloud. It seems to me that you are able to deconstruct a rational production principle through the visual complexity of its result, in the same way that the drawings appear to undo the rigor of the ballet. Do you agree?

AS Yes, the drawing becomes a kind of liberated document. You are right in saying that knowing the process opens the interpretive door of imagination, but in itself it defines a rational production principle.

KG In your drawing machine projects, the drawings can't be dissociated from their production process. However, if we attempt to read what the *Device for Drawing the Movements of a Ballerina* says about dance, we notice that the trace of movement doesn't correspond to our perception of the dancer: the nervous, haphazard scribble is in strong contrast with the ballerina's graceful gestures and movements in the *Four Seasons*. Is the visual dissonance between two elements that nonetheless coincide a way for you to draw attention to other discrepancies?

AS Perhaps. It is of course conceptual to relate the line to her dancing, although it is derived from it—it is still only linked to the idea of a path.

KG Unlike your other drawing machines, *Device for Drawing the Movements of a Ballerina* doesn't use the impulse from a movement to trace the drawing directly: there is no contact between the mobile body and the drawing's support, as the movement is remotely transmitted. Wallace operates like an infrared graphics tablet pen, more than as a "living pen." Do you want to avoid drawing by direct contact with the human body at all costs?

AS No, not at all. It was simply a practical methodology to use as the tool or medium in order to draw the movement. I would disagree that although there is no physical contact between the dancer and the pen; she is still emotionally, gesturally, and inherently intrinsically attached by the input into the infrared emitter on her head, just as the hand may hold and have the direct input to the pen for the tablet. My subsequent work *The White Spider* (2010) had the dancer directly attached by strings to the drawing device.

KG Looking more closely at the drawing made by the ballerina and your ingenious "machine," we can detect the consequences of the protocol through the tracing: several lines seem to take the same paths. Why did you decide that the drawing of the choreography would be produced by a sequence of six evening performances on the same support?

AS It was somewhat incidental. I had planned on a new piece of canvas for each performance. The choreographer Jennifer Mascall was frankly a bit disappointed: the drawing lacked density and visibility after the first full dress rehearsal. A decision was made to add to the same drawing, each performance thereafter, and to use a different color pen each time. In doing this it extended the timeline/lifeline drawn in the *Four Seasons* to the life of the overall performance(s).

KG That means that your choices are also partially guided by the aesthetics of the final drawing. Is this the case for your other drawing machines? If so, what are the aesthetic data that you are looking for?

AS There is a certain aesthetic consideration in the setting up of the circumstances, but a lot is left to chance. What I am most interested in seeing in the line is the distinctive quality that expresses an action or interaction in an empathetic way: a line or squiggle that expresses the interplay of the external forces on the machine/device and its existence. Like an EEG machine or a seismograph, they are recording the signs of life in the nuance of the lines through pulses and vibration. It becomes even more aesthetically interesting when layers and other patterns start to emerge out of the apparently random action.

KG What kind of other patterns are you thinking of?

AS I think a lot about various apparent random actions, which inevitably develop into patterns that are not seen until the passage of a time interval and in the record it. This has a certain intrigue. Cyclical patterns that generate a whole new level of the "lifeform" and another layer of realization. Intertwined with this, I have an inherent interest and corollary response to patterns that come out of the ocean currents, the wind, the atmosphere, or even from the wheels of a car on a dirt road as it creates a ribbed "washboard" pattern on the road surface that also develops over time. I am intrigued by interference patterns that happen from overlapping wave forms, whether in fluid, or light, or sound formations, etc. for example a moiré pattern between two pieces of perforated metal panels—which can be seen in a few of my public works. But back to dance, similarly, I see the movement intertwined in the same way.

KG From a graphic point of view, don't the six repetitions of the drawing on the same support cancel the apparent spontaneity of the gesture, giving a mechanical quality to the living body's movements?

AS Yes, somewhat. It had some interesting aspects to it though, of self-referencing the consecutive performances. The machine started to delineate subtle variations in Makaila's movements on the stage and developed some interesting analytical processing as to her more refined movements. However the drawing became more muddled and "cloud-like" as you say as the timeline went on. If I were to do this work again I would limit it to perhaps two or three performances per drawing.

KG In *Device for Drawing the Movements of a Ballerina*, the drawing device is suspended above the stage during the performance, where it can be seen by the audience who only discovers the final drawing at the end of the choreography. As with the *Handle with Care*, where the drawings are shown after the crates have arrived at the dock, you reveal them once they are made. Why do you prevent the audience from following the drawing being traced as the dancer moves around?

AS I felt that seeing the drawing being done during the performance might trivialize the actions of both the dancer and the drawing device, and be a distraction to the dance and overall performance. We did in fact have the device start out in the lowered position for the first minute or so, so that the audience was aware of its presence. It was a dance performance with very distinctive music about a timeline of a life of loves and tragedy through the analogy of the four seasons. The dance was primary, and the real-time drawing was a complement to it to be revealed to her and the audience at the end, as an envelope of time looking back at the story/history.

KG What similarities do you perceive between drawing and dancing?

AS In the *Device for Drawing the Movements of a Ballerina* project it was more about the record of something, the timeline as the analogy of the seasons of life. It was not so much about gesture, but about the passage of a life.

Of course there are different dances and different drawings. Some similarities that I find are intertwined like when a gestural movement and a gestural expression in a line can evoke a strong emotional response. The line in its intrinsic formation from a defined input of expression can be very similar to the movements and gestures of the dancers' expressions of emotion, torment, love, etc. A big difference lies in the fact that when the dance is finished it is dispersed, or "gone."

In my other dance-related work for *White Spider* it is much more about the gesture and movement and about the ephemeral nature of the dance performance. During a three and half minute segment in this work the dancer Darcy McMurray was directly connected by several ropes from parts of her body to the drawing device, like a reverse puppet. Her movements were choreographed very specifically, and the seemingly very arbitrary and very gestural segment of the dance produced the word "GONE" on the paper. This was a very deliberate statement relative to the ephemeral nature of dance, in that it is performed in a flurry of emotional gesture and exhilarating effort (sometimes) and then it is gone.

There were many things in this project that were speaking to and about dance itself and about the medium as it is worked between performers and audience. The context of the work was in mountain climbing vernacular, so the dancer being attached to the drawing device up overhead by dangling ropes gives the work the appropriate notional attachment.

KG Philosopher Michel Guérin describes dance as a "recreation, a deliverance from goals."[1] It is based on the desire to explore movement for itself. Do you think that the drawing from *Device for Drawing the Movements of a Ballerina* captures this detachment by transposing the ballerina's journey while looking like "nothing"?

AS Yes, sort of. Indeed it is a "recreation, and a deliverance from goals," but recording the history of a dance as a gesture in a drawing process intrinsically brings a solution of some substance, even if just for a moment as they relate to each other. I think the second (dance) work, *White Spider*, is actually more about this. The drawing device fleetingly gives the seemingly arbitrary exploration of movement, choreography, and "nothingness" a rational moment in creating the word "GONE," which is produced by the drawing device from the very gestural and expressive movements just as the dance part disappears, and is in fact gone forever.

[1] Michel Guérin, *Philosophie du geste*, "Le génie du philosophe," Actes Sud, Paris 1995, p. 64. In comparison with other gestures (do/make, give, write) that the philosopher explores, dance seems to be the only gesture without a link to the external world; it seems to be "just expression; which does not mean it expresses something, even freedom," p. 63. Trans. Christian Roy.

From Movement to Line
An Interview with Laetitia Legros
Magali Le Mens

This interview took place by email between May and December 2014.

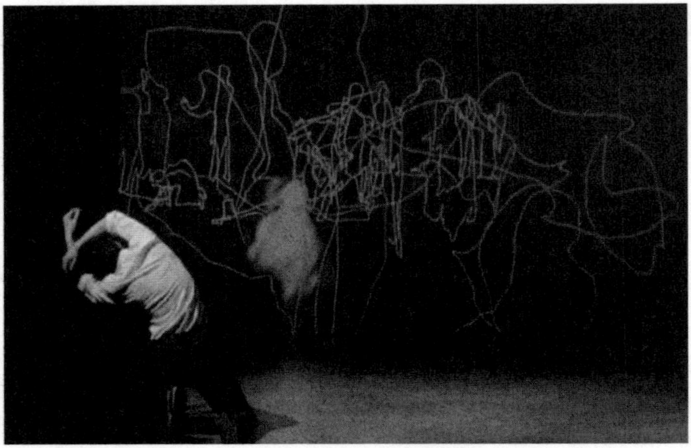

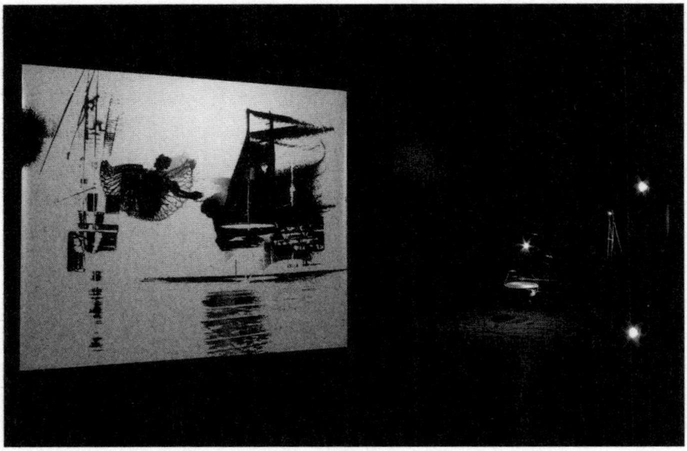

Laetitia Legros
Entre un œil et l'autre–Variation chorégraphique #1 pour tracé, 2007
Super-8 film, transferred to 35 mm film and Beta, black and white, 12'30
Choreography: Olivier Balzarini

Machine à dessiner, 2008
Installation, interactive drawing device; motor, metallic structure, leds, camera, image programming, projection on suspended screen

The artistic output of Laetitia Legros takes shape in different mediums. Through moving and still images, it is as if she were freeing herself from a long tradition of immobility in the visual arts, which is usually considered to reach as far back as one of the origins of art, when Callirhoe, the daughter of the clay modeler Butades, struck on the idea of fixing the outline of her lover's shadow onto a wall.[1] What was important was not the gesture of tracing the outline, but the possibility of conserving an image.

For Legros, the image (drawn, filmed, photographic, or digital) is just as important as the movement that summons or gives birth to it. That movement is visible even when it is fixed by a support, as in *Photogramme* (2003), in which she traces the outline of her shadow by hanging a sheet of light-sensitive paper on the wall. In her film *Entre un œil et l'autre – Variation chorégraphique #1 pour tracé* (2007), the artist follows the movements of a dancer with the tip of a pencil. *Machine à dessiner* (2008) features a film drawing, i.e., on a hanging screen, a play of marks and lines includes the visitor's movements in a graphic composition animated by the circular movement of a machine. In the photograph *IN FINE IN FINI – Templum* (2011–2012), the passage of a woman washing a tiled floor reveals the subtle geometrical balance of a building's architecture.

In each of the pieces mentioned above, it is movement—of the artist herself, the dancer, the visitor, or the subject of the depiction—that generates line. The movement's two graphic representations, that of the body, on the one hand, and of the drawing, on the other, engender a correspondence as if to extend one thing in the other.

* * *

MAGALI LE MENS In terms of *Machine à dessiner*, I can't really grasp in what way it has more to do with the drawing than the recording of the digital image. You say that it is a machine that composes a drawn transcription of the filmed space in real time.

LAETITIA LEGROS *Machine à dessiner* is the title of the piece. Whereas the drawing takes the form of a digital image, that title consciously raises the question of what is being shown, while choosing to make the piece resonate with what is usually understood by "a drawing machine."

The drawing does partly involve a mechanical process that operates directly in the image through a camera and a certain treatment of the filmed image. The sculptural light device installed on the floor is the key component of the image-drawing. Mounted on a kind of turntable that turns one complete revolution per minute, the sculpture consists of a play of metallic lines articulated around a single axis; outside its perimeter it bears a vertical rod that will cyclically sweep the image with a light reflection. Conceived as something between an opening out and a flattening of a spatialized drawing, this structure was designed to support and generate a light scan sweeping the room thanks to three LEDs distributed around the metallic axes. In the foreground of the shot, the light machine produces lines in the image thanks to its circular movement and the play of its light. The camera is positioned on the floor so that it favors a juxtaposition of the different components of the image: the machine in the foreground, the visitor in the middle ground, the architecture in the background. *Machine à dessiner* is also a machine for transposing space onto a flat surface, a plan view, and plays with that flattening to compose the image-drawing. Here the drawing is thought of in terms of the construction of space, both by the lines of a particular architecture and our own movements. It is conceived by considering the stable and mobile constructions of the space. The machine comes to occupy that in-between place, as if to question this complicity and sharpen our perception.

It is also about exploring what we understand by "drawing," advancing several questions or positions. To what extent can a digital texture generated by an image-recording device become a drawing? That is what motivated my research and the development of this device, but I also sought to allow the image to "emerge" thanks to the process that was used. The drawing is what is playing out in the image. In the established storyline, at first it is line, which then tends toward a photographic process, before finally dissolving in a play of digital texture. It is then an experience of line, at the meeting point of a mechanism and a piece of image-processing software. The drawing goes through several states that can produce connections with its history and run through different concepts of it, or even invite us to place certain experiences that concern the image in the field of drawing. I'm thinking, for example, of the work of Étienne-Jules Marey, in particular *Man With a Silver Button—Stereoscopic Trajectory of a Bright Point Placed at the Lumbar Vertebrae of a Man Who is Walking Away From the Camera, a Slow Trot and a Slow Walk, Stereoscopic Photographs* (1884)—a photographic experiment in which the constant movement of the reflecting point in dark space produces an enigmatic linear trace simply through the absence of any other element except the fluid line; or the chronophotograph of the *Man in a Black Suit* (1883), the graphic division of the movement of a man seen in profile showing straight lines attached to his clothes running between the main joints. The treatment of the image generated by the *Machine à dessiner* might suggest these initial photographic experiments but also, in specific instances, digital textures akin to certain video experiments of Nam June Paik, for example.

In *Machine à dessiner*, the drawing goes from a sensation of a line drawn with a brush to dark patches of black, verges on a pictorial line, or conjures up different technical gestures, from the fluid elasticity of an India ink to the denser stroke of an ink used in printmaking. There is something of a tactile and gestural relationship with a black pigment that is consumed as it is applied, leaving the line in a state of beginning. The body can leave a short-lived print or a series of lines similar to a breakdown of movement. The line is produced by light; it points us to the experience of photography (in an etymological approach, "writing with light"). Occasionally there is that feeling of an image being slowly revealed in the chemical bath. I am also thinking of *Light-Space Modulator* (1922–1930) by László Moholy-Nagy, and his experiments in comprehending space through light, movement, and rhythm in a relationship of construction or dynamic composition between space and the pictorial ground.

In the *Machine à dessiner* installation, it is the experience of space that causes an experience of line. I create a distance with the mechanical drawing machines like the ones introduced by Jean Tinguely, while inserting a small-scale mechanical sculpture at the heart of the device. Its tracing out of lines, however, occurs through considerations of parameters that are more about a transcription of space. Installing the device therefore requires a certain conformity with a chosen space. The arrangement of the various elements with respect to one another, the intervention of light, and the framing of the scene by the camera all have their importance.

MLM Does the captor only record certain aspects of the movement of the subjects and objects present?

LL Yes, but there isn't any captor other than the camera, whose images go through a combination of treatments, a programing—like a score I've composed that matches the pace of the machine's sweeping light. That sequence lasts around nine minutes; it begins with a blank screen on which the light machine, sitting on the floor, activates short-lived traces. Treatment of the image depends above all on the lighting of the room, so I decided to push that condition to the extreme by starting from a dark space in which I compose using points of light that are either fixed or in motion. The nature of visitors' inscription depends on the moment they arrive and the different parameters linked to their presence in the field covered by the recording (positioning in space, light, speed).

MLM Is it the machine's continuous movement that makes it similar to the line of a drawing since it works on the recorded image?

LL Yes. It is really the machine that generates the line in the image, by setting the points of light and the lines in motion. The continuous movement of the machine interacts with the parameters of the programming and lends a constant, perceptible graphic transcription in the meeting points of the light, the tool doing the recording, and the narrative of the graphics.

MLM When we see you in your film *Entre un œil et l'autre – Variation chorégraphique #1 pour tracé* drawing the outlines of a dancer and his gestures transparently on a vertical piece of glass, it is a continuous line. Could you clarify what that continuous line represents for you?

LL That continuous line links space and time in the same visual unity. While it pursues and delineates the dancer's shifts and movements, it seems to be running after time and looking to catch in the same net what is playing out before our eyes. It's like a screen capture, a way of recording. But what interests me is that contradiction between a continuous recording in real time, fully anchored in the present, and a transcription that is open to the imaginary and the improbable. That line is deployed through a device that is specific to the issues raised by representation (see the artifices for creating perspective described by Jean Du Breuil in his book *La perspective pratique*, notably a schema entitled "Une très belle invention pour faire naturellement de la perspective sans en garder les règles" [1679][2]: which shows a draftsman sketching a perspectival view using a transparent device). However, it would be hard to view the result as a representation. It is rather a translation, a recording whose length and process of outlining a silhouette in motion breaks down and juxtaposes events that could, by their sequence, conjure up a narrative or storyline. The continuous line weaves an invisible, nonexistent scene, despite a form of recording that aims to be as close as possible to the subject.

Lines are a supple, malleable form of delineation, which the body is led to direct and work on. In the film, the dancer in a way sculpts his dancing through line; he produces a double graphic representation, of the body in space and of line. The important point about this constraint binding us is that the drawing going on at the time influences the choreographic representation and vice versa.

The continuous line is a way of communicating with the dance. The line is a graphic representation that is divided between dance and drawing. It is the record of a movement from one place to another inscribed in a space, and it is the method that generates the form. The performance produces a line that develops like a landscape sculpted by the body.

This method can give rise to multiple variations, including on the basis of the same scenario; the whole interest of this performance was to foster an experience involving two people.

Thanks to its length, this line also gives us an indication of time. In this case, it corresponds to the length of time of the film sequence, give or take a few seconds.

MLM In your film *Entre un œil et l'autre – Variation chorégraphique #1 pour tracé* and in the *Machine à dessiner* installation, could we say that the final image is of little importance?

LL In both cases the drawing is elaborated by a device that is developed through an attentive and permanent back-and-forth shift between graphic restitution and work on the space (storyline, staging, light, distances, movement of the body, speed). The time of the drawing becomes a material that is active in a search for complicity between a graphic method and an arrangement of elements, actions, or phenomena that are fully part of the process of drawing the line.

The device is designed for the cinematographic image in both cases. Existing between dance and drawing, and conceived in terms of filming for *Entre un œil et l'autre …* , the performance yields the creation of a drawing that becomes part of a whole. *Machine à dessiner* produces an image in which the drawing comes to be understood in a perpetual renewal. What is at stake in the drawing is the enigmatic character of its development, the unforeseen part that can occur in a "result" whose process is worked out before our eyes. The drawing is a quest… It tends to capture what slips away. It takes shape in the present and is inscribed in an activation of thought and images.

MLM So it is not only your hand that allows itself to be carried along by the movement, since your eye also allows itself to be surprised by the gesture of the cleaning woman wielding a mop to clean the floor (in the photograph *IN FINE IN FINI – Templum*). Seen from above, it is no longer as if she were looking to clean a surface, but rather to gradually cover it with a reflecting substance that reveals the geometrical qualities of the architectural space. A square appears within the square. Could you come back to that mobility of gestures and the gaze? Or to the question of the freedom from immobility, as you see it?

LL In the film *Entre un œil et l'autre …* when I draw the movements of a dancer as he glides around a set I record the outlines of his silhouette, yet my eye at some point might also be carried away by another drawing, the invisible drawing that the dancer seems to trace in space, the line stretching between the points he makes with his gestures and movements (the tips of the feet, hands, or joints). The choreographic representation plays out in an awareness of three main pictorial planes, the drawing created on a transparent plane, the surface of the ground, and the filmed image.

I was fascinated by the gesture of that woman cleaning the floor because both my point of view at that moment and the distance from the subject put me in a situation of observation that allowed me to appreciate at once the cadence of the movement, which a pictorial gesture entails. What is playing out from my position opens that short scene to questions of a plastic, pictorial, performative, and choreographic nature, which are activated in the need to do the various shots.

The photograph is installed on site, hung on the wall of an old factory in a building of the Direction régionale des affaires culturelles Nord-Pas-de-Calais. It calls for a certain mobility of the eye on the part of the employees or the public in the venue, who can also take the point of view of the sequence. From one side of the passage, the photographic image is located within the tangent of the eye and from the other, the void, the space that simply drops off, and the tiling of the ground floor, whose reflection is regularly reactivated by an employee on duty in an established time slot.

This reflection places the body on the edge of an "opening" that suggests certain views of archeological digs that have fed into a project developed in the context of an art commission. The body seems to be laid down within the grid. The object of the photograph is not only what is playing out in the reflection, it is also the mobility of our bodies, the finality of our movements, the way our body bends to the space, our activities, and how it comes to punctuate space and time with a certain precision.

By going from a dance-drawing-film relationship to *Machine à dessiner*, and then to the photography of a gesture that generates line while underscoring and participating in the rigor of an architectural motif, I point drawing toward space, the contact of the body, and movement.

I can't say if I'm looking more to free myself from immobility or to work with mobility, but I think it is the latter hypothesis that leads to the former. My work has developed in that sense from the moment I did a drawing experiment with the constraint of not lifting the pencil from the paper. Three 1 × 1 m drawings were done on the same subject. Experiencing the continual movement of the point of a felt-tip pen tracing out a path over a large-format sheet of paper offers a feeling of freedom that is questioned at the same time. This method based on an uninterrupted trace involves an immediacy and a kind of letting go while questioning the line's destination constantly, combining anticipation and adaptation to what is being built, in view of an overall intention bound up with representation.

This experience led me to work using transparency, vertically, and on large plastic surfaces, confronting a situation of observing movement as part of a class offering art students an approach to contemporary choreography. The experiment came fully into its own in that unexpected and stimulating connection with the present and with movement.

That question of mobility also runs through the subjects or the form of the artworks realized, not as an objective, but as a consideration that is inescapable because it animates the work and forces it to find a form of stability. It is about working with the subject's mobility as much as the observer's. The recording devices installed in the venue are often questioned in their intention to freeze an image or their capacity to do so. This empty intention cultivates a necessary pursuit, through that which is going to generate the impermanence of the subject in the graphic representation underway.

[1] See Pliny the Elder, *Natural History*, vol. XXXV, paragraph 15. Butades is sometimes called Dibutades; Callirhoe is also known as Core or Kora in various versions of the story.

[2] Jean Du Breuil, *La perspective pratique, nécessaire à tous Peintres, Graveurs, Sculpteurs, Architectes, Orphèvres, Brodeurs, Tapissiers, & autres qui se meslent de desseigner, Par un Religieux de la Compagnie de Jésus. Première partie. Seconde édition. Reveuë, corrigée & augmentée par l'Auteur en plusieurs endroits…*, Antoine Dezallier, Paris 1679.

EXPLORING

Dancescaping. Anna Halprin

Sarah Burkhalter

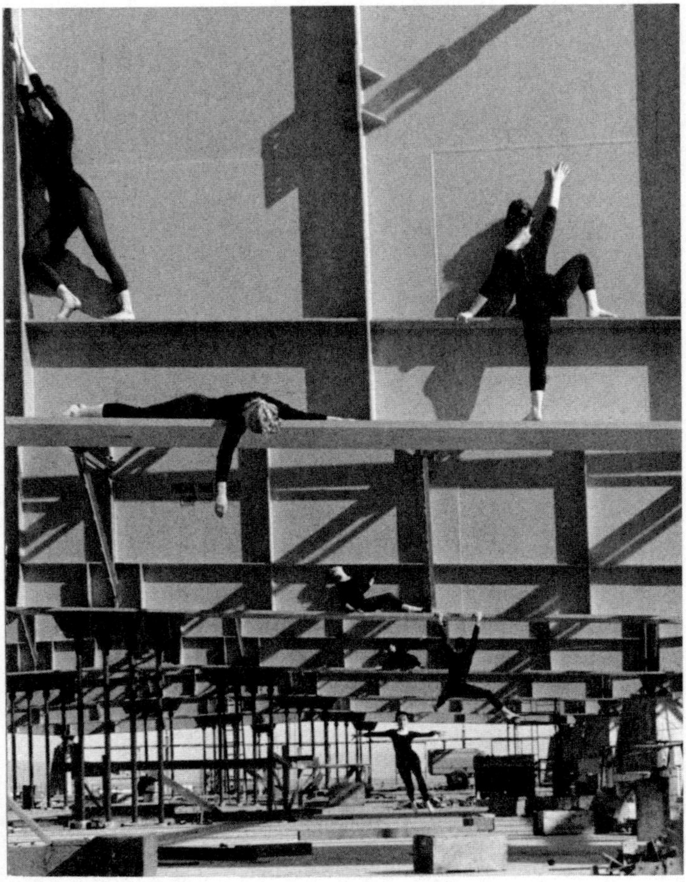

Anna Halprin
Hangar, San Francisco airport, 1957
Improvisation by Anna Halprin, Simone Forti, John Graham, Jenny Hunter Groat, A. A. Leath, Norma Leistiko, and an unknown dancer
Black and white photography by William B. Heick

In the spring of 1945, Anna Halprin[1] excitedly envisioned her future as a dancer in the uncharted territory of northern California. On the West Coast of the United States she was about to join her husband, Lawrence Halprin, who would eventually pick up his work as a landscape architect once again after serving in the Pacific during the War. Writing from New York City, she confided in a letter to a friend her hopes about the "wild open spaces"[2] promised by their move to San Francisco: "I want to be left alone, live a normal resourceful life with a connection to the soil and to the common pulse of the ordinary people," she stated. "I'm only interested in creating out of the soil and the people a healthy fresh dance that is alive and vital. I'm getting so sick and tired of New York dance—it's neurotic, eccentric, and in many cases stale, and in most cases uninspired. I'm not being smug—I don't say I can do better—but I do say New York itself breeds a warped kind of dance." In what stands as a sweeping diagnosis, Halprin was ready to escape the degenerative fate of her art, unsettled as she was by the American modern dance establishment in which aesthetic cloning and choreographic clans were thriving. She was eager to regenerate her dance from the ground up, away from formal preconceptions, amid a community of people, and in line with the land and its rhythm.

An outdoor dance deck came to embody this vision. Built by Lawrence Halprin and Arch Lauterer between 1953 and 1954, it fostered some of the most radical explorations in the fields of the performing arts, visual arts, pedagogy, therapy, and ritual, epitomizing the initiatory improvisations that grew into the Judson Dance Theater. It first and foremost expanded Anna Halprin's experience of dance and daily life. Here she was empowered to draw from the natural environment the articulations, figures, and textures she had longed for while living in the highly choreographed grid of Manhattan.

In 1954, Halprin once more relocated her research into movement from an urban setting, this time from San Francisco to the woods of Mount Tamalpais. She soon recognized how the surroundings affected her kinesthetic awareness. Dwelling with her family on the same compound as her dance studio, she tuned her artistic practice to the botanical and geological processes around her, crafting her movement much as a landscaper responds to the earth. The deck deeply reconfigured her subsequent use of space and force, task and form, improvisation and imagery—and ultimately, her sense of self. "It was the most marvelous space, and shocking, because I'd never danced in a space that wasn't rectangular," she observed.[3] "You just become part of that environment [...] It's your own nature being part of a larger nature [...] I find that this changes your internal sense of selfness."[4] Choreographic logic thus shifted from moving within a static cube to "movement within a moving space,"[5] which Merce Cunningham acknowledged in a lecture-demonstration on the deck in 1957, "There is no necessity to face 'front,' to limit the focus to one side."[6] The scope of action became all encompassing. In step with Halprin and those who worked with her, including Simone Forti (then Morris), Jenny Hunter Groat, John Graham, and A. A. Leath, it shifted from product and repertoire to focus on potential and process, thereby yielding participatory events.

To this day Halprin perceives the land through dance and sources movement material from it, in a practice akin to "dancescaping," which is understood here as a method of generating performance from the given dynamics of a place, the people who inhabit it, the images it instills, and the politics it channels. Of particular interest in this essay are the spatial and pictorial roots of this responsiveness. Although choreography now lies outside Halprin's value system,[7] the graphic medium has always remained at the core of her method, calling forth this study of pieces selected from seven decades of performance, as well as writings, recordings, and workshops. It appears that the "dancescape" quality of Halprin's work stems from the kinesthetic acuity she gained in Margaret H'Doubler's classes at the University of Wisconsin and from early exposure to architecture through her husband at Harvard University in the 1940s. It then developed throughout the off-stage and on-site experiments typical of the late 1950s and early 1960s summer sessions, which were seminal for a number of artists such as Trisha Brown, Ruth Emerson, Simone Forti, Robert Morris, and Yvonne Rainer. Finally, dancescaping indicates Halprin's reliance on scoring and drawing in relation to performance, both of which configure and reflect through word, chart, or image the performer's interaction with the environment, and continue to play distinctive roles in her creative process and pedagogy.

Making Space for Kinesiology, Aesthetics, and Tasks

Mining the body's articulation and musculature was H'Doubler's signature premise in bringing young dancers to kinesthetic awareness, as she did with Halprin, her student at the University of Wisconsin from 1938 to 1942. Modeled as investigations and empirical problem solving, the exercises led the dancers to think on their feet, freeing them from mirroring a set style, and prompting them to generate autograph movement. "She instilled in me a passion for true movement, and a fierce dedication to dance that people can do in their own way," Halprin has noted,[8] causing her in turn to "work from the bone," as Meredith Monk observed during the 1965 summer workshop in Kentfield.[9] Such sensorial probing, allied with clear motor instructions, led the way to the task-based aesthetics that permeated post-modern dance in the United States.

Halprin's assertions owe much to John Dewey's ideas in *Art as Experience* (1934). Dewey indeed valued the experiential substance of the arts, recognizing the indistinctness of mind and body, and their ensuing codependence in artistic activity. "When we view the arts from the standpoint of media of expression, the broad distinction that confronts us is between the arts that have the human organism, the mind-body, of the artist as their medium and those which depend to a much greater extent upon materials external to the body: automatic and shaping arts so-called."[10] Uniting dancing, singing, yarn-spinning, bodily scarifications, and tattoos under the same heading of "automatic arts," he continues:

> Modern taste tends to reckon as higher the fine arts that reshape material, where the product is enduring instead of fugitive [...] in contrast with the limitation of singing, dancing, and oral storytelling to an immediate audience. But all rankings of higher and lower are, ultimately, out of place and stupid. Each medium has its own efficacy and value [...] [The] movements of the individual body enter into all reshapings of material. When these movements carry over in dealings with physically external matters the organic push from within of an automatic art, they become, in so far, "fine." Something of the rhythm of vital natural expression, something as it were of dancing and pantomime, must go into carving, painting, and making statues, planning buildings, and writing stories [...][11]

Dewey's aesthetics of experience profoundly impacted Halprin through H'Doubler, who, as a pioneering educator herself, offered a counterpoint from her own field by publishing *Dance: A Creative Art Experience* (1940).[12] Tracing Halprin's aesthetic heritage to Dewey renders her dancescaping palpable, in so far as it can be seen as reshaping outer material through an "organic push from within."

A primal source of movement is the dancer's engagement with space and place. In Halprin's words, "I am very sensitive to the use of space—through my husband."[13] Architecture indeed proved to be a critical partner in her early intellectual culture, allowing her to further develop her understanding of the structural dynamics inherent in bodies, whether built or performing. At Harvard University, which Lawrence Halprin had entered with a scholarship in landscape architecture in 1941, she attended seminars in the School of Design, which Walter Gropius was reshaping as the head of the architecture department. Alongside her teaching dance to children in the college town, Halprin drew special inspiration from the general design seminar based on the curriculum Paul Klee had developed at the Bauhaus in Weimar and Dessau.

Klee's *Contributions to a Theory of Pictorial Form* (1921–1923), *Creative Mechanics (or Theory of Style)* (1924), and *Theory of Pictorial Configuration* (1925–1928) promoted movement as the matrix of artistic creation and aesthetic reception, a forceful insight he summarized in the *Pedagogical Sketchbook* (1925), which revealed the motor-tactile quality of line, form, and color. Music and nature, as well as dance, provided Klee with essential paradigms throughout his thought and practice.[14] Sharing this attention to process in form, both Halprins would seek a similar co-gestation of drawing, building, and performing. Thus, in her 1943 summer course entitled "Visual Design and Dance" in New Hampshire, Anna Halprin required her students to draw natural forms they found in nature, before dancing their impression of them; she likewise set tasks according to spatial concerns and integrated the lessons "learned from the architects,"[15] asking the participants to "design a dance in which they focused on the elements of planes in space." Lawrence Halprin later heralded Klee as a model in the methodology of *The RSVP Cycles* (1969).[16]

Situating Dance and Scoring Action

For Anna Halprin and her fellow dancers, stepping out of choreographic convention meant literally trespassing.

An airfield construction site just off the freeway at San Francisco Airport attracted them in 1957 to improvise with a raw, unfinished architectonic structure in a session that came to be named *Hangar*. Occurring between *The Branch* and *Flight* in Halprin's sequence of works that year, the piece is as pivotal in her collective dancescaping as it is in the simmering postmodern aesthetics of site-specific happenings.

The striking film and photographs shot that day invite clear readings of how the dancers, shifting from arboreal renderings on the dance deck to aeronautic decoding in the wasteland, first relate to the cargo hangar through crouching and beckoning. As they reach standing position, a number of them move into slow *pliés*, *développés*, and upward stretching, drawing their limbs into semaphore-like signals on the soon-to-be runway.[17] The sand and shrub below their bare feet are framed at grass level by the filmmaker and kicked up when the performers race toward the construction. There, the seven black-leotarded dancers lean against, balance on, and hang from the bright orange beams as each searches for his or her footing. Formal enquiry seems especially present, visible in the chromatic contrast of X-shaped figures that mingle among the steel shafts several feet above ground, creating score lines sometimes at the cost of ergonomics.[18] Working with and beyond such constraints lends *Hangar* a daredevil quality that would surface again in Halprin's use of a cargo net for stage action in *Esposizione* (1963), and by extension in Trisha Brown's teasing gravity in *Man Walking Down the Side of a Building* (1970) and *Floor of the Forest* (1970).

A tipping point in Brown's path as a dancer and choreographer came in the summer of 1960, when she enrolled in Halprin's workshop in Marin County. "Here I encountered, for the first time," Brown recalls in *How to Make a Modern Dance When the Sky's the Limit*, "the mercurial surges of an intuitive process where physical proposals and responses were dished and dashed on a whiz-by playing field."[19] What the outdoor location enabled was boundless experimentation with gesture and nature, thereby undoing precepts of cause and effect, and determining ordinary task as formal structure. Also, because it was off the radar of accepted dance training at the time, it brought out the most daring and resilient traits in bodies and characters. Fearlessness, a taste for edginess, and a genuine inquisitive attitude toward art making united the 15 participants in Halprin's 1960 summer session, which included, besides Brown, Simone Forti (then Morris) and Yvonne Rainer. All three artists would not only integrate their Kentfield experiments into their work once back in New York, implementing postmodern and minimalist aesthetics through the Judson Dance Theater, but also develop significant practices of scripting, notation, and drawing.[20]

It appears that sketching did not feature as such in the curriculum that year, but reliance on imagery and charting was encouraged. A sense of bodily outline and ligature was indeed imparted in the morning classes, through anatomical books and a skeleton model for movement analysis; in the afternoon ateliers, notation was examined in lectures on sound scripting given by La Monte Young.[21] Likewise, how to graphically summarize movement was instilled by the use of large charts, on which actions were jotted down in symbol and word form, a method favored by Halprin to break up stereotypical composition reflexes.[22] Improvisation thus coexisted with a peculiar corollary, that is, found movements could, and would, be fixed on paper. "Everything became arbitrary," Halprin explained in a 1962 interview with Rainer:

> I have a great chart on which I've taken every possible anatomical combination of movements, put them all on sheets of paper and given them numbers. One sheet had to do with flexion and different joints; another sheet had to do with extension. I would pick some elements and make a pattern. I tried to do them and I got into the wildest combinations of movements, things I never could have conceived myself. All of a sudden, my body began to experience new ways of moving. We applied this in bigger compositional ways. We would experiment with all the elements we worked with, even combinations of people. Even though I got the composition system formalized, we still worked it out with improvisation.[23]

Movement, no matter how unscripted it was when growing from the site and on the spot, nonetheless called for a written record. This would in turn provide another locale—the chart, map, or pattern—as material to act on.

Such material stands out in the score for *The Five-Legged Stool*, which premiered in 1962 at the Playhouse theater in San Francisco.[24] Stage action is distributed among the five protagonists—a woman, two men, a young girl, a stage hand—and drafted along what resembles musical staves, only in this case each line carries a spatial indication. A plan of the theater is provided above the code of symbols, and one is invited to read the actions horizontally, as they take place in the dressing rooms, backstage, in the pit, on stage, on the proscenium—and perhaps more strikingly, in the audience and in the lobby. Moving the outdoor experiments indoors resulted in embracing the entire theater as a potential dancescape. On paper, the performance unfolds as a 90-minute span marked by vertical shafts traced down the score at five-minute intervals, blocking out a series of gestural and aural *non sequiturs*.

The Five-Legged Stool, by all accounts, thoroughly tapped into the public's participatory instincts. Everyday moves were mixed with the spoken word, lending the piece an air of daily routine. Repetition undid all expectations of a narrative. Juxtaposition ensured sensorial surprise. "She wants most," Lawrence Halprin wrote in the *San Francisco Chronicle* during opening week, "to create an environment—a landscape, if you will, within which both audience and performers are part of the cast and the events are common to them both."[25] Events thus included strolling from lobby to stage with a radio at high volume, walking up and down a flight of stairs, handling empty wine bottles. The soundscape alternated between taped noises and live voices. For instance, a cryptic dialogue played out on stage: "Hum," "Take it," "Grin," "Grin," "Don't grin," "Don't please," "Please," "Stop it," "Stop it," "I am," "Ha ha." Prosaic utterances of all sorts pointed to shared experience, and it was precisely this choice that was intended to release poetic potential: the onlookers could craft their own stories through free association, channeling their own experiences into the performance proposal. In other words, the spatial continuum between audience and dancers stimulated the stream of thought, embracing chaos as much as flow. It especially captivated the composer Luciano Berio, who upon seeing *The Five-Legged Stool* instantly linked it to a taste for experimental, performative collage he shared with the opera singer Cathy Berberian—he proposed to Halprin that they collaborate on an opera, *Esposizione*, an endeavor that would eventually materialize at the International Festival of Contemporary Music in Venice in 1963. Such vocal indications, drawn as words in bubbles on the score of *The Five-Legged Stool*, experienced an interesting resurgence a few years later in Berberian's composition for *Stripsody* (1966), a riff on cartoon onomatopoeia and montage.

Much as Halprin searched for a renewed motor logic, scoring methods varied from piece to piece. The score of *Parades and Changes* reflects, in this sense, Morton Subotnick's input of a "cell-block" system: mapped out within a grid, each square (or cell) represents an action that a dancer, musician, stage designer, or sculptor may carry out. Duration is no longer indicated in a timeline, since the fulfillment of an action determines the articulation of the event. Sketches made by Lawrence Halprin in preparation for the Stockholm premiere in September 1965 indicate this shift from a linear model to a formal paradigm. Numbered squares and rectangles, for instance, are listed in the upper part of the sheet, complete with their respective action content, and assembled in the lower part of the page, in what resembles a floor plan of action units.[26] Here the pictorial reference is made explicit. A linear, free-drawn sketch suggests that the organic painting of Joan Miró helped visualize the idea of actions overlapping. This shift to figure over line and cipher is further supported by a cluster of arrows, this time reminiscent of Klee, which seems to comment on the sketch by adding direction to the overall shape.

If the purpose of *Parades and Changes* was to celebrate the sense of presence and genuine life situations inspired by Gestalt therapy—Anna Halprin met psychotherapist Fritz Perls in 1964—the score it evolved was indebted to principles of Gestalt psychology, namely that global perception of structured form precedes and determines its details. The Miró- and Klee-like drawings enabled exactly this.

The precedence given to the global view of the dance, or sense of a dancescape, surfaces in a commentary accompanying the two scores discussed so far. In Lawrence Halprin's words, "the choreographer establishes an environment and a generalized 'line of action,' but does not form the dance in the usual way of telling the group what the patterns should be. Instead, she invents specific kinds of interactions [...] It is safe to say that these theater pieces [*The Five-Legged Stool* and *Parades and Changes*] could never have been choreographed through the usual techniques—and the scoring technique influenced the results profoundly."[27] By "specific kinds of interactions," one understands that the scores could be open or closed, that is, the action could be more or less left open to chance. Anna Halprin herself recognized how the varying degree of openness affected her creative process. "I realized that there is so much power in being able to do a closed score, if you're doing it for the proper intention,"[28] she told Contact Improvisation pioneer Nancy Stark Smith. Improvisation—or exploration, as Halprin understands it—does not lose its resourceful impact if scored in a "closed" way, with a set sequencing or intention. Rather, through scoring the dance gains *Prägnanz*, that is, substance and point.

In considering how Halprin "establishes an environment" and "a generalized line of action," *Citydance* (1976–1977) offers yet another typology of graphic scores. *Citydance* unfolds along a scroll of paper, approximately 250 × 80 cm, mapped out with felt-tip pen and ink figures of people, vehicles, buildings, animals, parks, and natural sites. In the 1978 score, considered here in its 2009 reproduction housed in Halprin's personal archives, the color scheme verges on the psychedelic while the timeline takes on human attributes. The sun, whose course across the sky set the pace of the daylong and citywide event, is represented as a yellow clock face with arms and hands that signal various human gestures such as beckoning and pointing, reaching and pushing, eating and drumming. One of the score's most anthropomorphic details is at "Clementina [Street]," where a red-pillared structure morphs into a monumental pair of brown-skinned thighs, open wide yet non gendered, and over which circulate miniature automobiles. At once an overpass and a nude wheel pose, the vignette points to Halprin's larger investigation in *Citydance*, that is, how does the individual body relate to the collective body and they in turn to the body politic?

Urban dancescaping, in this case, entailed leading the public into participatory activity on a threefold scale: journeying across the city, carrying out activities at each of the nine locations, and performing scored dances within these activities.[29] It claimed the metropolis as partially charted territory where loosely outlined interaction could take place in the name of community building—characteristics that can be read in the 1978 scroll, which exudes playfulness throughout the city's skyline. Predominantly figurative, aesthetically close to naïve painting, it offers a counterpoint to the stave-based, cellblock, and floor plan models that favor graphic succinctness.[30] Significantly, it claims illustration as a heuristic method in dance making, which is precisely what Halprin seeks in her parallel use of portraiture.

Acting on Drawing

There is no room for mirrors at the Kentfield studio. The dancer's gaze is primarily guided into the natural environment, upon his or her fellows, and inward. Yet within the introspective loop that Halprin stimulates from the outdoor locale, mirror images do appear. In fact, the kinesthetic awareness thus assembled gives rise to a visual representation of oneself. With a pad of paper and crayons acting as additional tools for visualization, besides the skeleton, the self-reflective impulse is channeled through the exercise of drawing one's portrait.

In 1972, Halprin experienced a life-changing moment when she depicted herself with a tumor in her abdomen. Her survival of it and its recurrence three years later was entwined with the process of picturing her illness and overcoming denial and fear by dancing her self-portrait. The pictures she drew throughout the process, life-size and colorful, were shot through with the presence of cancer, but also conveyed the agency of her own healing resources. Halprin could recognize both aspects and thus act upon the image she had of herself, artistically and existentially. Her response exemplifies what the art historian David Freedberg has determined as "the power of images," that is, the "efficacy, effectiveness, and vitality of images," whether experienced or expected.[31] In Halprin's case, the response was dance, and the self-drawn image moved from being a palimpsest to a cathartic spark.

Before drawing became part of the curriculum at the Tamalpa Institute,[32] it appeared by chance to Halprin in her children's classes. "I knew that a lot was going on with these kids, but I didn't know how to access it, so one day I just brought some paper and drawings, and said 'Draw it!' That's how it started," Halprin recalls.[33] Accessing past personal experience through drawing went hand in hand with sketching natural forms for future choreography, as the courses at the Mettler Estate in the 1940s already suggest. Moreover, it eventually complemented the feedback process during scoring, when with adults Halprin noticed a wide discrepancy between what she had witnessed and what the performers were expressing in words.[34] Drawing, first introduced as a recording device, thus turned into a decoding tool. "I became interested in the relationship between movement and feeling, and then in the connection between movement, feeling, and imagery," Halprin explained to Smith. "Images and emotions were overwhelming the movement […] So then I thought, maybe we can understand this link if we start drawing it. We'll *draw* the images that are coming up. If you're crying and yelling, then put it back into movement, draw the image. [This] was one way of moving that material and keeping it within some sort of a process."[35] Interestingly, in this account, recycling the emotion into an image means "[putting] it back into movement," which elects drawing as productive decoder between motion and emotion.

The practice proved fruitful to the extent that it has been coined the Psycho-Kinetic Visualization Process, or Psychokinetic Imagery Process. It is premised on what Halprin deems to be the natural capacity to draw and is tied in with the task of scoring, which Lawrence Halprin named a "catalytic agent."[36] Kinesthetic and emotional information about oneself is derived through interaction with the environment, before being metabolized in a drawing; this in turn incites movement and acts as score, when the individual responds to the image through gesture or movement.

The drawn artifact is therefore a pivot in Anna Halprin's investigation of what moves people to relate—among each other and with the world—through dance. "Dance it!" is the obvious response to drawing—when it is not its instigator—in her holistic approach to artistic practice.

For all its openness, it is striking to notice how this process closes in on figurative representation. In the 2015 summer workshop I took part in, anatomical renderings of oneself spurred more discussion than abstract seismographic templates did. Tracings, cutouts, imprints drew less dialogue among participants than recognizable figures of nature, animals, or humans. In other words, the context Halprin establishes for the use of drawing favors iconicity over indexicality. The rhythm, energy, and perambulation of a line go unnoticed while pictorial completeness and accuracy to the model are celebrated. In what echoes a distant reading of the Gestaltian "good shape" principle, inchoative forms are side-lined. As a result, nondescript figures have little action within the process. Portraiture is understood literally and bears a prescriptive nature in the ensuing performance.

Self-portraits are generally presented for performance in a twofold procedure, first held up by a partner, then tacked up against the studio wall. Mirroring is clearly at stake. The image looks back at the observer/dancer in both cases, as a *sudarium* or a portrait in a gallery. Just as the hand is the overwhelming operator of the drawings, these tend to be full-length and are meant to be seen by standing viewers. Such devices for depicting and displaying dance thus borrow from the iconography and museum traditions. In doing so, they acknowledge the negotiation between formal and motor logics that is at work in dance. In fact, the performative reading of the portrait in a collective arena dramatizes, even exacerbates, the co-gestation of kinesthetic sensation and visual perception. In short, it materializes the workings of aesthetic experience, during which muscular knowledge is activated and empathy with form unfolds.

A parallel may be drawn here with the anthropological perspective on dance and drawing proposed by the anthropologist Alfred Gell. He defines drawing as a "ballistic" activity,[37] in which comprehension arises once the act is performed. What unites the two practices, according to his analysis of "drawing as akin to dancing," is a "cognitive indecipherability manifested in performance," that is, both "tantalize our capacity to deal with wholes and parts, continuity and discontinuity, synchrony and succession."[38] Halprin has embraced a principle of indecipherability since promoting indistinctness between art and life, which Robert Morris described in the 1960s as her blurring of performance, preparation, and process.[39] Moreover, in breaking down the body's capacity into anatomical and articulatory units, that is, in deciphering the somatic and visual logic at work in dance making, she ultimately maps out a greater sense of initiation and wholeness:

> I am interested in a theater where everything is experienced for the first time, and I have stripped away all ties with conventional dance forms: in the lives of individual performers, their training, rehearsals, and performances form a process which in itself is an experience. I have come back to the ritualistic beginnings of art as a sharpened expression of life, extending every kind of perception. I want to participate in events of supreme authenticity, to involve people with their environment so that life is lived whole.[40]

In Halprin's work, "feeling into" or "feeling at one with" a self-made image stems from her kinship with nature.[41] In so doing, she pursues the empathic sourcing that early 20th-century dancers Loïe Fuller and Isadora Duncan, in particular, exercised with natural phenomena, such as botanical growth or oceanic undulation, occasionally at the expense of authorial signature,[42] and places the dance deck within a larger cluster of heterotopias[43] that fostered performative contestation and renewal in outdoor settings, such as Monte Verità (Ascona, Switzerland) and Black Mountain College (North Carolina). The empathy she scores and enacts belongs to the genealogy that the dance historian Susan Leigh Foster describes as proceeding from a time when "land was measured and carved up into portions" and when "the individual experienced sympathy as the inherent connectivity among all humans constructed by their common location."[44] Such connectivity is rooted in a belief in the universal human condition, where it is "the tensile drama progressing through the individual body itself [that conveys] the human predicament."[45]

For Halprin this drama is interrelated with the land, to such an extent that she has scored her withdrawing into the soil, sand, roots, or water in the *Still Dance Series* (1998–2002).[46] Yet inherent to her dancescaping is a demand for efficiency. Indeed she recognizes the agency of natural matter and of image, and draws alternately on both to infuse her dance with action and meaning. In her experience, dance and drawing make sense of each other only when they arise in a live environment.

[1] *Née* Ann Schuman, Ann Halprin changed her name to Anna Halprin in 1972. While documentation may indicate this shift, we have opted for the unified spelling of "Anna."

[2] Anna Halprin, letter to Julie [family name unknown] (April 1945), Anna Halprin's archives, quoted by Janice Ross, *Anna Halprin. Experience as Dance*, University of California Press, Berkeley 2007, p. 69. All subsequent quotes in this paragraph are from the same book.

[3] Anna Halprin, in Joan Saffa, prod./dir., *Lawrence and Anna Halprin: Inner Landscapes*, video recording, San Francisco: KQED-TV, 1991.

[4] Anna Halprin, "In the Environment," video recording, in Baptiste Andrien and Florence Corin (eds.), *Anna Halprin, Dancing Life/Anna Halprin, Danser la vie*, DVD-ROM, Éditions Contredanse, Brussels 2014.

[5] Lawrence Halprin and Anna Halprin, "Dance Deck in the Woods," in *Impulse*, no. 24, 1956, quoted in Janice Ross, *Anna Halprin. Experience as Dance*, p. 106.

[6] Merce Cunningham, "Excerpts from lecture-demonstration given at Anna Halprin's dance deck (July 13, 1957)," in David Vaughan, *Merce Cunningham: Fifty Years*, Aperture, New York 1997, p. 100.

[7] "*Choreography*—I don't use that word anymore, because I don't do it anymore. I just use process." Anna Halprin, summer workshop, Kentfield (CA), June 23, 2015. Choreography, both as a precept and a notational device, faded from Halprin's dance making when improvisation/exploration took precedence in the 1950s.

[8] Richard Schechner and Anna Halprin, "Anna Halprin: A Life in Ritual. An Interview," in *TDR–The Drama Review*, vol. 33, no. 2, Summer 1989, p. 67–73; reprinted as "Anna Halprin: A Life in Ritual. Interview by Richard Schechner," in Rachel Kaplan (ed.), *Moving Toward Life. Five Decades of Transformative Dance*, Wesleyan University Press, Middletown (CT) 1995, p. 244.

[9] Meredith Monk, interview with Janice Ross (Palo Alto, CA, March 1, 2000), quoted in Janice Ross, *Anna Halprin. Experience as Dance*, p. 181.

[10] John Dewey, *Art as Experience*, Perigee, New York 2005, p. 236 [1st ed.: 1934].

[11] Ibid., p. 236–237.

[12] Janice Ross, *Anna Halprin. Experience as Dance*, p. 29. Ross adds to this genealogy by entitling Halprin's critical biography *Experience as Dance*.

[13] Anna Halprin, interview with the author (Kentfield, CA, June 24, 2015).

[14] Reto Sorg, "Dance and 'The Law of Movement' in Paul Klee," *Paul Klee: Theater Everywhere*, exh. cat., Hatje Cantz, Ostfildern 2007, p. 220–226; Régine Bonnefoit, *Die Linientheorien von Paul Klee*, Michael Imhof Verlag, Petersberg 2009; Sarah Burkhalter, *Vers une kinesthétique: danse moderne, arts visuels et perception (1890–1940)*, PhD dissertation, Université de Genève, 2012 (forthcoming publication, Les presses du réel, Dijon).

[15] Anna Halprin, interview with Janice Ross (March 12, 1994), in Janice Ross, *Anna Halprin. Experience as Dance*, p. 59.

[16] Lawrence Halprin, *The RSVP Cycles. Creative Processes in the Human Environment*, George Braziller, New York 1969, p. 12–13.

[17] Editor's note: See Alexander Schwan's discussion of semaphore movements in Trisha Brown's work in this volume, p. 60–73.

[18] For a discussion of the apparent paradox between Simone Forti's recollection of discomfort in performing *Hangar* and Halprin's belief in allowing movement to emerge organically from the site, see Janice Ross, *Anna Halprin. Experience as Dance*, p. 130–131.

[19] Trisha Brown, "How to Make a Modern Dance When the Sky's the Limit," in Hendel Teicher (ed.), *Trisha Brown: Dance and Art in Dialogue, 1961–2001*, exh. cat., The MIT Press, Cambridge (MA) 2002, p. 289.

[20] "We knew that what we were doing had nothing to do with dance anymore […] We knew that our grandfather was Marcel Duchamp and that we had links with Dada. We situated ourselves in that family." Simone Forti and Jacqueline Caux, "Entretien avec Simone Forti," in Jacqueline Caux (ed.), *Anna Halprin. À l'origine de la performance*, exh. cat., Editions du Panama, Paris 2006, p. 144. For an account of Halprin's legacy in Simone Forti's dance and visual arts practice, see Simone Forti, *Handbook in Motion*, The Press of the Nova Scotia College of Art & Design, Halifax 1974, p. 29–33; Simone Forti, "From Animate Dancing to Writing," in *Oh, Tongue*, Beyond Baroque Books, Los Angeles 2003, p. 129–142; and Simone Forti and Sabine Breitwieser (eds.), *Thinking with the Body*, exh. cat., Hirmer Verlag, Munich 2014. Editor's note: see the essays by Pauline Chevalier (p. 130–145) and Susan Rosenberg (p. 74–87), and interview by Catherine Quéloz (p. 16–27) in this volume.

[21] In *Lecture 1960*, La Monte Young spoke of "entering the sound." See La Monte Young and Jacqueline Caux, "Entretien avec La Monte Young," in Jacqueline Caux (ed.), *Anna Halprin. À l'origine de la performance*, p. 132.

[22] Janice Ross, "Atomizing Cause and Effect: Ann Halprin's 1960s Summer Dance Workshops," in *Art Journal*, vol. 68, no. 2, Summer 2009, College Art Association, New York, p. 68.

[23] Anna Halprin, "Yvonne Rainer interviews Anna Halprin (1965 [1962])," in Rachel Kaplan (ed.), *Moving Toward Life*, p. 81.

[24] The original score is stored in the Anna Halprin Papers, Museum of Performance + Design, San Francisco.

[25] Lawrence Halprin, quoted in Janice Ross, *Anna Halprin. Experience as Dance*, p. 162.

[26] The original score is stored in the Anna Halprin Papers, Museum of Performance + Design, San Francisco.

[27] Lawrence Halprin, *The RSVP Cycles*, p. 35. See Gabriele Brandstetter's essay on notational systems in this volume (p. 40–59).

[28] Anna Halprin, "After Improv. Interview by Nancy Stark Smith (1987)," in Rachel Kaplan (ed.), *Moving Toward Life*, p. 198–200.

[29] Anna Halprin, "A Report on Citydance (1978)," in Rachel Kaplan (ed.), *Moving Toward Life*, p. 171–172.

[30] Beside *The Five-Legged Stool* (1962) and *Parades and Changes* (1965), such scores include, among others, *Esposizione* (1963), *Procession* (1964), *Ten Myths* (1967), *Animal Ritual* (1971), *Initiations and Transformations* (1971), and *Circle the Earth* (1986ff.). See exhibition *Mapping Dance: the Scores of Anna Halprin*, at the Museum of Performance + Design, San Francisco (March 17–May 31, 2016), curated by Elliot Mercer and Muriel Maffre.

[31] "We must consider not only beholders' symptoms and behavior, but also the effectiveness, efficacy, and vitality of images themselves; not only what beholders do, but also what images appear to do; not only what people do as a result of their relationship with imaged form, but also what they expect imaged form to achieve, and why they have such expectations at all." David Freedberg, *The Power of Images. Studies in the History and Theory of Response*, The University of Chicago Press, Chicago 1989, p. xxii.

[32] Tamalpa Institute was cofounded in 1978 in Kentfield (CA), by Anna Halprin and her daughter Daria Halprin. A nonprofit organization, it offers "training programs and workshops in the Life/Art Process®, a movement-based expressive arts approach that integrates movement/dance, visual arts, performance techniques, and therapeutic practices. This approach supports personal, interpersonal, and social transformation, teaching new models for health,

psychology, art, and communication." www.tamalpa.org and printed leaflet information. With branches in Korea, Latin America, Germany, Great Britain, and France, it offers MA and PhD certifications in partnership with the European Graduate School (Leuk-Stadt/Loèche-Ville, Switzerland) and Meridian University (Petaluma, CA).

[33] Anna Halprin, interview with the author (Kentfield, CA, June 24, 2015).

[34] "Then I began to notice that when we had discussions after a creative dance experience, it was just horrible to listen to people try to talk about what had happened […] It was so boring and [it seemed] so dumb. It didn't have anything to do with what I was witnessing, I didn't know where they were coming from. So one day I just said, 'Oh just draw it, don't talk about it!'" Anna Halprin, "Importance of Imagery," in Baptiste Andrien and Florence Corin (eds.), *Anna Halprin, Dancing Life/Anna Halprin, Danser la vie*.

[35] Anna Halprin, in Rachel Kaplan (ed.), *Moving Toward Life*, p. 195–196.

[36] Lawrence Halprin, *The RSVP Cycles*, p. 1.

[37] "Drawing, and most other artistic skills (carving, etc.) are what are known as 'ballistic' activities, muscular performances which take place at a rate such that cognitive processing of the 'outcome' of action only takes place after the act is complete, not while it is in progress. (The archetypal 'ballistic' behaviour is throwing.)…" Alfred Gell, *Art and Agency. An Anthropological Theory*, Oxford University Press, Oxford 1998, p. 45.

[38] Ibid., p. 95.

[39] Robert Morris, quoted in Janice Ross, *Anna Halprin. Experience as Dance*, p. 65.

[40] Anna Halprin, "Creation," quoted in Lawrence Halprin, *The RSVP Cycles*, p. 31.

[41] Simone Forti has described its application to dance: "We worked in nature and it was a true enchantment. If, for instance, I was looking at the bark of an old tree, my hands immediately did such and such a gesture, my body and my face began to move in such and such a way. Later, I could forget the tree, but I kept the memory of the movements I'd done. Anna didn't only teach us how to move, she also taught us how to observe and to absorb our observations." Jacqueline Caux, "Entretien avec Simone Forti," in Jacqueline Caux (ed.), *Anna Halprin. À l'origine de la performance*, p. 144.

[42] On the syllogism between the female body, nature, and dance in Duncan's choreographic thinking, and the ensuing evacuation of individuality that echoed Fuller's disappearance in costume and stage effects, see Mark Franko, *Dancing Modernism/Performing Politics*, Indiana University Press, Bloomington (IN) 1995, p. 9–15. In Yvonne Rainer's words: "That summer workshop was where I was first exposed to movement in relation to objects […] I knew even then, however, that the nature-and-dance combo was not for me, a bias that the women's movement of a decade later would only confirm." Yvonne Rainer, quoted in Janice Ross, *Anna Halprin. À l'origine de la performance*, p. 150.

[43] As defined by Michel Foucault: "There are also, probably in every culture, in every civilization, real places—places that do exist and that are formed in the very founding of society—which are something like counter-sites, a kind of effectively enacted utopia in which the real sites, all the other real sites that can be found within the culture, are simultaneously represented, contested, and inverted." Michel Foucault, "Of Other Spaces, Heterotopias" [1967], trans. Jay Miskowiec, in *Architecture, Mouvement, Continuité*, no. 5, October 1984, p. 46–49.

[44] Susan Leigh Foster, *Choreographing Empathy. Kinesthesia in Performance*, Routledge, Oxon 2011, p. 176. Editor's note: for a sense of how agricultural thinking can be echoed in choreographic mapping in Anne Teresa De Keersmaeker, see the essay and interview by Julie Enckell Julliard in this volume, p. 148–162.

[45] Susan Leigh Foster, *Choreographing Empathy*, p. 178. The universalism of such a view can be critiqued, yet as Dee Reynolds and Matthew Reason point out, "the discourse of kinesthetic empathy is constantly being (re)constructed in different contexts and also involves negotiation across differences, respecting otherness, rather that eliding the other in the self-same." Dee Reynolds and Matthew Reason (eds.), *Kinesthetic Empathy in Creative and Cultural Practices*, Intellect, Bristol 2012, p. 20.

[46] Photography and film by Eeo Stubblefield. See chapter "Choreographing Disappearance: Dances of Aging, 1992–2006," in Janice Ross, *Anna Halprin. Experience as Dance*, p. 331–357.

"Dance is Hard to See." The Judson Dance Theater and the Visual Arts

Pauline Chevalier

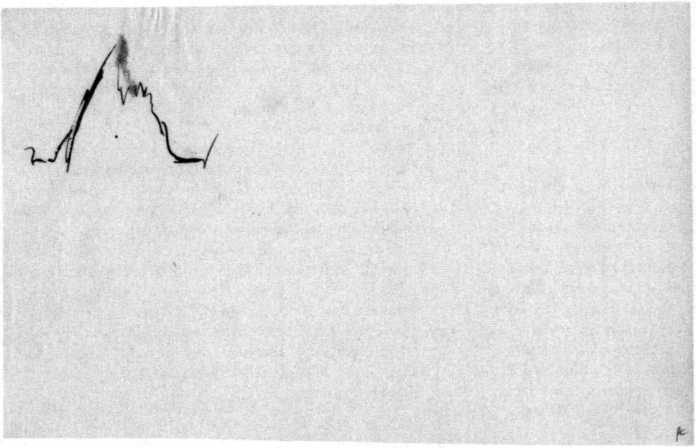

Philip Corner
Flares, 1963
Ink and pastel crayon on paper, dimensions unknown
Fales Library and Special Collections, New York University Libraries, New York

In the field of dance as in the field of the plastic arts, the Judson Dance Theater constantly fostered practices that would later contribute to a rereading of a pivotal moment in the history of American dance and art.[1] Often, of the eclecticism of the forms developed by the collective in the early 1960s, there remains but a singular view of their heritage, that of postmodern dance from the 1970s. In 1982, 20 years after the first "Concert of Dance" performed by the Judson Dance Theater, Barry Laine described the evolution thus: "As the years since Judson's heyday have passed, we have lost touch with some of the real detail of the period. We have tended to confuse the Judson's 'offspring'—the austere, formal mechanics of the 1970s postmodern dance—for the original aesthetic. While pedestrian movement and uninflected performance, for instance, *were* concerns of some of the choreographers at that time, outrageous theatricality and multimedia sensation were equally the rule. The appellation 'dance theater' has also obscured the degree to which nondance artists contributed to the Judson experience."[2]

The Judson Dance Theater was not only dance, and the share that the visual arts, notably the plastic arts, enjoyed was particularly substantial thanks to certain individualities (e.g., Robert Rauschenberg, Robert Morris, and Carolee Schneemann), as well as in the common perception of gesture, theatricality, space, and the temporality of the works. Between 1962 and 1964,[3] the Judson Dance Theater presented dance pieces and performances that combined movement, sculpture, environments, films, and lighting effects in a range of forms and practices. Sally Banes, whose works form the core of the Judson Dance Theater historiography, describes the collective in these terms: "It was a vital gathering place for artists in various fields who exchanged ideas and methods, seeking explicitly to explore, propose, and refute definitions of dance as an art form. The issues that concerned the group ranged from training and technique to choreographic process, music, performance style, and materials. There was no single prevailing aesthetic in the group; rather, an effort was made to preserve an ambiance of diversity and freedom."[4]

The very involvement of painters like Alex Hay and Schneemann, and sculptors like Charles Ross and Morris, ensured the eclecticism of the Judson Dance Theater's practices. Elaine Summers was of course a dancer but also a filmmaker, and she contributed to the development of an intermedial aesthetics. Philip Corner, the composer and musician for many of the company's dance pieces, worked on graphic systems of notation, sometimes projecting the scores on the church walls. These were literally experiments in vision that were carried out by the initial members of the Judson Dance Theater, which "became a metacommunity of sorts where the different communities revolving around single arts disciplines coalesced and where interdisciplinary imagination flourished."[5]

The experiments had had precedents in the very same church, for it was indeed in this venue, in the Judson Gallery, which had been installed there in 1959, that the first Happenings had been presented. Claes Oldenburg, Jim Dine,

Red Grooms, and Daniel Spoerri had already worked in the space.[6] Along the same lines, a poetry collective as well as a theater company had performed in the space, which was normally devoted to religious worship. The artistic tradition of the Washington Square church did not date from the 1950s, but in fact went back to the early years of the 20th century.

"God doesn't disappear when you don't talk about him."[7]: The Judson Memorial Church and Robert Dunn's Workshop

Built in 1892 by Edward Judson in honor of his father Adoniram Judson—one of the first American missionaries in Burma—the Judson Memorial Church had been featuring painting exhibitions in the building itself and on its outside railings since the 1920s. Besides a commitment to the arts, the church also stood out for its political commitments when, in the 1930s, various labor unions held meetings there, or when, in the 1960s, Howard Moody, the minister from 1957 to 1992, developed many liberal social programs in favor of drug addicts and women's rights. A defender of church autonomy and a freedom of thought that ran from the arts to civil rights, Reverend Moody recruited Al Carmines as his "associate reverend" in 1962. Carmines took charge of coordinating the theater and poetry programs, setting two simple rules for himself, namely, to apply no censorship once he had agreed to add a piece or performance to the program, and to show no religious works. These rules were likewise in force when the dancers from the workshop given by Robert Dunn came to him and proposed to perform in the church in the spring of 1962.

Dunn, who had studied under John Cage at the New School for Social Research in New York, gave a dance class at Merce Cunningham's studio and his instruction used some of Cage's precepts. Sally Banes also points out that the class Dunn attended between 1956 and 1960 at the New School included Jackson Mac Low, Dick Higgins, and Al Hansen, as well as Allan Kaprow and Toshi Ichiyanagi. All of these men had ties to the New York Happenings scene from the late 1950s,[8] and had created Happenings in both the Reuben Gallery and the basement at the Judson. Initially a course in choreography, Dunn's class focused its exercises on the constraints and structures of improvisation, regularly using pieces by Erik Satie, and the graphic score of Cage's *Fontana Mix* (1958).[9] These elements were reused, moreover, during the first concert of dance given at the Judson in 1962. Inspired by the Bauhaus, Dunn did not limit his teaching to dance or music. Western and Eastern philosophies, literature, and painting had a place in the work and discussions.

There was, however, a thread running through most of the exercises, namely, notation that was written out or drawn during the process of composing. In an interview he gave in 1980, Dunn insisted on this point, "Graphic notation is a way of inventing the dance. It is part of the conception of the dance. What the choreographer has to do is to choose a world of movement ... to invent or choose the graphic side and invent and choose the correlations."[10] Use of a drawn or written support would accompany the Judson Dance Theater collective's practice both in the transmission of gestures and choreographed pieces, and in the process of creation itself.

A "Concert of Dance"

Dunn's first students included Steve Paxton, Yvonne Rainer, and Simone Forti, the latter married to Robert Morris, who was himself associated with the group from very early on. Morris and Forti, who had arrived in New York in 1959, were regularly seen at the Reuben Gallery and attended the Happenings that Dine and Oldenburg performed there. Dunn's class drew other students as well, mainly though not exclusively dancers, and included such figures as Trisha Brown, Alex and Deborah Hay, Fred Herko, Carol Scothorn, and Summers.

A few dance pieces were initially performed in the studio, in a building the dancers shared with the Living Theatre (founded in New York in 1964 by Judith Malina and Julian Beck), but it was Rainer who suggested they go and knock at Al Carmines' door for the chance to perform at the Judson Church. Rainer had attended several evening events of the Judson Poets' Theater[11] and the venue, so unconventional, seemed to her like a favorable place for hosting the experiments coming out of Dunn's workshop. The meeting with Carmines was short—a ten-minute audition[12]—and the first "concert of dance" took place on July 6, 1962.[13]

More than four hours of performances and some 20 dance pieces made the news at the time. The *Village Voice*'s Jill Johnston, a regular at avant-garde venues, defended the young choreographers, and Allen Hughes, *The New York Times* music critic and a novice with regard to the dance avant-garde, penned an enthusiastic account of this first production of what was to be called, beginning in April 1963, the "Judson Dance Theater." Hughes described a "concert of 'movement,'"[14] an event that had "hardly anything conventional about it."[15] The press release stated that each event sprang from a process of improvisation and a love for a certain liberty left to chance and indeterminacy.[16] Hughes noted that, "for this reason, the same group may appear together on another occasion, and have a total flop. The chances are, however, that their experiments will influence dance development in this country and because this seems likely, they are worth watching."[17]

If the concerts produced between 1962 and 1964 cannot be reduced to a particular aesthetic, the first of them certainly set the tone for the productions that were to follow. Analysis of the various narratives and descriptions of the 23 pieces on the program of July 6, 1962, shows the extent to which the visual arts occupied an important place in the group's creative process. First, the viewers took their seats during the screening of a film, *Overture*, which Summers edited together from rushes she had shot herself and excerpts of a comedy by W. C. Fields, *The Bank Dick* (1940). The film ensured that viewers were already confronted by the situation of the show and displayed a few recurrent characteristics of the practices that Dunn's workshop adhered to, i.e., use of chance in the editing, "cut-up" assembly, and desynchronization. Summers and Scothorn offered performances inspired by photographs, words, and topographical maps. Whether still or moving, image combined with gesture in the creation of sets, lights, and costumes.[18] For example Alex Hay, both a painter and a sculptor, showed his piece *Rafladan*, a joint work with Deborah Hay and Charles Rotmil, at the closing of the first concert of dance. The light of a flashlight was used in the dark to capture snapshots of the dance movement, suggesting a practice like painting or photography. Likewise, the fact that Schneemann took part in the group's rehearsals suggests both the eclecticism of the collective's practices and the not insignificant place that visual arts practices enjoyed. While Schneemann recognizes there was a certain difficulty with producing her work during the first concerts of dance, she does describe the atmosphere of the collective as a source of inspiration for broadening her medium of choice, painting.[19]

Environment, Lights, and Intermediality: Collaborations

Schneemann, for example, used her dancer colleagues in a performance in which each person took the role of a body part. Seeing the collective as a "physical palette," she created *Newspaper Event* for *Concert no. 3* (July 6, 1962). The dancers seemed to melt into an environment of newspapers, a transformable plastic environment. Schneemann laid out the general principle of the performance: "I was thinking of an organism interchanging its parts. I noted five principles: 1) the primary experience is the body as your own environment. 2) the body with the actual, particular environment. 3) the materials of that environment—soft, responsive, tactile, active, malleable (paper ... paper). 4) the active environment of one another. 5) the visual structure of the bodies and materials defining space."[20] Each dancer was associated with a body part that had to move according to precise indications, transforming the setting at the same time. The ten-minute performance was supposed to show an unstructured collective body, applying the cut-up technique at the scale of the group. Schneemann is especially attached to the perception of her performance work as an extension of a gestural painting, and many of her later creations like *Up to And Including Her Limits* (1973) indeed seem like a continuation of the Judson Dance Theater experiments, combining dance and visual arts, and making the performer a "randomized drawing machine."[21]

The creations of the Judson took place many times with dancers and visual artists working closely together in the settings and environments. It is widely known, for instance, how important Rauschenberg was in the treatment of the lighting and occasionally costumes. We should also recall the unforgettable participation of Charles Ross, a young sculptor and great lover of mathematics who would later produce a number of Land Art works. *A Collaborative Event*, which took place on November 19 and 20, 1963, proved to be a more direct affirmation of a certain identity of the Judson that particularly emphasized collaborations of the sculptor and the dancers. Several metal ramps crossed the space of the stage in the church, some of them linking the floor with the balcony. Sheet metal, chairs, ropes, and tires had been added for the different dance pieces to be performed. The environment was both a work of art and a stage set. Rainer mounted *Room Service* in this space, using a mattress moved to the stage area, a gesture she was to employ in several of her following dance pieces, notably *Parts of Some Sextets* (1965). Carry, transport, manipulate—the choreographer saw in this taste for plays of weight, force, and dynamism of objects being moved a kinship with the teachings of Anna Halprin.[22] It was a matter of showing the body at work, the deploying of muscles during a precise task, work that could also be observed in certain *Equipment Pieces* by Brown, or in Forti's *Slant Board* (1961), even in Morris and Schneemann's *Site* (1964).[23] The environments and the literal presence of objects and practical gestures fostered the "anti-illusionist" project championed by Rainer, the dancers of the Judson, and the practitioners of minimal art.

The following year, in 1964, Summers took this fusion of installation and gesture a bit further when she created *Fantastic Gardens*, a piece that combined film, singing, piano, percussion, dance, painting, sculpture, and lighting. *Fantastic Gardens* was indeed an intermedial event produced by the woman who had founded the Experimental Intermedia Foundation in 1968, and it invited viewers to participate by using mirrors and walking around the objects and sculptures. The variety of the supports employed, along with their combination, sprang from an urge in Summers' work to multiply viewing possibilities. Dance, a fleeting art form, cannot be captured twice, and drawing, photography, and film function both as extensions of the gesture and tools for seeing. "*Fantastic Gardens* was made with the rather bitter acknowledgment that you can't see in the back of your head. You were not meant to see everything."[24] Because it could not let us see everything, the intermedial work of art had to be able to "make us feel," to multiply sensory experiences, not fulfilling all the perceptual frustrations that a viewer might experience, but creating a total work focused mainly on treating light and movement, generating a haptic view of the work of art shared by most members of the Judson.

Fantastic Gardens, a work of art that is emblematic of the collective, was the climax of the first two years of the Judson, and paved the way for intermedial practices[25] that widely flourished in New York at the end of the decade and more widely still in the 1970s, alongside the postmodern dance of a collective like Grand Union, another emanation of the Judson's eclecticism. The large part granted to the plastic arts within the collective was due to the varied interests of some of its members, combining the practices of the painter, filmmaker, sculptor, and dancer; and to many collaborations that defined both the creative process and the aesthetic of the first concerts of dance. Among the fertile fields of collaboration between dancers and visual artists figured a connection with line and graphic practices.

Lines, Maps: Graphic Processes

In keeping with Dunn's precepts, some dance pieces—notably those by Emerson and Scothorn—were imagined from Labanotation plates. The elements of the dance piece were separated into different categories (movements, spaces, geometrical motifs, parts of the body, qualities of movement) and combined in a random and shifting way every five or ten seconds. The cut-up exercise proposed by Dunn had led Emerson to work with combinatorial grids and the logic of series starting from a distortion of von Laban's notation. Dunn encouraged his students to work with the "structures," i.e., the frames of logic, often taking a rhythm, score, notation, or drawing as the basis for a work.

In her piece *Isolations*, which she presented at the first concert, Scothorn used Cage's graphic score for *Fontana Mix*, but also combined it with the Labanotation plates. The vertical lines of the latter crossed the curves of *Fontana Mix*, which indicated the quality and value of the movements (quick, slow, increasing, decreasing), while their intersections with von Laban's verticals indicated the different parts of the body to be moved. Scothorn recalls the great difficulty posed by a choreography based above all on graphic and theoretical principles: "There were no horizontal lines on the *Fontana Mix* score, so no movement 'chords' were produced. Everything passed rapidly from one part of the body to the other. There were long periods of silence (when no line was crossing the staff). The score was assigned a time value of 1 second to the square."[26]

This use of the page, lines, even images was not the sole province of Scothorn and Emerson. Corner, who occasionally composed for the "concerts of dance," produced a series of stencils and watercolors that functioned as both scores and images, which were screened during the concerts. *Flares* (1963)[27] is doubtless one of his best known creations. It seems to be freely inspired by Cage's experiments for *Fontana Mix*. The lines, colors, and shapes that served to structure the music were much freer, however. Made up of a group of pages, the score could also suggest the play of light in the church. Corner describes the piece in its "visual and sonic aspects" as an "alternation of silence and immobility, luminosity, sound, and movements."[28]

Colors and lines of force guided the interpretation. The spatial writing of sound, in the work of Cage and Corner, makes use of line, line that is common to the dance gesture. The colored sound maps formed by the scores display the gestures of the hand, the dynamic that is at work in the drawing as prefiguration of the sound gesture and the dance movement. Corner's drawings for *Flares* (1963) use not only different colors, but also different pictorial techniques. The line may be heavily emphasized or hazy, in pastel or ink. As a visual work, it leaves the reading of the piece open by returning to the line its dimension as both a trace—of a completed gesture—and a map—for a gesture, i.e., a route to come. While the dancers sought to break the "personal link between the manual gesture and graphic inscription"[29] by deconstructing the scores and visual supports, it was the musicians who enriched it at the Judson Dance Theater. Music ensured one of the literal bridges between the practices of dance and drawing.

Several of the Judson artists then envisioned the stage space in its connection with the page, reminding us in passing of the very etymology of the term "page," that is, "trellis," "real demarcated territory." It bears the spatial points of reference transposed to the scale of the body, proposes lines, columns, words to interpret, and images to reproduce. Summers used the newspaper page, though transformed into a choreographic matrix. With *The Daily Wake* (1962), which was presented for the Judson's first concert, Summers made use of both words and photographs. From the front page of the *Daily News* laid out on the floor, the choreographer set up a structure that took the words, paragraphs, and photographs as a vast map for her dance. The graphic support offered a grid structuring the choreography, while the photographs presented the poses to be reproduced (two people holding hands, a dancer posed as a bride, and another imitating the model in an advertisement for Pantino tapering trousers, etc.). Three levels of correlation between gesture and graphic representation were used. The structural framework of the page served as a frame and a matrix, in a relationship of *analogy* with the space of the stage; the word is a *description* of the gesture, whereas the image is a *depiction* of a pose.[30]

The transfer from the page to the gesture was realized through line and map, through a *representation* and a codification, shifting expression to the background through gesture. Despite its aesthetic diversity, the first concert of dance displayed a clear-cut partiality for logical operations, grids, and combinations.

A Community of Views

Dunn's teachings indeed championed the use of a graphic support and a combinational sensibility that suggests the logic at work in minimal art, which was taking shape around the time of the Judson's initial experiments. As in minimal art, certain pieces of the first concert can claim logic—and not rationality—as their operating mode, an essential distinction made by Sol LeWitt.[31] In an interview with Liza Bear and Willoughby Sharp in 1972, Rainer evokes the fundamental influence of minimalism on her work, as well as on the work of other members of the group, notably in the relationship to the object, the reified body, and the performer's relationship to the viewer.[32] The artist's "tasks," objectivity, and new definition of "work" developed by the sculptors of the minimalist generation are echoed by the

Judson's creations, and in the collaborations that fostered a certain minimalist aesthetic.

If it is hardly rare to see collaborations between dance and minimal art, and artists' freely recognizing borrowings and common inspiration, all of which is tangible proof of a community of practices, it is worth recalling, too, that dancers and sculptors frequently shared work and living spaces in Downtown Manhattan. Artists and inhabitants of Greenwich Village were involved for a time in a fight to prevent the destruction of the neighborhood,[33] and that struggle had united a good number of artists defending a way of life grounded in the proximity of individuals and art practices. The Judson Church was a nerve center, a meeting place, a place for coming together, having fun, and exchanging ideas and opinions; it served to unify a community of artists who were no longer looking to differentiate between artists, dancers, painters, or sculptors.[34] Thus it was a community with a certain way of life and a community with a certain way of practicing art and seeing the world, which flourished at that time in New York.

Combinational sensibility, however, was not the only common ground for sculptors and dancers of the New York scene; there was also a certain relationship to the stage and the viewer that was to bring the practices of the Judson and the visual arts of the period closer together. Minimal art managed to grant an essential role to the visitor's position, to the viewer in the space of the sculpture, to "the actual circumstances in which the beholder encounters literalist work."[35] Yet while the work of the Judson dancers ran counter to any theatricalized form of dance movement, it would attempt to fuse two distinct temporalities, the viewer's and the performance's. It was paradoxically the rejection of theater that more closely united dancers and sculptors looking to put on an equal footing the space and time of the work of art and the viewer.

In a dual article that appeared in *Artforum* (January and February 1974), Annette Michelson develops this particularly significant problem in Rainer's work. Establishing a new temporality, one modeled on the real execution of gestures and daily activities, constitutes the basis of the performance and the very possibility of interlinking dance and reality.

All action outside the choreography had the potential to be included in the semi-improvised performance. Rainer, however, remained in control of the movements, which were sometimes accelerated and disjointed, as if to remind the audience of the necessary distance between performance and the day-to-day world.

"Using found materials and found or rule-generated movement, using techniques of disjunction, setting movement against sound, sound against music and against speech, operational movement against recorded movement (that of film) and the image of movement in arrest (slides), it distended the arena of the organized temporality, installing within the dance situation a real or operational time, redefining choreography as a situation within which an action may take the time it takes to perform that action."[36] Just as the space of sculpture (like that of dance) is shared and conceived by the viewer's very position, the temporality of the dance gesture is inscribed in real time introducing a continuity between two normally separate temporal regimes.

The sculpture of Donald Judd, Carl Andre, and Morris raises questions concerning not only the temporality of the work of art but also the very place of the viewer with respect to that work of art, the two questions being closely associated. Spaces of visibility and instants of viewing intersect in the dance and sculpture of the first half of the 1960s. Exchanges were indeed fostered between the two, but the artists were also accompanied by sources they had in common. And at the forefront of those sources was the French philosopher Maurice Merleau-Ponty, whose *Phenomenology of Perception* was published in the United States in 1962. Merleau-Ponty's book appeared at just the right time for the concerns of the Judson dancers and the sculptors of the New York scene. The philosopher's analyses of space and motor skills were part of the reading of the dancers and sculptors alike. The body "*inhabits* space and time," " … each instant of the movement embraces its whole span, and particularly the first which, being the active initiative, institutes the link between a here and a yonder, a now and a future which the remainder of the instants will merely develop. In so far as I have a body through which I act in the world, space and time are not, for me, a collection of adjacent points."[37]

This spatiality of the body and the continuity of the gesture are indeed common to the works and writings of both Rainer and Morris.

Sequential Photography and Plasticity of Time

Rainer is probably one of the choreographers of the group who has most closely worked with this question of temporal continuities and discontinuities, both in her dance pieces and her films. Carrie Lambert-Beatty has studied the difficult visibility of dance, between arrested and continuous movement, and analyzes the options that then arise in the work of a choreographer like Rainer: "She could try to make performance less ephemeral, as she herself had done in 1961, when in her dance *The Bells* she repeated a short sequence of movements while facing in different directions, 'in a sense allowing the spectator to "walk around it,"' like an object. Or she could exaggerate the problem of dance's disappearance, as she had just done with an elided continuum of unique movements in what would become her most famous dance, *Trio A.*"[38] First presented in 1966, *Trio A* displays no break within the gesture, wiping out the gap between performance time and lived time, and making us sense that "shifting milieu" described by Merleau-Ponty.

This connection between dance and the temporal continuum is of course linked to the perception of time and space in contemporary sculpture, but also to a more unheralded approach of sequential photography both in the work of the dancers at the Judson and in minimalist sculpture. From the first lines of his 1965 essay called "Notes on Dance,"[39] Morris insists on the recurrent presence of movement in his work, movement of the body, movement of the performer and the viewer, movement of objects. Nevertheless, movement was not Morris's main interest, but rather a medium allowing him to question the relationship of the work of art to space and temporality.

"An element of the work as persistent as the use of objects is the coexistence of the static and the mobile—e.g. a sequence of ten Muybridge slides of a nude man lifting a stone followed by a similar movement by a nude male performer executed in the same space and illuminated by the beam of a slide projector (*Waterman Switch,* 1965); or the rotation of the upper torso through 90° over a five minute period—the movement itself being imperceptible—accompanied by a taped description of strenuous movements (*Arizona*, 1963), or a taped verbal description of actions which occur at a remove in time (*Waterman Switch*); or the illumination of a runner with stroboscopic-type light which, because of the briefness of the illumination, gives a static image (*Check*, 1964). In one form or another the static coexisting with the mobile occurs in every work."[40]

What Morris describes with respect to his dance pieces reveals a dilemma between the perception of a continuous time and the urge to seize the moment. Sequential photography, and its use in the field of dance, points up the relationship between real time—lived, continuous, and indivisible—and the time of the gesture, that of succession, immediacy, and instantaneity. The trace, whether photographic or graphic, is that of the instant, a reproducible instant evincing the urge to seize an objective time "with its fixed positions."[41] And yet "time, in our primordial experience of it, is not for us a system of objective positions, through which we pass, but a mobile setting which moves away from us, like the landscape seen through a railway carriage window."[42] The use of drawn lines notably in *Flares* or *Fontana Mix* and photography play on that dilemma.

The early years of the Judson Dance Theater were a period of a consciously overt eclecticism and radical experimentation with the creative processes of choreography and the collective as both a way of making art and a way of life. While this eclecticism sprang largely from a community that brought together dancers, sculptors, painters, musicians, and filmmakers, it drew sustenance from shared readings and a common wish to break with the past. The viewer's place, the environment of bodies and objects, and the fundamental unity of that environment were all rethought. The dance gesture was understood in its visual perception, an aporia that came to mean a challenge that required the artist to turn to the photographic image, the line, the page, light, even text. Beside the most obvious collaborations then, it was graphic processes and spatial and temporal logic that brought together visual artists and dancers in a community of viewpoints.

[1] The quotation in the title is from Yvonne Rainer (1966) cited by Carrie Lambert-Beatty, *Being Watched, Yvonne Rainer and the 1960s*, The MIT Press, Cambridge (MA), 2008, p. 3.
[2] Barry Laine, "In Search of Judson," in *Dance Magazine*, September 1982, p. 81. Judson Memorial Church Archives, Fales Library and Special Collections, New York University, New York.
[3] The Judson Dance Theater's activities continued after 1964 with a new generation of artists and dancers, but it is above all those key early years that drive my argument here.
[4] Sally Banes, "The Birth of the Judson Dance Theater: 'A Concert of Dance' at Judson Church, July 6, 1962," in *Dance Chronicle*, vol. 5, no. 2, 1982, p. 167.
[5] Sally Banes, *Greenwich Village 1963: Avant-garde Performance and the Effervescent Body*, Duke University Press, Durham (NC) 1993, p. 73.
[6] The basement areas of the Judson were indeed the site of a series of Happenings, a few images of which have come down to us, notably of the activities of Jim Dine (*The Smiling Workman*, 1960) and Claes Oldenburg (*Snapshots from the City*, 1960). See Olivier Lussac, *Happening et Fluxus, Polyexpressivité et pratique concrète des arts*, L'Harmattan, Paris 2004.
[7] Al Carmines, the pastor who welcomed the dancers of the Robert Dunn workshop, in an interview with Sally Banes (July 1, 1980), in Sally Banes, "The Birth of the Judson Dance Theater: 'A Concert of Dance' at Judson Church, July 6, 1962," p. 171.
[8] Sally Banes, *Democracy's Body. Judson Dance Theater, 1962–1964*, Duke University Press, Durham (NC) 1993, p. 1.
[9] Ibid.
[10] Robert Dunn, interview with Sally Banes (May 16, 1980), in ibid., p. 7.
[11] An initiative on the part of Robert Nichols that flourished from 1961 to 1981.
[12] See the interview between Sally Banes and Ruth Emerson (June 10, 1980), in Sally Banes, "The Birth of the Judson Dance Theater," p. 170.
[13] Entitled *Concert of Dance*, this first event featured the following program: "By Ruth Emerson: *Shoulder. Timepiece. Narrative* (J. Dunn, McDowell, Paxton, Rainer, E. Summers). By Fred Herko: *Once or Twice a Week I Put on Sneakers to Go Uptown* (music: Satie, pianist: Robert Dunn, costumes: Remy Charlip). *Like Most People* (music: Cecil Taylor). By Steve Paxton: *Transit. Proxy.* (Paxton, Rainer, Tipton). By John Herbert McDowell: *February Fun at Bucharest* (music: Marc-Antoine Charpentier). By Elaine Summers: *The Daily Wake* (structure created with the following performers: Emerson, S. Gross, McDowell, A. Williams, E. Summers). *Instant Chance* (Emerson, D. Hay, Herko, MacLane, Paxton, McDowell, Rudy Perez, E. Summers, Carol Scothorn. Music: Robert Dunn, John Herbert McDowell, Elaine Summers, Arthur Williams). By David Gordon: *Helen's Dance* (music: Satie, pianist: Robert Dunn). *Mannequin Dance* (music: James Waring, costume: Barbara Kastle). By Deborah Hay: *Rain Fur. 5 things*. By Gretchen MacLane: *Qubic*. By Yvonne Rainer: *Divertissement* (Rainer, Davis). *Ordinary Dance. Dance for 3 People and 6 Arms* (Davis, J. Dunn, Rainer). By John Cage: *Cartridge Music.* By Carol Scothorn: *Isolations*. By William Davis: *Crayon,* (music: The Volumes, Dee Clark, The Shells) By Alex Hay, Deborah Hay and Charles Rotmil: *Rafladan*." From the press release, Judson Memorial Church Archives (subseries Judson Dance Theater), Fales Library and Special Collections, New York University.
[14] See Allen Hughes, "Dance Program Seen at Church," in *The New York Times*, July 7, 1962, p. 9. Judson Memorial Church Archives (subseries Judson Dance Theater), Fales Library and Special Collections, New York University, New York.
[15] Ibid.
[16] Conserved in the Judson Dance Theater archives: Judson Memorial Church Archives (subseries Judson Dance Theater), Fales Library and Special Collections, New York University, New York.
[17] Allen Hughes, "Dance Program Seen at Church," p. 9.
[18] The press release mentions Carol Scothorn and Alex Hay as being in charge of lighting, and "advisor for costumes: Ruth Emerson."
[19] See Carolee Schneemann, *More than Meat Joy, Performance Works and Selected Writings*, McPherson & Co Publishers, New York 1997, p. 32.
[20] Ibid.
[21] Carolee Schneemann described herself as a "randomized drawing machine" in *Up to And Including Her Limits*. See the performance script, a copy of which is stored in the Lucy R. Lippard Papers, Archives of American Art, Washington, D.C.
[22] See Liza Bear and Willoughby Sharp, "The Performer as Persona: An Interview with Yvonne Rainer," in *Avalanche*, no. 5, Summer 1972, p. 54.
[23] The share of manipulating objects in dance sparked a debate between Monroe Beardsley and Noël Carroll and Sally Banes, the latter two writers defending the choreographic qualities of *Room Service* from criticism in an article by Beardsley in which he asserted that Yvonne Rainer's work did not in fact rise to the level of dance. See Noël Carroll and Sally Banes, "Working and Dancing: A Response to Monroe Beardsley's 'What Is Going on in Dance?'," in *Dance Research Journal*, vol. 15, no. 1, Autumn 1982, p. 37–41.
[24] Elaine Summers, in an interview with Sally Banes (March 15, 1980), in Sally Banes, *Democracy's Body*, p. 188.
[25] Dick Higgins theorized the notion of intermedia in 1965.
[26] Carol Scothorn, correspondence with Sally Banes, April 12, 1982, in Sally Banes, "The Birth of the Judson Dance Theater," p. 199.
[27] *Flares* was performed for the first time at the "Concert of Dance" number 8, June 25, 1963, with the following performers: Philip Corner, Malcolm Goldstein, Dick Higgins, Norma Marder, Elizabeth Munro, Max Neuhaus, Arlene Rothlein, Beverly Schmidt, James Tenney, and Vincent Wright.
[28] The individual sheets of the score and the description of the piece are conserved in the Judson Memorial Church Archives, Fales Library and Special Collections, New York University, New York.
[29] Tim Ingold, *Lines. A Brief History*, Routledge, London and New York 2007, p. 38.
[30] See the range of notations theorized by Nelson Goodman in *Languages of Art. An Approach to a Theory of Symbols*, Bobbs-Merrill, Indianapolis 1968.
[31] "In a logical thing, each part is dependent on the last. It follows in a certain sequence as part of the logic. But, a rational thing is something you have to make a rational decision on each time … You have to think about it. In a logical sequence, you don't think about it. It's a way of not thinking. It's *ir*rational," Sol LeWitt, quoted in Frances Colpitt, *Minimal Art: The Critical Perspective*, University of Washington Press, Seattle (WA) 1990, p. 58.
[32] Liza Bear and Willoughby Sharp, "The Performer as Persona," p. 50 and 52. On minimalism: "It was a movement, and it seemed very vital—phenomenology and objecthood … in terms of dancing and performing it took the form of (and I wasn't alone in this), it took the form of non-theatricality. A refusal to project a persona, but thinking of oneself in dancing as simply a neutral purveyor of information." And "it *was* influenced by the minimal art thing in its anti-European, anti-decorative, anti-cultural, in some way, attitudes. It led me more toward making dance that was involved with task, work, rather than with exhibition."

[33] Greenwich Village and what was to become SoHo were in the crosshairs of Robert Moses, who was defending various large-scale town planning projects that included an expressway, against which artists and inhabitants, led by Jane Jacobs, were protesting. Those years of protest and civic activism proved especially unifying for the early-1960s art community that was installed in the neighborhood's legal and illegal lofts.

[34] Legalization of lofts brought with it the need to define the activities of "artists," which raised problems of its own. Eventually it was declared that any creative activity was enough to qualify one as an artist, even for a law that was mainly concerned with the visual arts. This evolution of the definition tells us quite a lot about a state of mind attuned to the diversity and freedom of art practices: "The definition of an artist, as stated in the Multiple Dwelling Law for the Visual Arts, is in the process of being changed for expansion, and will apply to all A.I.R.'s as well. Filmmakers, weavers, ceramists, happeners, choreographers, composers, are among those to be included—in fact, anyone doing any CREATIVE work who needs the space will be back with the A.T.A." Artists Tenants Association Records, Archives of American Art, Washington, D.C. Editor's note: see essay by Alexander Schwan in this volume, p. 60–73.

[35] Michael Fried, "Art and Objecthood," in *Artforum*, vol. 5, no. 10, Summer 1967, p. 15.

[36] Annette Michelson, "Yvonne Rainer, Part One: The Dancer and the Dance," in *Artforum*, vol. 12, no. 5, January 1974, p. 58.

[37] Maurice Merleau-Ponty, *Phenomenology of Perception*, trans. Colin Smith, Routledge & Kegan Paul, The Humanities Press, London and New Jersey 1978, p. 139–140 [1st ed.: Paris 1945].

[38] Carrie Lambert-Beatty, *Being Watched, Yvonne Rainer and the 1960s*, p. 3.

[39] Robert Morris, "Notes on Dance," in *The Tulane Drama Review*, vol. 10, no. 2, Winter 1965, p. 179.

[40] Ibid., p. 183.

[41] Maurice Merleau-Ponty, *Phenomenology of Perception*, p. 420.

[42] Ibid., p. 419–420.

Visualizing Voids and Measuring the Earth: The Raison d'Être of Drawing in the Choreographic Work of Anne Teresa De Keersmaeker

Julie Enckell Julliard

This essay is followed by an interview which took place in Paris on November 29, 2013.
The author would like to thank Nicolas Julliard, Federica Martini, and Stéphanie Serra.

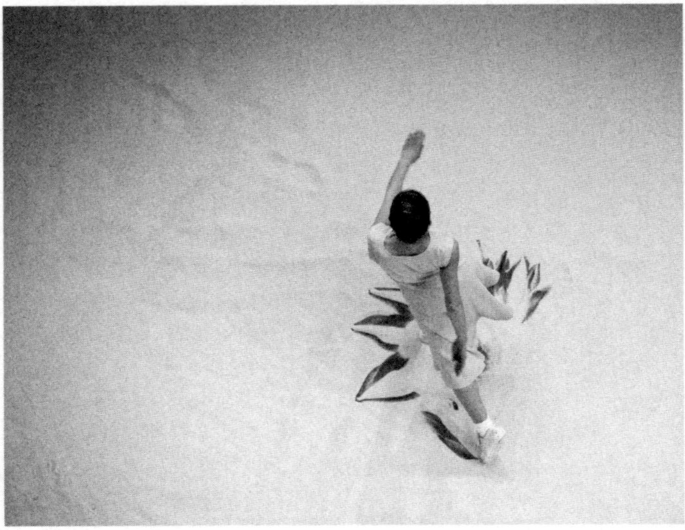

Anne Teresa De Keersmaeker
Violin Phase from Fase: Four Movements to the Music of Steve Reich, 1982
Created by Anne Teresa De Keersmaeker on the occasion of Beursschouwburg, Brussels, March 18, 1982; here as performed on the occasion of *Performance 13: On Line/Anne Teresa De Keersmaeker*, The Donald B. and Catherine C. Marron Atrium, The Museum of Modern Art, New York, January 22–23, 2011
Concept and direction: Thierry De Mey; choreography and performance: Anne Teresa De Keersmaeker; music: Steve Reich; violin: George Alexander van Dam

There are certain tropes in the work of professional historians of the arts that only artists manage to thwart. Because we understand far too little of the history of dance and kinesthesia, and our field limits itself quite frequently and almost exclusively to the field of the plastic arts, there is an initial automatic response that consists of immediately looking at choreographers' drawings to find reference points in the formal language of the art of their day and age. This probably springs from the fact that the two disciplines of dance and the visual arts have maintained close ties throughout their history, and that, for several decades now, bridges have been built between them, in particular through performance art. Anne Teresa De Keersmaeker is above all a choreographer who is respected in her milieu. Her practice is accompanied and enriched by work in drawing, which she does not show in art venues or exhibit independently from her dance research.

The drawings are essentially abstract; they are made up of simple geometrical motifs—circles, spirals, rectangles, lines, etc.—generally accompanied by various annotations in words, letters, and numbers, referring as much to the nature of the movement as to the identity of the dancers and the length or different phases of a dance piece. Colors are rarely employed and when they do appear, they are often uniform—the dancer limits herself most of the time to using just one of them. In some cases, the drawing pops up on stage—as a circular diagram traced out on the floor—when not emerging from the dance itself. With the exception of the drawings produced by or for her dance pieces—with *Fase* (2002/2011), but also *Elena's Aria* (1984), or more recently *Cesena* (2011)—drawing is far from constituting a work of art in and of itself. It is first of all a tool of dance notation and cannot be considered independently of what it is bound up with—a sequence of movements, a given period of time—and which the dancer has used from the outset to realize her projects. When I met the choreographer in Paris for an interview in the fall of 2013 [see p. 156–161], I learned, moreover, that the drawings, once they had been worked out, were often given and explained to the dancers to enable them to visualize for themselves the sequences envisaged by the artist. This approach did, therefore, have pedagogical virtues that are hard to see at first. That is, drawing is abstract and that abstraction possesses an inner logic that is not accessible to all without explanation.

Attention to any kind of structure or layout that the choreographer's drawings denote, the working out of a motif according to precise rules and proportions, the minimal character of the vocabulary—all of this invites us from the very outset to seek formal echoes in the artistic developments of the decades that witnessed the birth of her succeeding dance pieces in the United States and Belgium. The first of these, created in 1982 when De Keersmaeker was studying at New York University's Tisch School of the Arts (*Fase: Four Movements to the Music of Steve Reich*), is indeed built around a piece of music that Steve Reich composed in the 1960s, a time when John Cage was elaborating his first musical score drawings, and American abstraction was striking out in new directions in the plastic arts, mixing ever more frequently with other disciplines.[1] This founding reference fosters the idea that the dancer's formal vocabulary—her circles, spirals, parallel lines, pentagons, and other abstract signs—may have been influenced by the practices of abstraction that emerged in the 1960s. The drawings of Mel Bochner, for instance, thematize the measure of space. Beside posing the shift of numbers to spatial reality as an articulation, for some they summon a series of abstract signs that play on different types of relationships, whether symmetrical or tangential, among geometrical shapes that are at times formally akin to those produced by the Belgian artist.[2] The works of artists for whom the body in motion acts like a vector are sometimes a distorting mirror of the presence of drawing on stage and its integration in the choreography. The Japanese artist Atsuko Tanaka, a member of the Gutai movement, for instance, recorded herself tracing a temporary mind map on the sand in a filmed self-portrait. This performance brings to mind the piece that De Keersmaeker created in the sand for *Violin Phase*,[3] which gives rise to a traced circular figure beneath her feet at the end of the performance. In 2011, the choreographer brought the project to the exhibition *On Line. Drawing through the Twentieth Century* (2010–2011) at The Museum of Modern Art in New York. This time viewers watched the birth of a drawing through dance directly from the museum's upper floors. Shown as part of the exhibition's thematic framework, De Keersmaeker's work fully participated in the realm of contemporary plastic arts. The museum setting became the space of the stage, the very stage where a dance piece also played out as a fully-fledged work of visual art in the sense above.

Integrating the dance piece into the overt theme of *On Line* might suggest that the choreographer's predilection for drawing should be viewed first as a piece of formal research that is closely related to the experiments of visual artists. I went to meet with De Keersmaeker, filled with the thoughts voiced here, and with the idea that her drawings bear witness to a kind of permeability—conscious or not, although rich in meaning—in relation to the visual arts of her generation. During our discussion, the artist nonetheless pointed out that she did not necessarily connect her drawing practice with contemporary forms. I understood then that my initial postulate about the formal echoes of her art with that of visual artists who had also developed a body of work in drawing would prove insufficient for comprehending the meaning of her work, and that I needed to search elsewhere, and in a different way, to locate it. First of all, because De Keersmaeker's drawings, which are constructed like arrangements of geometrical motifs, are characterized by a clear form of atemporality. This atemporality offers the possibility of connecting them with art forms of all periods and cultures. The recurrent motifs of the circle, spiral, and pentagram, the network of perpendicular lines, and finally the arrows touch on a universal form of visual language, transcending both borders and time.

It is important to note, moreover, the words chosen by De Keersmaeker to describe the act of drawing. Above all, it is a "way of organizing the space and time" of the choreography, as well as a means "of visualizing its empty spaces." The approach thus had to go beyond simple dance notation, and the terms used underscored something more fundamental, something having to do with her understanding of the world. To determine if that intuition was correct, I returned to De Keersmaeker's thought as she had articulated it in her interviews with Bojana Cvejić,[4] her understanding of existence and the world, her beliefs, and her points of reference. How does the choreographer envisage the space and time of being on earth? In what ways do dance and drawing reflect those ideas? All of that was precisely expressed by the dancer and was expanded on in our exchanges. What emerged was a great sensitivity to the functioning of the world overall, to the physical laws of nature constituting higher invisible forces that are liable to influence our existence. For De Keersmaeker, this conception of things is fostered by Far Eastern philosophies, Taoism in particular, of which the choreographer has had a detailed and precise knowledge for the last 20 years. Without delving into too many details, we might simply recall here that in those philosophies the world is considered in terms of complementarities (yin and yang) rather than Manichaeisms, and that reality finds itself endowed with an infinite power to transform. The choreographer's knowledge thus allies in a surprising way a rigorous pragmatism and a belief in transcendental or esoteric forces, all of which fosters a profound quest for harmony, through the need to feel in sync with nature and its vital forces. Formally this need results in great attention being paid to the relationships of proportions. "With practice I became more and more convinced that if you put it in a drawing, the drawing has to be beautiful. It has to be well proportioned."

The dancer borrows the principles of proportion from medieval mathematics, working out her dance pieces according to the golden ratio as it is applied in the principle of the Fibonacci sequence.[5] This series of increasingly larger integers, which had already been discovered in ancient India, bears the name of its Western theoretician of the 13th century. The sequence can also be seen in nature—its exponential logic underlies the pedigree of honeybees, the structure of DNA molecules: "I use the Fibonacci sequence as a temporal spiral. The dancers calibrate, for instance, their entrances in proportions of 1, 2, 3, 5, 8, etc. Or I divide the length of the show or the music according to that series, and I observe what happens at the traversal points."[6] The combination of numbers is also developed on the basis of a magic square, in this case serving to structure the movement in three-dimensional space.[7] Thus the choreographer constantly makes appeal to sacred geometry, that ancestral thought founded on the correspondences between the macrostructural forms of the universe and those of human nature. Such principles govern the spatiotemporal construction of the choreography and serve as the basis for elaborating the drawing. Their use reached an apotheosis in the Middle Ages, while among Christians, art forms are never understood independently of Christian thought and its codes. Each iconographic choice has its explanation in a symbolism established by the Church Fathers; each measurement or proportion refers to those mentioned in the Scriptures, with art always appearing as a materialized form of the sacred.

While conveying a highly personal vision of existence, De Keersmaeker thus revives this perception of art, whose form perforce weaves a play of symbolic correspondences between the tangible world and the spiritual. "How can I use abstract ideas to [sic] concrete movements?"[8] This concern is the same that underlies the initial dance pieces. Through the repetition of the gestures, and their extreme simplicity—they are inspired by children's first danced movements—with *Fase* the choreographer found the means to link the first intuitions about the movements of human beings to the mathematical structure of the music: "When I created my first dance piece—*Violin Phase*—I looked for a plan that could govern first my movement and my inscription in space-time; this involved two interdependent registers. It was Thierry De Mey who suggested to me that I observe the laws of growth in nature, the biological and mathematical models that account for the natural phenomena of expansion."[9]

At this point in my reflection, the links between the choreographer's drawings and other forms of art seemed clearer to me. First of all, in the elements borrowed from sacred geometry, there were numerous echoes to be found in the thinking of medieval theologians, for whom art forms are above all tokens of a precise organization of space-time. Without subscribing to the same worldview, De Keersmaeker's drawings also chart such an organization through diagrams and symbolic forms.[10] These affinities with the Middle Ages fueled the projects *En Atendant* (2010) and *Cesena*, the latter performed in 2011 at the Festival d'Avignon in the *court d'honneur*, the main courtyard, of the Papal Palace. At the time De Keersmaeker had joined forces with Björn Schmelzer, the director of the vocal ensemble Graindelavoix, to create a dance piece sung according to the rules of 14th-century *ars subtilior*. Formed from a circle, the geometrical configuration of *Cesena* played out on the ground like the rose window of a cathedral, bearing at the center a star, which was in turn inscribed in a pentagram.

Other parallels point to drawings on black paper by Rudolf Steiner.[11] In compositions that were also created for educational ends, the anthroposophical conception of astral bodies is expressed through a play of spirals based on the Fibonacci sequence, or by complementary eccentric and concentric forces, tokens of a constant search for an articulation between the material and the spiritual body. It is energy flows that govern the composition as much as they locate the being within the universe. Here drawings go beyond the simple need for notation to incarnate a harmonized vision of beings, space, and time. They play the part of an interface between the visible and the invisible, embody the place where two complementary parts of the world succeed in uniting. Beyond their mission as notation, for Steiner drawings represented a vector that renders a component that escapes our sensorial perception of the world visible to one and all.

During our exchanges, De Keersmaeker remembered the drawings that her grandfather, an agricultural engineer, did of farmland and its distribution by owner. These drawings point to a macrostructure, a geometrical order of the world, as much as they reflect the daily life of the population. De Keersmaeker is so fond of them because they indicate the articulation of an abstract geometrical principle and its embodiment in nature. The dancer also brought up the pleasure she felt when she discovered ceramic kitchen utensils decorated with geometrical drawings at the Mycenaean archeological museum. Like the structured fields of the Belgian countryside, the ancient vestiges embody that articulation between a superior order of the world—of which drawings are an imprint or relic—and human civilization, guided in its daily life by needs as basic as feeding oneself.

De Keersmaeker's drawings thus call for a reading that is based not solely on a play of formal kinships, or that echoes with the art that emerged at a certain period, but also that based on a homothetic relationship with intangible forces, whose translation in numbers or geometry refers us to a universal codification, i.e., drawings as the mark of a form of abstraction of the world, which they enable us to experience on a human scale. The measure is done first on the page and then by the body in space, "When you work with geometry, with geometrical patterns, what you are actually doing is is measuring the earth."[12] In drawing and dance, De Keersmaeker sounds the limits of space; she comprehends it in view of lending it an outline, imagining its beginning and its end. The fundamental principles of the Christian liturgy offer keys for evaluating the scope of this expression. Through rites and processions, the liturgy places Christians in eschatological time, and helps them experience the "organization of time and space" dictated by God. It officiates as the means for envisioning the fate of beings, visualizing their trajectory, anticipating their end and their rebirth in Paradise.

By the intermediary of drawing and dance, De Keersmaeker both revives and embodies that appropriateness of beings with the world, thought with the body, the abstract with the concrete, which formally is translated by the fitting measure of things. Drawing is not limited, however, to bringing to light a way of locating oneself in the world. Through its encrypted language it still possesses a symbolic force whose depths the choreographer and her dancers alone have plumbed. It reminds us that the role of dancers was always that of the ferryman, in the sense of those who, in sacred dances, play out once again the key stages of human destiny, connecting beings with a transcendental order of the world.

* * *

JULIE ENCKELL JULLIARD Let's start with general thoughts about dance and drawing: both are related to childhood as the very first intuitive and simple ways to express creativity. Do you remember yourself drawing as much as dancing as a child? How important was it for you to draw?

ANNE TERESA DE KEERSMAEKER It's funny, no one has ever asked me that question … When I go back in my memory, yes, I liked to draw and paint a lot. Maybe also because my mother, who was a teacher, could draw quite well. My grandfather also, an agriculture engineer, was an amateur painter and draughtsman. He drew a lot.

JEJ Do you remember watching him draw in his atelier?

ATDK No, he was already too old when I was born. He made a lot of drawings of landscapes and of his children. He was a soldier during the First World War. In the trenches, he drew the army. Then afterward, as agriculture engineer, he wrote a book based on the history of agriculture in the lowlands of Belgium. He interviewed a lot of farmers and also studied old paintings to collect information. But he also drew a lot of agricultural tools and plans of how the farmers divided up the land around the villages. These drawings of how land was mapped are really beautiful. When I was working on the *Choreographer's Scores* (2012),[13] I moved house and I came across these drawings again. I was extremely touched by seeing my grandfather's drawings, which were very much articulated and detailed, but also half scientific and half artistic.

JEJ Do you remember your mother drawing?

ATDK Yes. She was not an amateur painter like my grandfather, but she would draw a lot of things for us. I remember that.

JEJ Do you think you began to feel like moving at the same time that you felt the desire to draw?

ATDK [Long silence.] I think that drawing was something that was very much related to childhood, to school. It was encouraged, and I did it, but then once you get to a certain age it's not encouraged anymore in the educational system. I began to draw again when I started to be a choreographer. Then I began organizing time and space, I would make drawings mainly of geometrical patterns. To organize a time span. I never do them to remember things. They are schemes and scores.

JEJ Would you say then that these appear at the very beginning of the creative process?

ATDK They help to articulate thoughts. I must say that the last time that I was involved with drawing on a daily basis was in the education of my children. They went to a Steiner school, where they were encouraged in a very active way. Even for mathematics. I liked it a lot.

JEJ Some children use geometrical patterns very early in their drawings. Did you?

ATDK [Long silence.] That's a difficult question. I don't know. I have more memories of narrative paintings and drawings, and these are the ones that I still have. I do very much like the idea of drawing as an origin of something. A couple of years ago I was in Greece, in Mycenae, in the archaeological museum. I was looking at the tomb of Agamemnon (also called the Atreus treasury [1250 BC]).

These ceramics hold some of the earliest drawings. They're all geometrical forms, patterns, with a lot of spirals. It's all designed geometry. These objects combine the function of a tool, say for cooking, with drawing. Which I like a lot.

JEJ What is it that you like?

ATDK That the use of geometrical drawing is so old, and that the very origin of drawing is based on something that has to do with nourishment.

JEJ Would you say that you use drawing to trigger your thoughts about dance?

ATDK Yes, you could say that. The fact of visualizing. A lot is about proportions when you organize movement in time and in space. I became more and more convinced the more I drew that if you put it in a drawing, the drawing has to be beautiful and well proportioned. Which is the same thing in Eastern calligraphy.

JEJ Here the brush has to be held vertically, perpendicular to the paper, like the body on the stage.

ATDK Absolutely. And in those drawings, it's about the organization of space, about what is full and what is empty. It's not much about what you draw, but rather which spaces you don't draw.

JEJ Is drawing a way for you to see voids, too?

ATDK Yes, exactly. To see voids, and of course they are an extension of an energetic flow and a movement.

JEJ On the other hand, they are maps, and an abstraction of all that you put in your choreographies. They don't give any information about color for example.

ATDK Yes, they are a kind of reduction of the choreographies.

JEJ Do you begin to think of your choreography with this opposition between full spaces and emptiness?

ATDK No, I don't think so. There is more a general idea. I have a time span in my head. That generally comes from music. Of course music has a drawing, a notation. I first see the total time span and in that time span I organize divisions and energetic tension lines. Intensities. And then it is about special organization.

JEJ Would you say that drawings give structure to your thoughts?

ATDK Yes.

JEJ Do you ever come back to them? How do you use them?

ATDK Yes, of course. I will make a timeline and a spatial organization. Then we will start to make this material and I have this structural draught. Then we dance it and sometimes things don't work out as you planned them. We look and I ask: "Could you please count once, this is supposed to be 20 minutes. How much is it in reality?" Then you draw the real time span and see how the proportions are, if they are out of balance.

JEJ Is it a tool?

ATDK Yes. For example, for *Partita 2* (2013), it's very clear there is a geometrical pattern that underlies it. There is one point. Then there are two points, which make a line, so we draw a line. From that line we have a circle and from that circle we make a curve into it and then we go on to a pentagon and then we wipe it out and then we retrograde back. It's all very designed.

JEJ Sometimes a drawing comes from a choreography, for example at The Museum of Modern Art in New York (2011): would you say your path in the sand made a drawing?

ATDK Yes. It's writing movement in the sand. As if you draw with your finger in the sand.

JEJ Did it feel different to dance in the sand? Was it as if you were carving something in the clay?

ATDK Yes. It has technical consequences, such as stability, but also the fact that people could see the movement from above. The frontal view was gone and the design emerged from the movement. The fact that you leave an imprint, traces. Literally inscribing dance itself.

JEJ Could you say that this was the first time your choreography had drawing as a consequence?

ATDK Yes. Well in all the pieces, from the very beginning, there were always geometrical patterns or designed frameworks that underlined the choreography.

JEJ We could then say that there is also an invisible drawing.

ATDK Yes.

JEJ Do you know contemporary artists that draw? What is your perception of them?

ATDK Only a few, it is very intuitive. The daily practice of drawing is a kind of handwriting. The fact that our practice of writing by hand is disappearing has consequences on our thoughts.

JEJ What would you say about the presentability of your drawing practice? We know the drawings of Trisha Brown quite well, for example. What are yours like?

ATDK [Long silence.] I never thought of commercializing them. It's different because Trisha really made drawings for their own sake. The drawings I do are always working material. There are always tools.

JEJ Some artists show their sketchbooks, even if they are not finished works.

ATDK They are visual artists, aren't they?

JEJ Yes. You are a kind of a visual artist, too.

ATDK I think it's different. I write with bodies.

JEJ If someone proposed to exhibit your drawings, how would you react?

ATDK As I say, they are working tools. I have seen people sell the drawings they've made on a tablecloth in a restaurant. I'm not so much in favor of that.

JEJ I understand. But would you say that it could add something to our perception of the way you work?

ATDK The *Choreographer's Scores* are the most honest way to do it, I guess. They are a way to clarify the way I work.

JEJ Are you surprised to realize how important they are in your life and work?

ATDK [Long silence.] The question is about what remains. It is so different with visual arts or literature. For choreography, this is something that could remain from inscribing the movement which disappears. But I find it difficult, a constant dilemma. [She opens a copy of *Choreographer's Scores*.]

JEJ Would you say that your drawings have evolved with your choreographies?

ATDK Oh yes. I'm working on *Drumming* (1998) now and *Rain* (2001), and underlining geometry can sometimes become more complicated.

JEJ Some look like spines. Are you the only one who understands or reads them?

ATDK I use the drawings to explain things to the dancers.

[1] Anne Teresa De Keersmaeker and Bojana Cvejić, *Carnets d'une chorégraphe. Fase, Rosas danst Rosas, Elena's Aria, Bartòk*, Rosas and Mercatorfonds, Brussels 2012. On Cage, for example: John Cage, Jeremy Millar, Lauren Wright, and Roger Malbert, *Every Day is a Good Day. The Visual Art of John Cage*, Hayward Press, London 2010.

[2] Mel Bochner recounts the origins of these drawings as follows, "After [the] September '73 exhibition of *Non-Verbal Structures* (RYB), the shape of drawings returned to the center of my attention. The charcoal drawings in that exhibition had dealt with quite basic types of relationships, generally axial symmetries, tangencies, and simple counting structures—triangle (3), square (4), pentagon (5)." Mel Bochner, *Solar System & Rest Rooms. Writings and Interviews 1965–2007*, The MIT Press, Cambridge (MA) and London 2008, p. 120.

[3] Anne Teresa De Keersmaeker and Thierry De Mey, *Top Shot*, 2002, video, 16'04".

[4] Anne Teresa De Keersmaeker and Bojana Cvejić, *En Atendant & Cesena*, *Carnets d'une chorégraphe*, vol. II, Rosas and Mercatorfonds, Brussels 2013, especially p. 26 to 37.

[5] This is also the case of Mario Merz, who introduced the Fibonacci sequence into his works in 1970, not only as a ratio, but also to symbolize the flow of energy in organic matter.

[6] Anne Teresa De Keersmaeker and Bojana Cvejić, *Carnets d'une chorégraphe*, vol. II, p. 36.

[7] Ibid., p. 32–33.

[8] Said by the artist in English in the interview in the DVD accompanying ibid.

[9] Ibid., p. 34.

[10] Kinships exist with the musical notation from the Romanesque period—with the *Liber divinorum operum* of Hildegard of Bingen, for example—where a concentric structure governs the different levels of visible and invisible reality.

[11] During the interview the choreographer mentioned how much her connection with drawing was revived through the Steiner school, where she sent her own children. The Steiner-Waldorf teaching method is based on the theories of Rudolf Steiner and his conception of education.

[12] Ben Coccio, assisted by Cal Robertson, *MoMA "Online" Series: Anne Teresa De Keersmaeker*, 3'24", 2011: https://www.moma.org/explore/multimedia/videos/136/902.

[13] Anne Teresa De Keersmaeker and Bojana Cvejić, *A Choregrapher's Score*, Yale University Press, New Haven and London 2012.

The Structure of Signs, The Lines of the Body An Interview with Cindy Van Acker

Nolwenn Mégard

This interview took place in Geneva between May and November 2014.

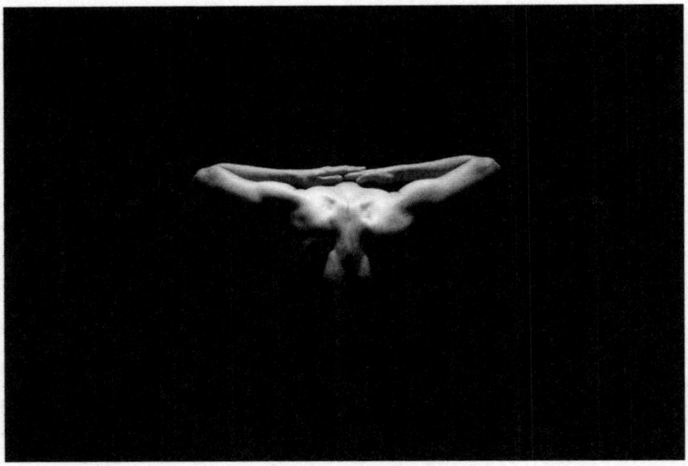

Cindy Van Acker
Monoloog, 2010
Created and performed by Cindy Van Acker, on the occasion of Festival Électron, Alhambra, Geneva, April 1, 2010

Points, lines, grids: the choreographic scores created by Cindy Van Acker—the Belgian dancer and choreographer who has been living and working in Geneva for over 20 years—reveal a passion for structure. These notations govern a number of her pieces, and each of them has its own code, which does not extend either the movement of the performer or the hand drawing them. Rather, each individual code is built up like a graphic representation, a species of writing that is influenced by the visual logic of the signs. Lines are likewise present on stage when the bodies of the dancers of Cie Greffe, founded in 2002 with the solo *Corps 00:00*, become the vectors of geometric motifs. That is, they propagate forms and directions in space that resonate with the rigorous minimalist stage installations, like the *Nine Tubes* machine created by Victor Roy for *Diffraction* (2011).

In Van Acker's work, powerful electronic sounds, precision in the composition of the dance, and great mastery of the body exist alongside moments in which the body becomes an art material and summons forms that upend perception and stimulate the imagination. The suggestion of potential images and the experience of losing one's sensory reference points are thus central concerns of the choreographer, whose world is marked by a keen interest in the visual arts and film. This inclination leads the artist to create sorts of tableaux vivants and guide the eye of the viewer as a camera would, but also to use the pictorial medium directly on stage in the piece entitled *Helder* (2013), for example.

* * *

NOLWENN MÉGARD Working with Victor Roy, in 2012 you mounted an exhibition for the Genevan art space Le Commun at the Bâtiment d'art contemporain. *Score Conductor* presented your choreographic scores to the public for the first time.[1] The notational systems invented for your pieces took concrete shape in different ways, notably thanks to machines or objects executing the scores and revealing the structure of the graphic system, for example, a giant piece of knitting for "Étude M" of *Fractie* (2003). Did the scores as such, which were exhibited as prints on panels designed by the graphic artist collective Akatre, have the status of works of art at that moment? Could you have defined them as "drawings?"

CINDY VAN ACKER They have the status of graphic artworks in the context of that exhibition, but their essence only takes shape when resonating with the materialization of their content. You could say that they are artistically translatable and reproducible inductions, generating multiple interpretations. So I wouldn't want to characterize them as drawings for exactly that reason, because they play a role that goes beyond themselves as objects.

NM In general, can we speak of a practice of drawing within your work as a dancer and choreographer?

CVA I use drawing when it's a question of researching solutions for thinking of the stage space or when I work *without* a score to identify the movement on paper in a way other than with coded signs; I draw forms that the bodies take, the lines of the dancers and their movements. My notations though are clearly more akin to writing than drawing.

NM In the exhibition catalogue *Traces of Dance* (1991), the dance historian Laurence Louppe suggests that the movement of the body is linked to the movement traced out by the hand in the practice of notation through the idea of a flow joining them.[2] In your work, however, it seems to me that the signs of the scores are neither an extension of the danced movement, nor the opposite. How do you see yourself in the history of choreographic notation, for example, with respect to systems that have influenced the whole of the 20th century, like Rudolf von Laban's system?

CVA The invention of a tool like Labanotation that enables you to note each movement, position of the body, or shift is extraordinary and gives access to an archival space besides the recorded image, as well as various possibilities for developing the idiom of choreography. However, the objective of my scores does not fit the idea of an idiom as such. I use them if a project demands it and invent tailor-made signs when I feel the need for composing in the work. This involves an occasional, compact use in the graphic representation. The notations are accordingly illegible to anyone who doesn't know the codes for deciphering them. They give me the chance to move the choreography along, on my kitchen table, without the dancers' presence.

NM Some of your scores generate motifs through alignment, repetition, and the arrangement of the signs forming them, like the pyramidal construction of the "Étude M" of *Fractie*, or the incredible patterns of the conductor's score of *Diffraction*. Do you work out these notations according to graphically oriented considerations?

CVA The graphic forms often appear by themselves because it is the logic of the choreographic composition as such that is visually taking shape. That introduces a dialogue between signs and the danced movement, which may command the graphic forms or, on the contrary, may be diverted by the representation. I like to pay attention to chance and the unexpected incidents that arise in that confrontation between logic and aesthetics.

NM In some of your pieces, including *Fractie* and *Kernel* (2007), the choreographic score is written directly on the body of the performers or on the floor. In those cases, as Tamara Bacci, who has danced in your pieces since 2004, explains, reading the signs takes place at the same time as the movement and freezes the performer in the "present of the execution."[3] Does the difficulty seen in the codes of your notations play a part in the performer's concentration?

CVA Difficulty is never an objective in and of itself. However, inscribing these signs in the space of the stage most certainly implies a state of being in the moment that is different from when you know the score by heart. Reading the score occurs in real time and as a result the performer must be simultaneously a transmitter and a receiver; the information is absorbed in the present of the action.

NM The straight line dominates in your work, notably through the force and importance of horizontality and verticality. In *Diffraction*, the movements of the performers' arms might suggest semaphore signals at times, communicating information from one point to another. It seems natural here to bring in Tim Ingold's *Lines: A Brief History* (2007), a book you are quite interested in and which begins with this question, "What do walking, weaving, observing, singing, storytelling, drawing, and writing have in common? The answer is that they all proceed along lines of one kind or another."[4] At other moments, your pieces offer very organic and ambiguous configurations, for example, through a fusion of bodies. Is playing with visual perception important for you?

CVA It's very important. It's about disturbing or shifting perception to open up imaginary spaces. I like to work with the idea of a new organicity, that is, compose with movements that are not organic, or common, and work them until a new truth appears. Bodies have to be transparent and accept being transformed. That thought can be applied to the work done on space and light, too. In *Obtus* (2009) in particular, the space of the stage is crossed by a bank of light tubes (designed by Victor Roy) that moves forward from the back of the stage toward the audience over a distance of 6 meters during 25 minutes. This slow movement creates a total reversal of the space and thus in an almost indiscernible way works on the audience's perception throughout the piece.

NM I find your pieces have a great capacity for stimulating the imagination. The solo piece *Monoloog* (2010) allows us, for example, to see all kinds of forms in which potential images can be imagined from the dancer's moving back.

CVA Indeed, maybe it's precisely where we lose our bearings that the language of the body can sublimate the real.

NM In the book *Partituurstructuur* (2012) you assert the following idea, "I don't want any lyricism or romanticism. What dance alone can offer is abstraction."[5] Is the adjective "abstract" enough to characterize your work?

CVA Yes, insofar as I don't work in representation or narrative, and abstraction takes us out of reality. Maybe a certain degree of abstraction allows me paradoxically to spill my guts, and in return infuse these forms with a kind of human cruelty that might become excessive, even repulsive, with the restraint of abstraction. That's what I feel as a performer of my works.

NM Paint as a physical material applied directly to the performer's skin or costume is present on stage in your creation *Helder*. Why have you turned to this medium so directly and what does that give you the means to summon?

CVA Paint makes it possible to assert the body as a raw material, to underscore the lines I see in it, but also to bring relief and movement to the perception of the lines and directions, and create a resonance between those applied colors and the space enclosing them.

NM The piece entitled *Magnitude* (2013) is a work originally created for Geneva's Ballet Junior. Through its geometry and variations of color and light—generated by a number of things, including the movements of the dancers—it suggests a monochrome painting and could well be described as a tableau vivant. Is it pertinent, in this regard, to draw connections with the work of painters like Mark Rothko or Pierre Soulages, whose pictures have a great deal to say to you?

CVA Certainly. For *Magnitude,* I worked with the corporeal material of the 22 dancers as if they were a single body. The idiom and movements I offer demand an effort from viewers in terms of their attention. When there is just one body, viewers can remain focused on that one. I can only open up that attention and gaze by creating a new entity, a new homogenous material, a monochrome. Each dancer must accept being in the service of the work of art. There is no question whatsoever of being virtuoso or demonstrative. He or she has to be very precise for the whole to work. The movement of the light over a "static" materiality is equally important; it's what fascinates me in Pierre Soulages's work.

NM So you are looking to guide viewers' visual perception?

CVA Yes, in all of the solos you find a reflection on the idea of focal distance. I'm looking to guide the eye, and place greater intensity on one aspect or another through the proposed bodily forms and the mental work of the performers. They can hold the viewers' attention on one part of their body by increasing the intensity of the presence in that area; they look to shift the viewer's gaze by shifting their own, their inner gaze. That brings us to the idea that the mental can set in motion a shift of bodily habits. This concern often ends up defining the relationship between light, music, and the body. It's a question of framing, mental and visual.

NM Did *Films 6/6* (2014),[6] which Orsola Valenti made from your six solos (*Obtus*, *Nixe*, *Nodal*, *Antre*, *Lanx*, and *Obvie*), make it possible to do real zooms for that reason?

CVA Absolutely. Orsola Valenti went looking for details of the body, a shoulder, the skin. She chose very specific, evocative ways to frame the shot. She filmed around the dancers, scrutinized them, literally made the camera dance. When she was shooting for the first time, I realized it was important to free up the choreography for the film in terms of both the point of view (often straight on the stage) and the chronology of the dance. The filmmaker needed an altogether different relationship to time and rhythm, given that the medium of film fixes them on an unchanging support. In my pieces, even if the relationship to rhythm has been spelled out beforehand, the performer can render that time elastic on stage. Freed from graphic representation, the movement became the filmmaker's raw material in turn, and she could cut and mix it as she saw fit. Her films are true cinematographic interpretations of works for the stage. They are works of art in and of themselves. They tell a new story.

[1] The scores do not concern all of the artist's dance pieces (far from it) and do not strictly govern those that they do in their entirety. Created at the instigation of Michèle Pralong for the art exhibition *Score Conductor*, the piece entitled *Partituurstructuur* reproduced eight of them, from the first three scores for *Fractie* (2003) to *Diffraction* (2011). Michèle Pralong (ed.), *Partituurstructuur. Les partitions chorégraphiques de Cindy Van Acker*, Éditions Héros-Limite, Geneva 2012.

[2] "Why all these drawings, lines, layouts, grids, trajectories thrown down on the paper by a hand imparting its own movement, as if the movement had read the movement of the body and projected its flow?" Laurence Louppe (ed.), *Traces of Dance: Drawings and Notations of Choreographers*, Dis Voir, Paris 1991, p. 22. On dance notations and their history, see also Ann Hutchinson Guest, *Choreo-graphics. A Comparison of Dance Notation Systems from the Fifteenth Century to the Present*, Gordon and Breach, Amsterdam 1989; Hubertus von Amelunxen et al. (eds.), *Notation. Kalkül und Form in den Künsten*, with essays by Heidy Zimmermann et al., Akademie der Künste, Berlin 2008.

[3] Michèle Pralong, *Partituurstructuur*, p. 23.

[4] Tim Ingold, *Lines: A Brief History*, Routledge, London and New York 2007, p. 1.

[5] Michèle Pralong, *Partituurstructuur*, p. 18.

[6] The films making up *Films 6/6* were brought out by Cie Greffe in a DVD boxset in 2014.

EXPANDING

Figurae: Retranslating the Encounter between Francis Bacon, William Forsythe, and Peter Welz

Mark Franko

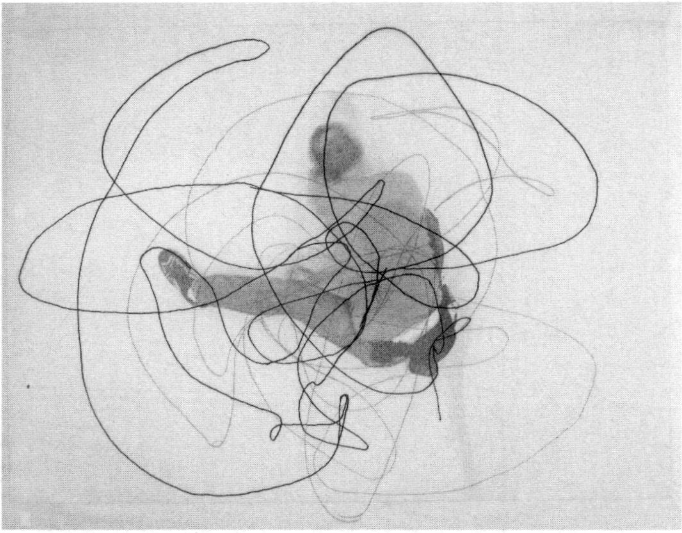

William Forsythe and Peter Welz
Study / Movement of the right hand (black) left hand (red) / Above, 2004
C-print on photographic paper, permanent marker, gaffer tape, PVC, 61 × 86 cm

In a gallery of the Louvre hangs a painting by Francis Bacon—the one said to be his final painting, found incomplete in his studio on his death.[1] Large white screens bisect the gallery where Bacon's *Untitled (Final Unfinished Portrait)* (1991–1992) is on view. Projected on the large-format screens is a male dancer dressed in black—William Forsythe—as captured on video against an entirely white background by Peter Welz; each screen offers a unique angle of perspective on the body moving on the floor.[2] The extreme contrast of black and white, and the difficulty of locating the dancer's body in a three-dimensional space lend the dancer's appearance a "graphic" quality. It is difficult to distinguish floor from ceiling, down from up. The large screens, positioned at oblique angles to the wall upon which the painting is hung, divide up the gallery, effectively creating pathways toward the painting, but also away from it. The dancer's movements are decidedly anguished and in themselves unfinished. Forsythe's performance could be characterized as expressionist in this instance, as indicated by his impetuous and discontinued impulses and rhythms, as well as by the placement of his palms on his head, recalling the performance of Paul Sanasardo in *Pain* (1969). Expressionism and Sanasardo's influence in Forsythe's early work *Love Songs* (1983) for the Joffrey Ballet are evident.

Yet, here we are in a decidedly visual art environment. What the portrait shows is a head painted in a warm ochre emerging from or embedded in a tangle of black and red trace marks through which the painter seems to have been deforming and remodeling this unfinished figuration of self. Hence a certain battle with figuration can be perceived in the movement of the painter's hand: the painter's action in process. In his masterful study of Bacon, Gilles Deleuze discusses at length not only the artist's struggle against figuration (illustration, narrative, story telling) so endemic to Western painting, but also Bacon's drive to materialize from the negation of figuration, the Figure. In this way Deleuze understands that Bacon still works with the human form, but also attempts to uncouple the human form from its normal associations with the pictorial representation of reality. In particular, Deleuze sees Bacon as investing the Figure with sensation, and in this way uncovering the *pictoriality* of the Figure. The relation of graphism to sensation is what distinguishes Bacon's *oeuvre* from abstraction, on the one hand, and from representation (figuration), on the other. Bacon, in other words, neither abandoned the body subject, nor engaged with abstraction, understood as the abandonment of subject matter altogether. "*A probably visual whole (first figuration) has been disorganized and deformed by free manual traits that, by being reinjected into the whole, will produce the improbable visual Figure (second figuration).*"[3] The manual provenance of these traits allies them with the dancer's action. There is a connection here—although Deleuze does not point it out—between the pictorial Figure and the dancing body.

It is not difficult to see why Forsythe was attracted to Bacon. The choreographer's project with respect to ballet could be considered a parallel project, one that attempts to remove figuration from the ballet body, and, ultimately, to return sensation to that body as a "logic" of proprioception: one that senses itself and senses its own movement as a way to conduct itself. Forsythe's question is how this logic can be seen. Indeed, such a "logic," if it can be called that, is one in which "[t]he body becomes the medium of a kind of perceptual work."[4] The visual technologies Forsythe has developed to teach improvisation (*Improvisation Technologies*, 1999) have also been used to document work, as for example in *Synchronous Objects* (2009). Hence, we see in the notion of the proprioceptive already both a creative and a documentary tool which, in its dual intentionality, creates a channel between dancing and drawing—between the performative and the visual—between seizing the moment in/as movement, and retaining its residue in/as drawing. Such a self-documenting spontaneity brings polar aspects of dance and notation, understood as the ability to trace dance's trajectory in the visual field, which is why they themselves might be referred to, borrowing Forsythe's term, as "synchronous objects."

This project has a historical context: it is the character of dance to point to its own history as an element in its construction of expression and meaning, a character that distinguishes it broadly from performance art.[5]

Yet it is precisely because the portrait is unfinished that documentation is itself a gesture rather than a fact. In both Bacon and Forsythe a complementary logic of deformation or defiguration is at work: no deformation without proprioception.[6] Forsythe's move into intermedial installation can be said to reflect his concern with sensation and proprioception as engines of movement generation, display, and documentation.

Forsythe's opening into *Untitled* relies on the fact that the portrait is unfinished, existing as an operative gestural "work" the painter left behind, a potential area of contours and angles that are symptomatic as much of the defiguring process of the painter's hand as they are of a second figuration to come, in Deleuze's terms, as an artistic solution. Between this active process of the defiguration of the figure, whose result we can only surmise and the unrealized endpoint we will never behold, we also find the exposure of painting as a choreographic act. In this sense, Forsythe's contribution is a sustained commentary on the generation of the line in Bacon's painting as a choreographic act. Yet, is it also the case that Forsythe's response to Bacon extends the dancer's exploration of defiguration into new domains? The projection of *Untitled* onto the ground upon which Forsythe moves is both clarifying and limiting. From this perspective, Forsythe seems to be showing us choreography in the act of painting, but not painting in the act of choreography.

Untitled offers us a fragment of a body—albeit an important because centralizing one, the head—and an action of drawing that may be the forming or deforming of an incipient armature. Do these contours elaborate on or undo the figure? Do they reveal the contours of a body yet to be figured, a ramification of the body depending from the head in its ultimate distortion and dissolution? Colors (especially red, white, and flesh tones) contribute to the uncertain yet evocative interactions of figure and line. As Deleuze also wrote of Bacon's painting: "[T]hrough the membrane of the contour, a double movement is produced—a flat extension toward the armature and a voluminous contraction toward the body."[7]

The dancer, for his part, has charcoal affixed to his hands and feet thanks to which each of his motions is inscribed upon the ground. The results of the dancer's trajectories are displayed at one end of the gallery for the viewer to examine. The dancer, need it be said, has, or is, a body. S/he is forced into an existential relation to figuration. But, at the same time, because the dancer's body is here a body that draws, the dancer iterates the relation between armature, contour, and figure that is already patent in the portrait. The dancer's movement engenders traces left in movement's wake. In this way, the dancer is a (physical) volume in the service of contour. One could read the dancer as a drawing rather than as a body in three-dimensional space, as long as the pictoriality of his drawing body draws out the painter's unfinished gesture. More precisely, the dancer's movements *iterate* or *cite* the unfinished portrait as a process—this seems implied by a film that shows us Forsythe's movements as mapped onto the canvas itself—and hence "re-translate" it into movement, which itself draws. Although video as a medium tends to flatten the dancer out into two dimensions, Welz's camera angles resist this tendency by juxtaposing different angles of view, thus attempting to establish what he calls video-sculpture, an interaction of two- and three-dimensional space. This intent to discover within the otherwise flat medium of video the volume of sculptural space is facilitated by the presence of a dancing body that, although captured in the two dimensions of the video screen, provides a "figuration" of three-dimensional movement by virtue of the associations we have with dance, but which also diverts this perception toward the understanding of drawing as the dancer's path and ultimate destination.

It is well known that Forsythe's choreographic work began with an interrogation of the principles of ballet, and although later in his installation work ballet seems left far behind, traces of its presence remain in aspects of his work that seem the furthest removed from it. In this case, I would call attention to the way in which the drawing body Forsythe performs is also a writing body. Each of his moves is traced in black chalk on the white background and hence creates another network in relation to Bacon's *Untitled*. The line drawn on the floor recalls dance notation, which, in the early versions created by Raoul-Auger Feuillet and associated with the beginnings of ballet, recorded a trajectory through space. Of course, his trajectory is entirely indexical, yet it is still a documentation in that it is figural. The conceit is present in that the trace marks left behind might serve to reconstitute the dancer's movements: they are a kind of document inasmuch as they make reference to the documentary impulse of notation. The marks Forsythe leaves behind have a dual identity as a mimesis of the process of drawing and a documentation of the fact that the dancer moves. He creates in his wake a movement-writing. Of course, this leads not only to a path, which is fundamentally linear, but to the "glyph," or what Deleuze has called the diagram. Part of the notion of writing/notation that movement activates through its relation to drawing has to do with recording and thus rendering repeatable. What is bypassed here is the symbolic code of traditional dance notation and what is conserved is its relationship to the letter and/or the diagram.

Forsythe has remarked in interviews on the continuity between drawing, notation, writing, recording, and dancing, and this conjuncture is present as well in his *Improvisation Technologies* and *Synchronous Objects*, where the trail of movement is tracked visually as a stroke.[8] These three terms—movement, drawing, writing—mirror terms Deleuze employs relative to Bacon—armature, contour, figure—indicating the field in which dance operates to be its own pictoriality, understood as the aesthetic tools choreography aligns against figuration. Put otherwise, while the curatorial gesture of placing painting in the proximity of video allows for the participation of the dancer in the relation of choreography to visual media, the dancer's presence surreptitiously introduces the relation of the visual to writing through the historical motif of notating. Dance ushers writing into the visual and hence transforms the notion of drawing often detached from the body per se into that of a drawing body, which recognition implies that drawing is also scriptural once we acknowledge the bodily presence as self-documenting. The figure of the (written) word is the letter, the *gramma*, a figure whose manipulation in/as the human body engenders a transactional relation between dance and text to be seen and reflected upon in choreography. The index attains to the figurality of the diagram. By the same token, Bacon's final self-portrait may itself be a manner of self-documentation.[9]

So the question arises: what is the relation of documentation to figuration? How does a document configure a past once the death of the painter has foreclosed the possibility of completion: the finished work? How do we complete an incipient deformation, a deformation in progress? (That is, if we accept Deleuze's hypothesis that deformation takes place in "the act of painting" by expunging pre-given representations, called "figurations"). Forsythe seems to follow the trace lines of *Untitled* in the act of painting. He translates the painting back into the active process of its constitution. At the same time, his body occupies a space between that of the Figure, the object of figuration—"self"—and the painter's (discontinued) agency. This is necessarily a masochistic position to occupy (hence, its expressionism). The notion of deformation and/or defiguration invokes a blurring between these sorts of relations.

But what is implied in the idea of *re-translation* is the necessity to think all these elements at the same time, and this is how we escape from figuration in choreographic terms. Yet, at the conceptual level, movement as a proprioceptive residual is translated from the body to space where it makes its phenomenal appearance but also leaves its residual mark. That is, movement is always already not only translated from sensation to motility, but is then also re-translated into a visual artifact: this work focuses on a "second" translation or a translation "back into." It is this double or tiered translation that appears to collapse its levels into simultaneity. The contribution of Forsythe and Welz is to prise them apart and expose them conceptually in the museal space. Drawing, writing, moving, documenting, and translating are all proprioceptive acts and, understood as such, they reject figuration while conserving the Figure, in that re-translations are attempts to render the changed as the transformed same.

[1] This painting is part of the collection of The Dublin City Gallery The Hugh Lane, in Dublin. See Marcella Lista, "Avant-Propos," in Marcella Lista, *Corps étrangers: danse, dessin, film*, exh. cat., Musée du Louvre/Fage éditions, Paris/Lyon 2006, n. p.

[2] *Retranslation/Final Unfinished Portrait (Francis Bacon)* was an installation in the Louvre as part of the show *Corps étrangers: danse, dessin, film* curated by Marcella Lista (September 13, 2006–January 15, 2007).

[3] Gilles Deleuze, *Francis Bacon. The Logic of Sensation*, trans. Daniel W. Smith, University of Minnesota Press, Minneapolis 2003, p. 79 [1st ed.: Paris 1981].

[4] Sabine Huschka, "Media-Bodies: Choreography as Intermedial Thinking Through in the Work of William Forsythe," in *Dance Research Journal*, vol. 42, no. 1, Summer 2010, p. 67.

[5] I have argued elsewhere that dance distinguishes itself from other theatrical media through references to its own history. See my *Dance as Text: Ideologies of the Baroque Body*, Cambridge University Press, Cambridge and New York 1993.

[6] An article by Gabriele Brandstetter on Forsythe underlines the defigurative qualities of his work. "Defigurative Choreography. From Marcel Duchamp to William Forsythe," in *TDR–The Drama Review*, vol. 42, no. 4, Winter 1998, p. 37–55. See also my discussion of the figure in geometrical dance in Mark Franko, "Writing Dancing, 1573," in Mark Franko, *Dance as Text*, p. 15–31.

[7] Gilles Deleuze, *Francis Bacon*, p. 98.

[8] William Forsythe and Paul Kaiser, "Dance Geometry. William Forsythe in dialogue with Paul Kaiser," in *Performance Research*, vol. 4, no. 2, 1999, p. 64–71; see also Forsythe's discussion on universal writing in the CD-ROM *Improvisation Technologies* (1999). The discussion of dance as a "trace-form" was originated by Rudolf von Laban, and it engages as well with a discourse of architecture, of tracing in three-dimensional space.

[9] It seems to me there may be a precedent for this in Walter Benjamin's idea of "alphabetical script" in *The Origin of German Tragic Drama* (1928), because Benjamin broaches the intersection of the visual and the scriptural (in the sense of writing) as a choreographic phenomenon. Such a reference could serve to remind us that drawing, writing, and choreography (from the point of view of notation) can all be subsumed in "the allegorical attitude." "In the context of allegory," notes Benjamin, "the image is only a signature, only the monogram of essence, not the essence itself in a mask." See Walter Benjamin, *The Origin of German Tragic Drama*, trans. John Osborne, Verso, London 1977, p. 214 [1st ed.: Berlin 1928].

Channa Horwitz. Breathing

Catherine Wood

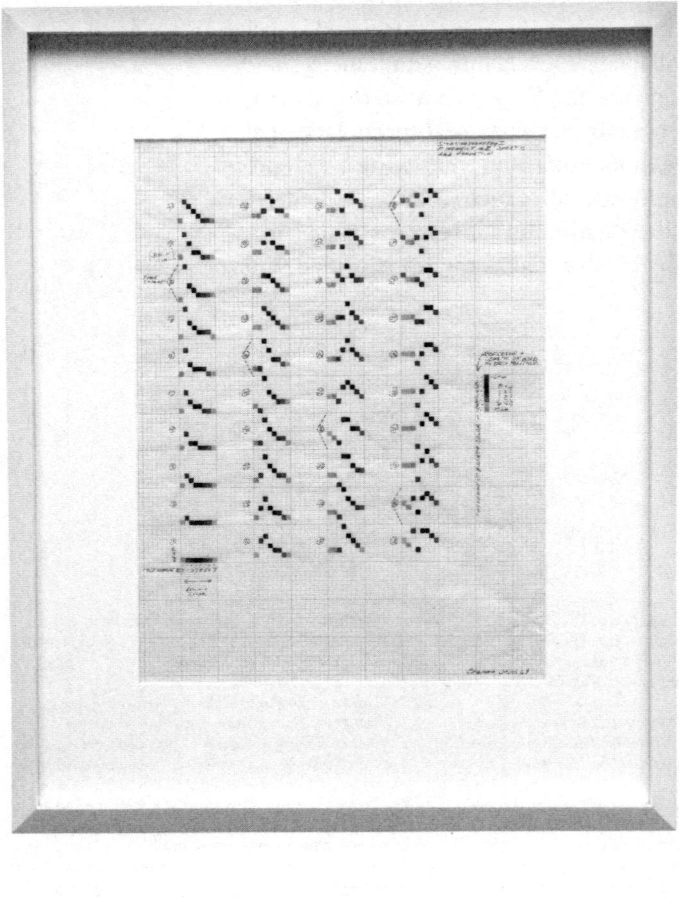

Channa Horwitz
Sonakinatography I, Movement #II, Sheet C, 2nd Variation, 1969
Plaka and pencil on graph paper [color drawing], 40.6 × 30.5 cm

In 1967, early on within her developing practice as an artist, Channa Horwitz (then Channa Davis) created a hybrid painting-sculpture construction that she called a *Breather*. It consisted of a white painted box, secured on top of another box made of Perspex, into which air could be pumped. The *Breather* was a form of hand-operated kinetic sculpture, resembling something like a rudimentary artificial lung. Having made this prototype, and tested its capacity to inflate and deflate, Horwitz subsequently had the idea to create an event: a concert of *Breathers* that would present six of these sculptures together, and animate them sequentially. The artist started to make small graph paper drawings to plot how the boxes could "breathe" in and out through time.

In 1968, Horwitz submitted a proposal to the Art and Technology Program at the Los Angeles County Museum of Art. Her proposal was for an experimental sculpture-performance: eight beams moving vertically out of sculptural bases over a ten-minute period, corresponding to a choreography of colored lights. These sculptures were never fabricated, but the idea is recorded in a complex score whose materials list comprises eight beams, two suspension poles, 16 lights, and which plots the movement of these elements. The surviving drawing tracks and notes the "location and position of the beams" as well as the direction they are moving in. On the other side of the work on paper that survives is a drawing that details the "suspension of vertical beams moving in space," and an accompanying diagram shows "varied positions of one beam as indicated in letters A through E."

Although neither of these early ideas—the concert for *Breathers* nor the "choreography for suspended beams"—materialized as events in the end, Horwitz's approach to the planning of them was highly significant for her subsequent practice, building upon her earlier drawings series—*Language* (1964–2005)—within which she had begun to use grids and graphs to explore patterns and movement.

The drawings that Horwitz made in order to map out the respiratory patterns of the boxes or the movement of beams and lights intended to underwrite the function of these kinetic sculptures, laid the foundations for what would persist as her primary work in itself: the drawing of score-like patterns. Horwitz's drawing practice thus emerged fully in the late 1960s as a system of composition called *Sonakinatography*, encapsulating *sound—motion—notation.* Working with graph paper, the artist drew black-and-white and colored squares, circles, and lines in ink to build complex matrices of sequential patterns. The figures 1 through 8 are the foci of the notation principle she created in these drawings, which visualize time, rhythm, and movement as graphic "beats." The use of the number eight was originally determined by the readymade graph paper—with eight squares to the square inch—and by the idea of the eight corners of a cube. *Sonakinatography* drawings, as they evolved, were both stand-alone works, and open to being performed or activated via dance, spoken word, or music.

In making these drawings, it became apparent that above and beyond questions of medium—painting, sculpture, drawing, performance, or even "the cross-disciplinary"—it was the question of *time*, and how to organize it, that was an ongoing obsession for Horwitz. Temporal structure, as a shared notion, is the invisible matrix that binds social relations, regulating the days, hours, and minutes within which we work, eat, sleep, play, alone and together. The communication grids of the apportionment of time—the clock and the calendar—infiltrate our consciousnesses (at least, in most parts of the world today) to an extreme degree. Against non-Western ideas of "task time" that have been identified in certain tribal situations by anthropologists (the time it takes to complete a task being understood as a measure of duration, e.g. "a rice-cooking while"[1]), the clock offers an ongoing succession of identical pockets of time to be filled, arbitrarily, and stretching ahead with an infinite regularity of repetition.

Yet time has remained—for art—somehow invisible in favor of the prioritization of space as the defining structure within which we encounter it. Space, whether it is architectural or the space of the canvas, page, or plinth, is to be articulated, filled, divided, or exceeded, but always the central consideration. The habitual architectural space within which art is shown, the "white cube" gallery, seems to exist, as Brian O'Doherty has described it, outside of the vicissitudes of time in a kind of a-temporal zone of immanence.[2] "Time-based" art—typically understood as film, video, and performance—is understood to demand a different kind of space: a black box within which theatrical elisions of real space-time can be created, manipulated, and fictionalized.

What is both curious and compelling about Horwitz's drawings is that while they sit on the walls of the white cube quite happily, at home alongside modernist sculpture or painting, they are, internal to themselves, essentially "time-based." For the purposes of display, they masquerade as drawings that deal with the space of the page, appearing as compositional patterns. But they also contain a world of movement, movement that is calibrated within the pace of the artist's decision-making manifest as marks and transitions, and which is suggested as something that might—from the drawings treated as "scores"—be "played," from a newly invented mathematical-cum-musical stave.

Sonakinatography I, Movement #II, Sheet C, 2nd Variation (1969), for example, uses the combination of this grid and inked-in squares in different colors from the spectrum to indicate different suggestive qualities, i.e. "length of hold" from "low to high." *Variation Inversion V* begins at the top with just one square of each color (from yellow via blues to orange, in eight shades) in the top right hand square of the 8 × 8 in graph paper, and as the grid progresses below this the squares increasingly fill up: with three colored in, then six, then ten, then fifteen and so on, progressively, until in the bottom squares they are entirely filled in with color. *Sonakinatography Movement 5#* (1973) is composed of black dots in her typical 8 × 8 in graph grid, progressing from the beginning with just one inked-in line of black (the bottom eight squares of the grid-square) to the displacement of first just one dot, moved up one square, then another, then another, up to the top, and then down again in sequence, to two squares moving up, then up again, and successively down, and so on.

So Horwitz's practice, at one level, seems to adhere to the logic of the given grid. Time to be filled, and she fills it with elaborating, progressive patterns and sequences. But considering the roots of her approach in the *Breathers*, the work seems to ask how to relate one's own bodily rhythm, the automatic activity of breathing, related as it is to heartbeat and pulse, to a representation of time that is constructed within apparent reality, and yet carefully calibrated. The work's grid-logic belies its fragility and relationship to the fallibility of the body, and the body's idiosyncracy, manifesting a poetic conflict between the handmade-ness, the body of the maker, the breathing body-in-time, and the rigor of the grid. Not just a score to spring from, to create movement external to itself. But it contains movement, registers it, internally.

The complexity of *Sonakinatographies* is also contained in the paradox that one can read or view them as a whole image. But since they also bring to mind musical notation, and invite being read as sequences, left to right, that dance on the page, moving in progression as they unfold in our reading of them. In contrast with later drawings such as *Patterns* (1982), however, in which the marks and lines on graph paper create a matrix that fills the page through the repetition of structure in such a way that it coheres as a singular totality, akin to a form of tapestry or chain-link mesh, the *Sonakinatographies* keep the eye moving and shifting as the differences are observed and we try to make sense of them. Instead of a coherent pattern of sameness and difference set out with regularity that allows the eye to rest on a sense of understanding the whole, the score-drawings imply and indeed encourage movement with the drawing's decision making as it unfolds. To the naked eye (without forensic testing!) there is nothing in the material trace of the drawing itself that tells us that Horwitz began at the top left and progressed toward the bottom right, but the way in which her pattern-sequences build implies this as a construction process, and encourages us to read it this way. While the later pattern drawings could extend outward in all directions, infinitely expanding if it was so desired to cover any extent of surface, the score-drawings occupy a clearly delimited bracket of space and time, with a beginning and end.

Horwitz's very earliest set of drawings, *Window Shades* (1964), depicted architectural interiors inhabited, in the artist's imagination, by a fictitious couple named Mr and Mrs McGillicutty. In these rooms—all similarly rendered with fabric swatches and stencils to depict a window and a shade—Horwitz seems to have been particularly fascinated by the changing position of the window blind, and how its lowering and raising alters the image. Critic Chris Kraus, who has written at length about Horwitz, observes that the "cute conceit"[3] of this series would soon be superseded by the rigor and pure geometries of the artist's subsequent work. But these fabricated scenes, with their partially obscured intimacy, also seem to anticipate the curious magnetism of the abstract grid drawings that would be the focus of much of Horwitz's career.

Horwitz's meticulously crafted, repetitive patterns evoke an image of the artist sequestered in her studio in the Hidden Hills enclave of Los Angeles; like a modern version of the sewn "samplers" of 19th-century ladies of leisure, working through seconds, minutes, hours, as an intricate daily practice. At one level, the drawings serve as evidence of her labor: they are finely woven tapestries of time spent.

On another level, they represent a basis in temporality that is outside of what artist Mike Kelley has termed the "love hours"[4] of craft's making. Resembling mathematical diagrams, computer punch-cards, or sewing patterns, Horwitz's drawings are modern hieroglyphs that compress the expansive dramas and effects of movement, music, and gesture into silent two-dimensionality. From the flat surface of her picture plane—as from a graphic rendering of a cube—the observer can infer a third and even a fourth dimension.

Activity is therefore folded into the construction of Horwitz's drawings and held there. They demand activity, also, from the viewer, in order to read them, to follow their patterns and progressions. But although Horwitz's conception was that her drawings, in their open simplicity, could somehow contain everything, and although she often gave her score-drawings to other artists to interpret, it is not necessary to see that movement or sound or gesture enacted literally. They possess an extraordinary self-sufficiency: they neither vie for attention nor attempt to entertain. They could be maps for new, abstract temporal territories, or diagrams of disturbances radiating among the air's atoms and wavelengths. Yet in mood, these cryptic drawings persist with the resistant, almost deliberately exclusive quality of strangers' rooms glimpsed from the street at night, rooms that are lit to expose the mystery of their interiors, but into which—tantalizingly—the viewer can never enter.

Although Horwitz's drawings thus communicate autonomously, and despite her early plans for unrealized performances, the relationship between the works on paper and actual performance is significant. In some of her early assemblage paintings that no longer survive, Horwitz simply drew attention to the changes in light throughout a day: in one case, for example, she affixed a small box to the canvas and painted its gray shadow, while also allowing for the play of actual cast shadows on its surface plane.

Movements (1969) is itself moving: a rudimentary animation film based on eight drawn circles on a grid-square, that are positioned in sequence, displaced one at a time, to create the appearance of movement. They almost have the figurative connotation of a group of people seen from above, switching positions in a dance.

In a 1978 performance, presented at the Palazzo della Cultura e dei Congressi in Bologna, dancers wearing black-and-white geometrically patterned costumes moved according to Horwitz's established graphic rules of circles and lines. After a 1978 performance of her *Poem Opera*, a work for eight vocalists (restaged as part of New York's High Line Art Performance program in 2012), Horwitz began to give drawings to performers to use as scores, without mandating how they were to be interpreted. When giving the scores to others to use she only said, "keep it simple." The scores were purely structures through time, rather than any description of what potential movement might look like, or sound might be.

Horwitz's drawings were again used as a score for choreographic interpretation in *Moments: A History of Performance in 10 Acts* (2012) at the Zentrum für Kunst und Medientechnologie (ZKM) in Karlsruhe, Germany—an exploration of performance in dance and art, curated by Boris Charmatz, Sigrid Gareis, and Georg Schöllhammer. The show included performances in which a rendering of Horwitz's drawn grid was taped onto the floor, a graphic-numeric structure that was activated by Charmatz and colleagues: standing within the floor grid, they performed sequenced gestures based on the other works featured in the exhibition. In this context, Horwitz's drawing thus served as a juncture where the radical origins of those performance works (now shown as static objects, videos, or documentary photography) met with live action, in the present tense; the four dimensional capacity of bodily reality at play with her two-dimensional structures. Through Horwitz's drawing —and other works on display by Marina Abramović, Anna Halprin, Reinhild Hoffmann, Adrian Piper, Yvonne Rainer, and others—Charmatz and his collaborators, including Meg Stuart and Jan Ritsema, transposed the entire contents of a complex historical show into a performed primary code, as though exposing its very DNA.

Horwitz's *Sonakinatographies* and other drawings have a significant place in relation to the work of other artists: as drawings, they resonate with the compositional strategies of her contemporaries Sol LeWitt and Agnes Martin. As notation, with the musical scores of Charlemagne Palestine and also with the abstracted scores of choreographic elders such as Mary Wigman and Rudolf von Laban. According to Mark Franko, “Laban’s meta-languages furthered what one could call abstraction in danced movement by allowing us to see how movement communicated harmonies and affective tendencies without the traditional theatrical signposts of character as dependent upon narrative”[5]: a drama not of character/narrative but of bodies in space. Horwitz’s drawings, similarly, create a drama of composition without narrative.

As works that encapsulate and compress the expansive notion of the time-based within stasis, Horwitz’s body of work makes new sense today. In the past decade, the relationships among image, object, and action in art have been increasingly complicated through the pervasiveness of lens-based technologies. Images are often understood not as ends in themselves, but as modes of translation or communication. Horwitz’s works occupy a unique place in this evolving territory, because they reject and at the same time embrace their own potential as conduits. They go beyond the question of performance and its material trace as instruction or documentation. Simultaneously, her works are end points: registers of the passage of time that imply acute concentrating and intricate work in their making, and potential beginnings: prompts that might open up movement, sound anarchic energy. But within this dual status they hold a mysterious self-containment: suspending a bracket of time from beginning to end they deny a before or after. In their nuanced calibration of a present passage of time, they are enough, a priori.

[1] See Carrie Lambert-Beatty’s discussion of task-time in her book *Being Watched: Yvonne Rainer and the 1960s*, The MIT Press, Cambridge (MA) and London, 2008.

[2] Brian O’Doherty, “Inside the White Cube: Notes on the Gallery Space,” in *Artforum*, vol. 14, no. 7, March 1976, p. 24–30.

[3] Chris Kraus, *Channa Horwitz: Full Circle, 1964–2005*, Solway Jones, Los Angeles 2005, p. 6.

[4] See Mike Kelley’s 1987 assemblage *More Love Hours Than Can Ever Be Repaid and the Wages of Sin* (Collection of the Whitney Museum of American Art, New York).

[5] Mark Franko, “Danced Abstraction: Rudolf von Laban,” in Leah Dickerman (ed.), *Inventing Abstraction, 1910–1925: How a Radical Idea Changed Modern Art*, exh. cat., The Museum of Modern Art, New York 2012, p. 294.

Break Down the Movement and the Drawing Takes Shape: Photography as Intermediary

Laurence Schmidlin

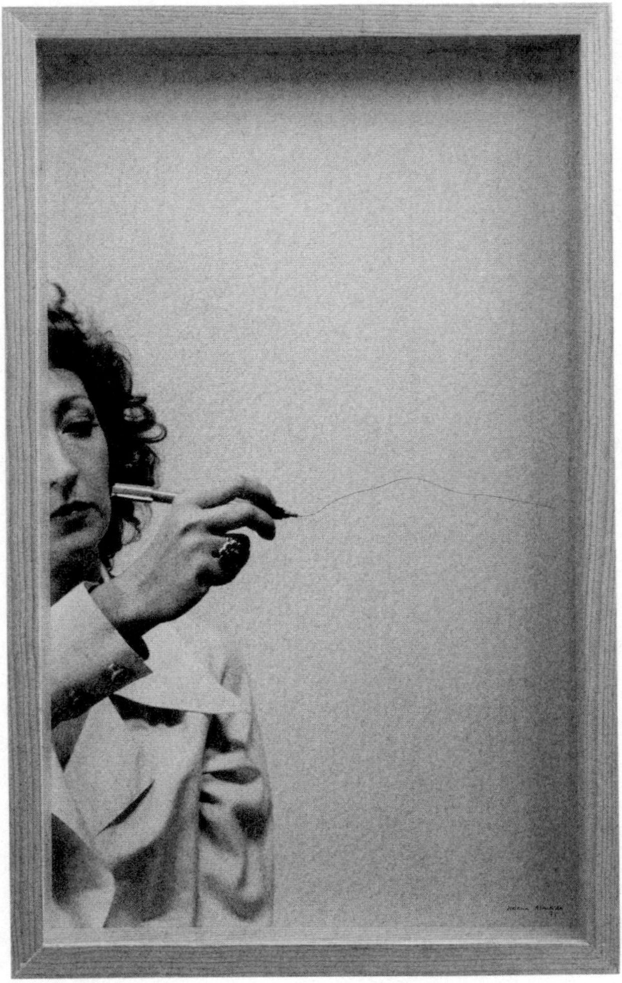

Helena Almeida
Inhabited Drawing, 1975
Black and white photograph, India ink and horsehair, 51.4 × 32.7 cm
Leal Rios Collection, Lisbon

Drawing is closely connected with the gesture that creates it. The hand, and more unusually the mouth or foot—or indeed any auxiliary (even a mechanical one) capable of holding and directing an instrument—objectifies a form or an intention by guiding a line-making tool over a support and leaving marks. This action sometimes transcribes a premeditated thought (we imagine ahead of time what we will draw); at other times, it originates from a more instinctive impetus (we imagine as we draw, or we move, tool in hand, and record each gesture). In the latter case, when the drawing results from a kind of spontaneity, the mental model that determines the composition recedes in favor of its kinesthetic and spatiotemporal incarnation.

Drawing is at once a movement (the act) and its index (the graphic vestige), whereas dance, which one might tentatively define as ephemeral writing executed in space, does not have the finality of inscription in the material sense of the term. A sensitive, or "prepared" terrain is required if the lines of dance are to be fully visualized. For example, *Violin Phase*, the second movement from *Fase: Four Movements to the Music of Steve Reich* (1982) by Anne Teresa De Keersmaeker, stages a dancer drawing a rose pattern with the tips of her toes, according to a precise diagram that governs the choreography.[1] In 2002 this motif was given visible form for the first time. De Keersmaeker danced on a layer of sand for a film shot by Thierry De Mey.[2] A number of dance pieces have made deliberate use of the ground and a lateral support, which are able to retain the memory of the gestures performed. For example, the sensitive surface in Compagnie Philippe Saire's *Black Out* (2011) is no mere element of the stage design. It is in fact part of the very mechanism of the work. Through their movement the performers' bodies etch the black granular material, which is altered by these imprints.

In the two examples above, the drawing is only a secondary objective, well after bodily expression, and notwithstanding possible plans involved in the conception of the pieces, plans that also show, especially in De Keersmaeker's case, that drawing determines the dancers' movements, that it is a tool enabling the artist to *draw on* (tap into) space.

On Certain Interactions between Photography and Drawing

In order to highlight the gesture/trace pairing particular to both dance and drawing, we can approach the question indirectly via photography. I will consider the different uses of this medium and, in particular, the way it has made it possible to break down movement and visualize the composition of drawing by means of fixed images. I will also consider how some artists have chosen photography as a way of showing off the graphic dimension of the body, and will conclude with the project of actually entering the drawing, which both visual artists and dancers have embraced.

This means automatically excluding another major aspect of photography's contribution as a medium to drawing, i.e., artistic practices in which it does not serve as medium or material, but provides an iconographic source that the artist appropriates by copying it—a way of altering it but also of reintroducing a kind of slowness into the work. In this register, one of the instances most representative of this movement/drawing articulation has to be Robert Longo's *Men in the Cities*. These large-format drawings show men and women dressed formally in suits and skirts frozen in contorted poses. They are adaptations of photographs taken between 1976 and 1979 at performances that Longo organized on the roof of a building in New York. He asked friends, including Larry Gagosian and Cindy Sherman, to jump into the air while exaggerating their leap as if they had just been hit by a projectile. The drawings made by Longo in the early 1980s based on these photographs, with no indication as to whether this was the final purpose of the performance, abstracted the surroundings and details, and kept only the artificial posture of the bodies fixed in the blank space of the sheet.[3]

The precarious and transient nature of the artistic forms developed in the 1960s led many artists to find ways of registering the existence of their works. This did not necessarily mean substituting one experience for another; it could be more a matter of passing on and disseminating information. Indeed, artists gave importance to photography because they could, thanks to it, document actions or artworks, and because they did not need to be professionals and could use it unconstrained by artistic tradition or technical accomplishment. They thus created by-products of the initial work that were present both in exhibitions and on the market, attributing to them either a subsidiary, purely informational status, or a role as real placeholders for the original work.

The need to record the existence of work that was by nature ephemeral established the use of photography in two modes, the documentary (photographs of performances) and the theatrical (performed photography).[4] Performance can be credited, first of all, with having renewed the resources of drawing, which lent itself to events of all kinds by the modesty of its simple, familiar techniques. Furthermore, it made drawing's realization visible.[5] Once drawing was perceived as the action that preceded the residual image or graphic trace, it became possible to consider it from the angle of process. To memorize a number of tasks—self-imposed on the principle of *task performance*—in order to break free of one's subjectivity, or to establish a set of constraints for the execution of a work, each prescription stressed the operational matrix that would fulfill it. By putting the body at the center of the apparatus, artists unburdened themselves of intellectual responsibility for the result, and renounced the speculative dimension of graphic activity. The resulting drawing was precisely the fruit of carrying these out.

Showing the Realization of the Drawing

The fascination with speed of execution, in just a handful of lines, and sometimes in just one continuous line, led to Pablo Picasso drawing in the air with light pens in front of Gjon Mili's lens (1949). The photographer adapted a trick that had already been tested with ice skaters.[6] The shutter was left open and the motif—in other words, the sum of actions that went into making it—was captured on film, while the position of the artist's body was that of the drawing's final punctuation, its full stop. There had been other, earlier experiments of this kind, not always with an artistic intention. Georges Demenÿ and Édouard Quénu sought ways of observing movement and resorted, for example, to a system of incandescent bulbs attached to the limbs of their models (*Étude de la locomotion humaine dans les cas pathologiques*, around 1889; the body is hardly visible in their study). Frank Gilbreth and Lillian Moller Gilbreth set about rationalizing actions in the workplace and, to that end, produced photographs of laborers at work, the trace of their movements being picked up from the miniature electric lights worn on their hands. The virtuoso violinist Jascha Heifetz played in front of Mili's camera in 1952. The light source was attached to his bow and made it possible to record the fleeting trace of his movements in the half-light of the studio. The difference between the way Picasso and Heifetz carried out this exercise was determined by the nature of their art. The former moved his hand in order to represent. Differences of materiality notwithstanding, the motif created would have "appeared" in the same way whether he was holding a pencil or a light brush. The latter brought into play his body to interpret a score. There was no graphic intention behind the coordination of his movements, i.e., the musician's sole reason for moving was to obtain sounds from his instrument. His choreography was not deliberate. Artists like Morgan O'Hara (*LIVE TRANSMISSION* series, since 1981) and Pierre Bismuth (*Following the Right Hand of…*, a series begun in the early 2000s) explore from other angles this project of transcribing human activity in real time, of mapping a succession of actions that are performed for reasons other than devising a graphic record.

Just as it served to break down movement in the second half of the 19th century (chronophotography, as developed by both Étienne-Jules Marey, who was assisted by Demenÿ and Quénu, and Eadweard Muybridge), photography made it possible to show how drawing was invented over time by revealing the phases of its realization. One unit in the chain of images, each photograph "iconographed" in documentary fashion a fraction of the movement that brought the drawing into being; it captured the kinetics of the body engaged in its elaboration, while the addition of these images described the progression of the graphic program. The fluidity of the accumulated gestures was glimpsed fragmentarily and stressed as much the birth of the form as the body at work and its motive dimension.

The rhythmic decomposition of gesture was not foreign to the practice of drawing. Certain artists rendered the flow of time thanks to this medium, each second being translated onto a sheet of paper, as a singular event lived by the observed subject. Ferdinand Hodler, for example, was constantly in search of form, as witnessed by the many sketches that preceded his oil painting projects. The series of images, each displaying minute differences, sometimes produce the illusion of movement when placed side by side, as if one could repeat an instant of life. The changing nature of all things also found a kinetic form of expression in the work of Henri Matisse. In the collection entitled *Thèmes et variations* (1943),[7] multiple studies of the same subject (the drawings are distributed among 17 series treating a range of themes such as the female model, the flower bouquet, an arrangement of gourds) seem more than ever to be animated as you turn the pages of the album one after the other.

In another instance of giving shape to movement, Hilka Nordhausen was to use photography to record both bodies in action and drawings in the process of being composed. The sequences the artist shot between 1974 and 1975 drew their subject matter from performances and were shown as *artworks* and not specifically as documentation. In the 26 drawings brought together under the generic title of *Untersuchungen zum Zeichenvorgang* (1973–1974), Nordhausen set for herself an operational framework (for example, cover a certain number of sheets of paper with lines, or use of a metronome to pace the gestures involved in doing a drawing in a fixed time frame[8]). After that series the sheets assumed increasingly larger formats and had to be hung on the wall. This gradual extension of scale seems to explain both her adopting these working procedures within the framework of performance art, and giving up the intermediary of paper, occasioning the use of photography in the absence of such a recording device, as if it were no longer the sheet of paper that was limiting the artwork but the amplitude of the body. For *Ohne Titel (Fixierstift auf Nessel)* (April 13, 1974, 11 images), which comes from the series *Untersuchungen zur Handreichweite* (1974), the artist drew an initial circle (an unbroken zigzag and not a straight line), while seated on the ground, then a second circle, a third one, and so on. When the shape had been sufficiently expanded to fit the artist's body at its center, Nordhausen placed herself in it and continued this spatial expansion as far as the length of her arm allowed. Finally, she no longer deployed her arm but her entire body as a compass and carried on drawing within these renewed limits. For *Ohne Titel (Kreidekreis)* (May 23, 1974, 18 images) from the same series, the device was simplified. Lying on the floor blindfolded, Nordhausen turned around horizontally while drawing chalk circles one over another. Before her one true public performance,[9] she stopped passersby in the basement hallway of Hamburg's Hochschule für bildende Künste (*A 18* from *Untersuchungen zum Zeichenvorgang*) over the course of three half-days.[10] She asked these participants to photograph her while she herself documented her mission, which consisted in covering 150 × 865 cm sheets with lines, using a different camera on an automatic setting every 15 minutes.

Ferdinand Hodler and Henri Matisse infused their subjects with movement, so to speak, by multiplying the number of sheets of paper. On the contrary, Hilka Nordhausen, by breaking movement down into several still images, sought to decipher the drawing gesture rather than to animate a motif by deconstructing its final form—the image sequence was to document the emergence of a motif, not its metamorphosis as a motif, moving from one potential image to another. The artist emphasized the laborious effort of carrying out the drawing task, a pretext for the performance in the service of which she placed her entire body.

Still another option consists in recreating movement on one and the same support by superimposition. In the early 1980s, Robert Janz adopted a drawing technique that integrated the evolving nature of a subject in a still image that fused different stages of the movement. What he called *redrawing*[11] consisted of partially erasing a motif and redrawing it over the subsequent traces. One of these drawings was done on the Berlin Wall in 1981: *Unclenching: 20 Days* showed a clenched fist over which were superimposed different intermediary states of the artist's hand right up to one that depicted it open. Janz moved back and forth constantly to observe his hand vis-à-vis the drawing in progress, then returning to the wall to pick up where he had left off with as great a degree of faithfulness to the proportions as possible.

An artist can thus lend an artificial rhythm to a series of drawings, which are enriched like so many points of view down to the very instant a given motif is sketched out, as well as the very emotion accompanying it at that time. Robin Rhode makes use of a similar process, but develops the motif laterally rather than superimposing it.[12] Since the early 2000s, working on the ground or on walls in the streets of Johannesburg for the most part, he has executed white chalk drawings with which a performer then interacts as in a game of hopscotch. The body enters a dialogue with an arrangement of forms that fade over time, the artist occasionally erasing them in order to recreate and infuse them with new energy from one state to the next. The forms develop in lines and deletions, graphic additions and subtractions. The drawing—of a range of motifs, including bicycles, characters, and turntables—is precisely choreographed beforehand. It is preserved with a series of photographs or a digital slideshow presentation. Gradually it takes shape, from one image to the next, while the movement of the body is broken down, showing it each time in a new physical configuration, a new posture that *represents*, even *becomes drawing*.

Showing the Body Becoming Drawing

Picasso adding the final full stop to a drawing. Nordhausen hardly varying her position as if she were a mere instrument. Rhode's performer frozen in a posture like one state of an action in progress. These freeze frames reveal the plastic presence of the individual in the act of creating—busy, involved, mediating. If the drawing is shown as it is being done, its sequencing sacrifices the fluidity of movement. The body thus expresses more than its plastic capacity, its capacity to create form. It expresses its "graphic capacity,"[13] its capacity to *become drawing* through the linearity of its limbs and its verticality. The body is the expression of a network of lines that is all the more obvious when it is *taken* in a photograph and the volumes and surfaces are smoothed out a bit in the image.

Nordhausen greatly stressed the notion of action as intrinsic to drawing. She had doubtless assimilated the thinking of Franz Erhard Walther, under whom she studied at the Hamburger Hochschule für bildende Künste (1970–1975), and who exploited the presence of the body, its plastic dimension and dimension as an accessory, in a participative conception of the work of art and the creation of "sculptural situations" in pieces like the 58 elements making up *1. Werksatz* (1963–1969).[14] In *Line Piece to La Monte Young II* (spring 1964), Yoko Ono introduced the linear axis of the body as an element in drawing. In this score, her direction reads "draw a line with yourself. Go on drawing until you disappear," as though we could renounce ourselves through the creative act alone. The body is always a performative subject; it is such from the very outset. Its actions and movements show it to be graphic matter, as when one forms letters with one's body. "Draw a line with yourself" indicates the completion of an artistic act, *a minima*, the smallest possible event in and of itself. All one needs to do is stand up straight with one's arms along one's sides, or lie down on the floor, with the ground as a support, and form a line. "Go on drawing until you disappear" is to never stop moving and follow one posture with another until one is no longer an individual but a form in constant metamorphosis. Dissolving the border between art and life can be achieved as much by devoting the latter to the former as the opposite, with one's own being as the means.

Entering the Drawing

With Ono's enlightening example, we have observed that the body, already material from the outset, can itself be graphic material. Photography, by breaking down movement and "freezing" bodies in action as Nordhausen and Rhode did, exalted this graphic dimension in the past. Photography is also a device for exploring space (consider the series of photographs by Michael Heizer, Jan Dibbets, Gordon Matta-Clark, and Mary Miss, which reformulate space), whether rendering the linearity of the real world visible, or being itself understood as a construction unit of a line. It was its technical resources that were put to flushing out illusions—including the illusion of the line that does not exist in nature—as well as producing them. Besides graphic installations on an architectural scale, it is notably thanks to photography in particular that artists made the attempt to literally enter drawing. The fantasy of integrating the space of drawing and interacting with it achieved its absolute fulfillment thanks to the medium of film.

To break up a space with a line, subdivide it and play with that limit, was also an attempt to renew what was a given for a site in terms of its space. Rosemarie Castoro realized that her living space and her studio physically coexisted, whereas their respective functions kept them separate. With this realization in mind, in 1969 she began a series of interventions she called *Cracking,* which took advantage of her practice involving the body in space.[15] She did not physically manipulate a site in the way Matta-Clark did with his *Building Cuts* (1974–1978)—cuts that were carried out in the architecture of a building in order to transform one's perception of it—but what she dubbed sculpture consisted of the display of a strip of aluminum through a given space splitting it in two—she was referring to seismic fault lines recreating spaces that were already demarcated.

The first *Cracking* was done in the streets of New York in April 1969. By encircling a city block,[16] Castoro aimed to make "an atoll of Manhattan ... "[17] She later photographed the site of her art piece in 2007 and discovered a genuine crack in the sidewalk as though she had provoked it herself, rather than anticipated it. She also applied this concept to people during performances (*Cracking People*, 1969), as well as to herself—thus anticipating by a few years Liliana Porter's photographic portraits, which showed the artist with a drawing of her face, contiguous to other surfaces such as a wall. The Polaroid photograph called *Cracking Self-Portrait* (July 1969) belongs to a group of "notes" in the form of images that constitute a kind of journal. The notes generally show her in a playful relationship with her body and artworks. In one self-portrait, we see Castoro looking at herself in a mirror, encircling her right eye with a piece of string. Her face is displayed as a puzzle whose pieces she can determine and reveal.

In Castoro's work, photography is merely the means for capturing a situation (for example, a face seen as detachable pieces, though solely in terms of the imagination). In Helena Almeida's series *Desenho habitado* (1975), photography was the very instrument of these "inhabited drawings," in that their aim "was to materialize the drawing, so that people could touch it, become part of it, live it. The drawing would materialize, come out, be transformed into something solid, and people would enter into it."[18] Some self-portraits of the series show the artist drawing "in the air" with a felt-tip pen. The black line seems to run to the edge of the image and was materialized in the space with a strand of horsehair. Almeida would interact with the elements of her media beyond the fiction of the image. The realities of the artist and the viewer were thus brought together, and the two-dimensionality of the drawing denounced as an illusion. In Almeida's case photography articulated the two sides of a relational situation. That is, if we grasped between our fingertips the line that reaches beyond the edge of the photograph, we would find ourselves in the same pose as the artist, standing opposite her and linked with her.

Once the desire to get into the work of art is materialized, only the moving image enables one to make the evolving dimension of the body and the drawing coexist, to give rise to their possible interactions. Suggesting animation in which one form summons another, with the constant transformation of the drawing contributing to the development of the fiction, Judith Wechsler demonstrates "how film realizes drawing and how drawing acts on film."[19] This is what is seen in Benoît Félix's output. Félix is developing a body of work in which drawing is a playful element that serves to produce reality. "Drawing, I lay down the preliminary trace of what will be a foreign body fallen into real space soon after, when I cut it out."[20] He himself can interact "at the juncture of the space of the image and the space of the body, at the point of articulation or passage where reality and the imagination constitute a threshold for one another."[21] In the video *Dessine ce par quoi tu passes/passe par ce que tu dessines* (2010), cocreated with Jonathan Sullam, Félix draws elements (for example, a door or a line) that "become" a reality that can be activated (the door opens or the artist can stand on the line).

In counterpoint to these examples that summon technology to create fictional situations and play with drawing, we could mention the ways in which dancers, too, have entered the space of the drawing, but with their bodies only. Whereas De Keersmaeker, in the dance piece mentioned above, created space through drawings, Trisha Brown produces one and the other simultaneously in *It's a Draw* (2002). The piece commits the dancer to a zone that is circumscribed by the edges of a sheet of paper; alternately seated, lying down, squatting on the support-constraint, pivoting around herself, moving back and forth, using her different limbs, Brown employs her bodily vocabulary to explore the surface. She marks each decision, each intention in pastel and/or charcoal, rubbing these materials in passing. Gradually they accumulate on the paper. In the 1980s and 1990s Brown adopted the relationship of an observer with respect to her own body, which she treated "like an object"[22] as Peter Eleey put it, drawing her hands and subsequently her feet in a utilitarian connection with the sheet of paper. She then embraced once again an inner point of view: "In moving the paper from the notebook or desk down to the level of the dance floor, these foot drawings put the picture plane at the mercy of Brown's entire body,"[23] and so "she began to treat the frame of the paper as a stage,"[24] analyzes Eleey.

Other dance pieces similar to Brown's allow us to understand how the body inhabits a drawing by producing it on the surface of the sheet of paper. Since the 2000s Katrina Brown, for instance, has been developing a corpus of performances that reconcile dance and drawing. In *Drawing In, As and After Performance: A Choreographic Investigation of Surface(s)* (2013), she seeks to connect her body and surface through the drawing, as if it were a tool for understanding the ordinary plane in which dancers operate: "What is surface, what does surface do, what can surface facilitate in relation to the choreographic processes and conditions of and between body-space-material-time? What becomes visible on the surface, what lies beneath the surface, what rises from surface?"[25] The device here is analogous to Trisha Brown's own approach (Katrina Brown explicitly refers to her fellow artist), i.e., seated at the center of a blank sheet of paper, holding a stick of charcoal, she relentlessly turns round and round, making half-circles and spirals, which she blurs a little more each time her body passes.

On the other hand, Tony Orrico's *Penwald Drawings* (2009–present) dwell on the impenetrability of the drawing space. During these performances, this former dancer (notably with the Trisha Brown Dance Company) executes geometric, often circular, drawings that display an extreme precision. His body is a kind of two-pencil spirograph; his gestures, rhythmically and regularly repeated, form great decorative compositions on the wall or floor. Knowing beforehand what he is going to draw subordinates the graphic result to the physical effort of the performance and that becomes the true finality of the piece. The density of the shapes and darkened areas bears witness to the artist's endurance as he draws to the point of exhaustion. The weariness of the body gives out before the infinity of the circular form. Where paper is for Orrico a support over which he passes again and again (his body is a tool, he is an agent), in the work of Trisha Brown and Katrina Brown it is a site, and the drawing a mediator between the body and the ground. Entering the space of the drawing in the dancer's work thus signifies understanding it from both a utilitarian conditioning of oneself. In the last examples we observed, the photographic and film media are involved as documentary tools.[26] Outside of possible film recordings, a piece of choreography is rarely recalled by a single photograph—such a photograph would evidence the dance piece as it would an event—but rather by a series of shots that serve to reconstruct the body's movements and gestures, their graphic result, and the intention of the project.

Photography helps to question the nature of what has been classified as an art of space (drawing) and an art of time (dance), which are not in the end reducible to one or the other dimension. The interdisciplinarity of dance and drawing has more than brought them close to one another throughout the last century: it has shown their similarities. Whereas until the 1950s only the residual graphic object was submitted to us, it eventually became clear that drawings emanated from movement, from a body fundamentally involved in its creation. Thanks to the photographic medium, which enables a deconstruction of drawing and allows it to be shown as it comes into being, drawing was notably understood as an action. Combined, photography, movement, and drawing emerged in their full operational dimension, the first of the three bringing to light the joint gestation of the two other media, which were closely wedded by their respective conquest of space.

[1] Editor's note: on this subject, see the essay by Julie Enckell Julliard and interview with Anne Teresa De Keersmaeker, p. 148–163 in this volume.

[2] In 2013, De Keersmaeker's piece *Vortex Temporum* made clear the governing geometric construction directly on the floor. That construction showed how it structured the space of the dance, but also how a form of beauty and liberty could emerge from this apparent rigor based on numbers and mathematical laws.

[3] Zaha Redman, "Tenir le vide," *LIGEIA. Dossiers sur l'art*, vol. 25, no. 117–118–119–120, July–December 2012, p. 133 and 135.

[4] Anne Bénichou, "Ces documents qui sont aussi des œuvres … ," in Anne Bénichou (ed.), *Ouvrir le document. Enjeux et pratiques de la documentation dans les arts visuels contemporains*, "Perceptions" series, Les presses du réel, Dijon 2010, p. 67.

[5] See Laurence Schmidlin, "L'événement du dessin," in *Roven*, no. 5, special issue on performative drawing, October 2013, p. 10–29.

[6] See Gjon Mili, *Picasso's Third Dimension*, Triton Press, Tudor, New York 1970.

[7] The collection features reproductions of 158 drawings done in Cimiez, a residential neighborhood in Nice, between 1941 and 1942.

[8] The instructions for doing the pieces were conserved and are available at the following site: www.hilkanordhausen.de.

[9] A drawing executed in the exhibition space of the Gruppe Grün in Bremen between 3 and 12 March 1975, on ten sections of wall, the last being done in half light.

[10] Nordhausen ended the experiment more quickly than planned because of a physical and psychological fatigue that obscured the initial raison d'être of her project even from herself.

[11] Patrick T. Murphy, "Forward," *Robert Janz. Moving Pictures*, exh. cat., Douglas Hyde Gallery, Dublin 1985, p. 3.

[12] Editor's note: See the interview with Robin Rhode by Anna Lovatt in this volume, p. 208–216.

[13] I have conceived and developed the notion of "graphic capacity" [*capacité graphique*] in my PhD dissertation, "'The Drawingness of Drawing.' La spatialisation du dessin dans l'art américain des années 1960–1970," Université de Genève, 2016. See especially p. 22–23, 121, 125–128.

[14] Erik Verhagen "The Work Can Never Be Finished. An Interview with Franz Erhard Walther," in Elena Filipovic (ed.), *Franz Erhard Walther. The Body Decides,* exh. cat., Wiels/Walther König, Brussels/Cologne 2014, p. 61.

[15] In the early 1960s, Castoro took part as a dancer in projects notably by Yvonne Rainer. She was also interested in choreography during her studies at Pratt Institute, in Brooklyn, from which she graduated in 1963.

[16] The block in question was formed by 13th and 14th streets between 5th and 6th avenues.

[17] "[…] making an atoll of Manhattan Island using the linear metaphor of aluminum tape chasing around a city block." Artist's statement, November 3, 2007, published online: http://www.galeriearnaudlefebvre.com/exhibit.php?exhibit=38.

[18] María de Corral, "Conversation between Helena Almeida and María de Corral, CGAC, November 25, 1999, Santiago de Compostela," in *Helena Almeida*, exh. cat., Centro Galego de Arte Contemporànea, Santiago de Compostela 2000, p. 173.

[19] Judith Wechsler, "Dessin et film d'animation. Ruth Lingford et William Kentridge," trans. Gérard Pecorari and Patricia-Laure Thivat, *LIGEIA. Dossiers sur l'art,* vol. 20, no. 77–78–79–80, July–December 2007, p. 189.

[20] *Drawing in an Expanded Field. 30 ans de l'atelier de dessin*, exh. cat., Presses de l'Académie royale des Beaux-Arts de Bruxelles, Brussels 2011, p. 55.

[21] Ibid.

[22] Peter Eleey, "If You Couldn't See Me: The Drawings of Trisha Brown," in Peter Eleey (ed.), *Trisha Brown: So That the Audience Doesn't Know Whether I Have Stopped Dancing*, exh. cat., Walker Art Center, Minneapolis 2008, p. 25.

[23] Ibid.

[24] Ibid.

[25] Statement by the artist, published online: http://sensingsite.blogspot.ch/2013/10/perfect-flat-circle-katrina-brown.html.

[26] For example, there are photographs and a film recording of the choreography. *It's a Draw [Live Feed/Overhead Camera]* (April 17, 2008) is an overhead view of Trisha Brown performing. In the exhibition setting, it is shown on a screen located on the floor, opposite the drawings hanging on the wall. As for Tony Orrico, the artist has regularly worked with the photographer Michael Hart since 2010. Images of the *Penwald Drawings* always present Orrico at the center of his drawing.

“Time Waits for No Line.” An Interview with Robin Rhode

Anna Lovatt

This interview took place by email in December 2014.

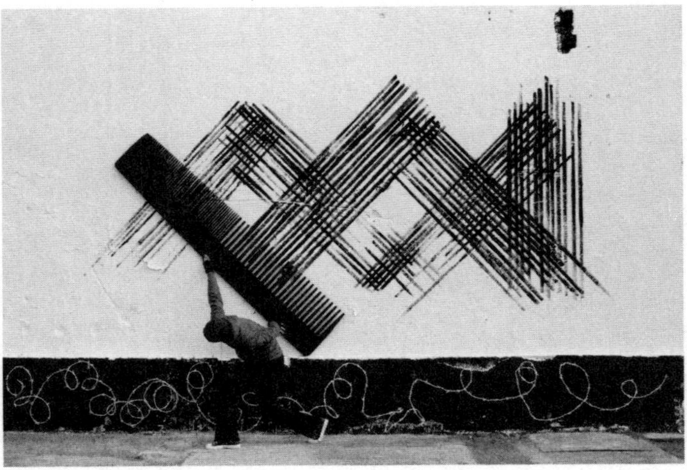

Robin Rhode
Almanac [detail], 2012–2013
Digital type C-print, 41.6 × 61.6 cm (framed)

Robin Rhode began working during the late 1990s while he was a student at the South Africa School of Film, Television and Dramatic Arts. His practice is thoroughly interdisciplinary in nature, traversing performance, drawing, photography, film, animation, sculpture, and the readymade. Once a breakdancer, Rhode's early work combined elements of graffiti—where the artist's identity is hidden or coded—with more performative modes of street art that hinge upon the artist's presence. Rather than tracing an absent body in the manner of the graffito, Rhode's images draw the body to them, eliciting interaction on the part of the performer and sometimes on the part of the spectator. Just as the body responds to Rhode's drawings, the drawings respond to the body in a productive dialogue that is improvisatory and open-ended. Perhaps this is why Rhode emphasizes the process-based nature of his work, likening his drawings to "verbs" (in the manner of process artist Richard Serra) despite their inclusion of recognizable objects and narratives.

In a series of works from 2004–2005 including *Untitled (Entry/Exit)*, and *Untitled (Skipping Rope)*, Rhode's mobile body and those of his audience served as frenetic instruments of inscription, leaving their traces on the walls or floor as they interacted with rudimentary images. Since 2006 Rhode has collaborated with the professional dancer Jean-Baptiste André on more structured performances such as *Frequency* (2007) and *Light Giver Light Taker* (2015), which reference various choreographic, theatrical, and cinematic traditions. What these two distinct series and the rest of Rhode's practice have in common is an emphasis on the temporality of drawing, which unfolds and transforms before the viewer's eyes (whether in a live performance, a film, or a series of photographic frames). Resisting fixity, Rhode's shape-shifting works capitalize on the inherent restlessness and dynamism of drawing. In the words of the artist: "time … waits for no line."

* * *

ANNA LOVATT Growing up in Johannesburg you encountered activist mural paintings; you have also spoken about an initiation rite whereby older schoolboys would force younger ones to interact with objects drawn on the bathroom wall. In both situations, the wall is a site of interpersonal or political struggle. Does this extend to your own practice?

ROBIN RHODE Both these factors have had an enormous impact, not only on my working process, but also in terms of shaping the way I understand art. From the perspective of mural art, these crude rudimentary painted wall works embodied a very strong sociopolitical theme. These themes either embodied religious iconography, or were a collage of distant lands or cities, such as a Venice lagoon in the foreground coupled with a New York skyline in the background. All painted with the intention of projecting society away from its current social and political predicament. In a way, the murals functioned as windows onto an imaginary world. This is how I understood these mural artworks, or how I intended to understand them. My work functions in more or less the same way, projected worlds composed through a combination of theoretical, lived, and imaginary understandings, viewed from a world that is both inclusive in one instance, and exclusive in another.

The second point, regarding the high school drawing initiation, has developed into an urban myth. These sub-cultural rites of passage embodied so many art historical references, from the early primitive Bushmen cave paintings depicting the desires and practices of everyday life, to the Dada actions of the 1920s, as well as to performance art in the 1960s. In many ways I consider myself a nomadic Bushman, painting on the walls of a 21st-century reality.

AL The mural and the initiation rite are both collaborative, but not without friction. Is collaboration an important aspect of your work, and what challenges does it pose?

RR Collaboration in the working process develops rather organically, as it is the work, or rather the idea, that calls for a collaborative response. My doppelgangers are my collaborators, as is the photographer who captures the imagery, as well as the painters, street vendors, shopkeepers, neighbors, street hoodlums—basically everyone who has access to the process. I develop an intuitive mechanism to draw influence from the witnesses that view the process. I see them as active participants with whom I can engage and who will challenge my initial idea of what the artwork means. This grassroots level is of fundamental importance to the meaning of the artwork, before it even reaches the art world.

AL Please talk me through the process of making one of your photographic series. What comes first—a narrative, a location, a bodily gesture, a drawn or readymade object—or does it vary?

RR The process seems to shift from time to time. There are considerable variations in the photographic series. What comes first could be the desire to generate a particular line or shape. I then research how I could develop that particular mark-making process into a more cohesive narrative. Sometimes what comes first is a particular object that has some kind of sociopolitical significance. I then attempt to weave a mark-making process into or around the object in focus. My work definitely involves the desire to realize an aesthetically compelling wall painting, drawing, etc. My process also involves very basic principles, such as: "If the drawing is great ... the piece is great ... no matter the strength of the concept or idea." And I will know immediately whether the piece is developing strength by the reaction of the people around me to the drawing or wall painting. My band of collaborators tend to respond immediately to the mark-making process, and this response gauges the strength of the piece. My intention is to create beautiful poetic imagery that conjures a reaction from those who view it, no matter what their social or economic backgrounds. Art should break through these existing barriers. My work is never governed by politics, but rather expresses a freedom from it.

AL Some of the objects deployed by your doppelgangers are fairly generic, such as a bicycle or a feather, but others have more specific cultural connotations, such as an Afro hair comb or a Gerrit Rietveld chair. How do you select these objects?

RR My objects are selected on a narrative basis. Or according to how I am able to conjure a narrative-based drawing from the object in question. Certain objects are cultural phenomena from which I am able to extract narrative rather easily—a good example of this is the comb in the works *Almanac* (2012) and *Blackness Blooms* (2012), which is based on a story told to me by the South African poet and political activist Don Mattera. His story involves his political detention and subsequent torture by the Apartheid police. He speaks of being incarcerated in a pitch black holding cell, and over a period of two weeks he began to imagine the darkness as a kind of wound in the sky, as if a wound was dripping pitch-black darkness onto the concrete surface of the cell's cold ground. I adapted this story by using the comb to denote blackness, and my wall painting is reminiscent of a flower, blooming in the sky.

In the case of the chairs by Gerrit Rietveld, *Arm Chair*, *Military Chair*, *Kinderstoel*, and *Berlin Chair* allowed me to investigate these particular thematics, using, for example, the inherent form of the *Zig-Zag Chair* (1934) to develop a formal composition that is visually engaging, and at times provocative, as in the case of *Piano Chair*, where the pianist petrol bombs his wall-painted image of the musical instrument.[1]

AL Do the actions staged for the camera in your photographic series constitute a performance in their own right? And are you interested in the afterlife of the drawings once they have been photographed?

RR The actions staged for the camera are exactly that, staged, almost choreographed. Depending on the location of these photographic series, especially in a very specific location in Johannesburg, I see the process of the photographic series as theatrical, like a kind of theatrical rehearsal that evolves live, within the public realm. Here my audience becomes the school kids on their way home from school, the neighbors who peep over walls to see the wall painting and performance evolve, the daily passersby on their way to and from work, local gangsters, and drug addicts who enjoy their high watching a very peculiar street narrative unfolding before their lucid eyes.

I am not concerned with the afterlife of the wall drawing/painting. I mostly "bomb" (paint out) my own drawings so that local graffiti artists can access the wall after my work is documented. I will then return to the given wall at some point in the near future and "bomb" the existing graffiti in order to create my new concept. This process has at times created friction between graffiti crews and myself. My understanding is that no one should claim ownership of the walls.

AL Photography enables you to extract drawings and gestures from the contexts within which they were made and to display them in very different contexts. What is the role of location in your work?

RR The context is very important. In my early pieces I would choose a wall due to its particular surface, smoothness, to allow me to draw with chalk or charcoal very rapidly. The notions of speed and energy were very important in that period of production.

Then I shifted to a very specific wall in Berlin that had a more controlled air to it. The space was rented and cordoned off, allowing me complete freedom and access to the space without any fear of police harassment or public accessibility. This context allowed me to produce work over longer production time periods, therefore producing work that had a greater investment in drawing detail, costume, etc. The context allowed for a more theatrical approach. My wall in Johannesburg is completely exposed to the public so there is a greater interaction and accessibility. This allows for exterior elements to influence the work—whether these are comments made by the public or various fear factors or criminal influences that pervade the working area, such as robbers in the vicinity, or individuals under the influence of drugs who attempt to engage with the work, to perform or even to interact with the wall drawing. These exterior elements definitely influence the working process and are crucial to the context within which the work is created.

Until now, I would say that my work in Johannesburg has greater resonance, while working in Berlin allows for more conceptual consideration. Both contexts are important for me as an artist, to have this counterbalance between my past and my present.

AL Are you interested in the work of other artists who have worked/are working in the interstice between performance, drawing, and photography or film, such as Helena Almeida,[2] William Kentridge, or Arnulf Rainer?

RR I have no interest in other artists working with this process. My path seems to be set in a different direction, created by having lived in a very specific generation with new social and political influences. I know William Kentridge personally and have immense respect for him living and working in South Africa, when most artists there feel that leaving the country gives one a greater shot at success.

AL During the 1970s Richard Serra said that drawing had become "a verb," a process freed from any representational function. But there has since been a return to depiction and narrative in contemporary drawing, causing curator

Laura Hoptman to argue that drawing has once again become "a noun."[3] Where does your work fit within this trajectory?

RR My work definitely fits into the category of "a verb." The act of "doing" is the overriding factor, sometimes "doing" intuitively, rather than waiting, for too long. Time waits for no line.

AL Your sequential images arranged in a grid bring to mind the 19th-century chronophotography of Eadweard Muybridge, as well the serial logic of conceptual photography. How did you come to this mode of presentation?

RR This logical concept came about through my brief studies in film school where I majored in production design. My role was to sketch the storyboard for my fellow film director colleagues. It was during this storyboard phase that I realized I could adopt this same process for my own work, and fragment the performative aspect of the idea into individual frames that capture the narrative progression. This process allowed me to step away from the live aspect and to focus on a more complex wall-drawing process. It also allowed me to choreograph more performance-related pieces. This low-fi approach is a hallmark of early cinema processes and has very organically developed the discourse of my practice in fascinating ways. My artistic practice is "formed" by cinema, not "informed" by it.

AL The giant compasses in your 2013 show at the Lehmann Maupin Gallery implied that the body is analogous to a drawing instrument, and vice versa. How do dance and drawing converge and diverge in your practice?

RR Dance and drawing converge and diverge through rhythm. Drawing is dependent on a rhythmic approach so as to project a physical output, lines, and mark-making that become an extension of the human form. Here tempo is just as important as dance and physical movement. Dance allows the body to shift through an invisible physicality of time and space. Drawing allows for the same to occur but on a given surface. Our bodies react instinctively to space, conjuring rhythms unconsciously.

AL You often use the term "choreography" to describe the construction of narratives in your work and the way in which actions are presented to the camera. Are you interested in the work of specific choreographers and performing artists, or particular genres of dance?

RR No, I cannot say that there is a specific reference to any choreographers in my work. My work tends to construct itself in the given moment. The body reacts to the drawn narrative, its contours, shapes, forms, and meanings, rather than any rehearsed choreography. My street pieces function as intuitive responses to the space/reality in which they are engulfed. The physical movement is taken from the people that inhabit those spaces. This brings the artwork's physical attributes toward the common person—an any day, anyone inclusion that allows the artwork to relate on a more physical level to the viewer.

[1] Editor's note: *Arm Chair*, *Military Chair*, *Kinderstoel*, *Berlin Chair*, and *Piano Chair* are part of a series of six video animations made by Robin Rhode between 2010 and 2011, collectively entitled *Variants*. In citing the chairs created by the Dutch designer and architect Gerrit Rietveld, the animations subvert the formal modernist ideology anchored in the pieces of furniture. *Piano Chiar* is a homage to fellow citizen and the artist's contemporary, South African pianist and composer Moses Molelekwa.

[2] Editor's note: see the essay by Laurence Schmidlin in this volume, p. 202–203.

[3] Laura Hoptman, "Drawing Is a Noun," in Laura Hoptman (ed.), *Drawing Now: Eight Propositions*, exh. cat., The Museum of Modern Art, New York 2002, p. 12.

"If You Know What It's Going to Be, It's Not Interesting." An Interview with Paul Kaiser from OpenEndedGroup

Nadia Peručić

This interview took place in New York City on December 20, 2013.

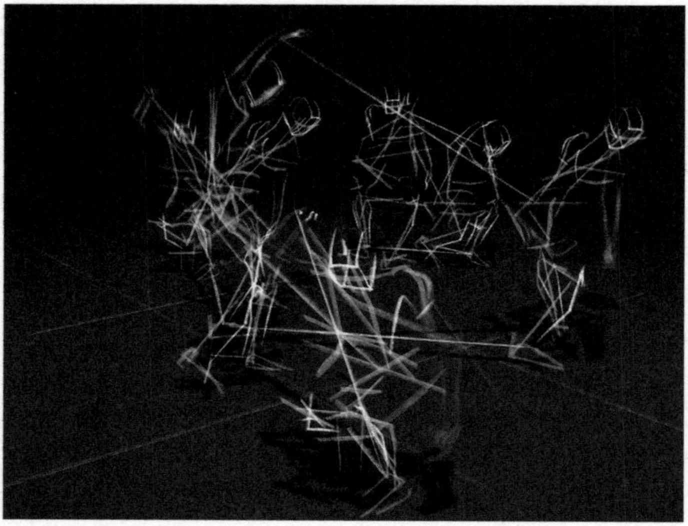

OpenEndedGroup
Ghostcatching, 1999
Digital art installation
Choreography and performance: Bill T. Jones
Visual and sound design: Shelley Eshkar and Paul Kaiser

The digital art collective OpenEndedGroup includes Paul Kaiser (1995–present), Marc Downie (2001–present), and Shelley Eshkar (1995–2014). Although they have worked in a wide range of disciplines, notably dance, music, film, installation, and public art, this interview with Kaiser focuses on their multi-media collaborations with contemporary choreographers. Some of the choreographers with whom they have worked closely are Merce Cunningham (*Hand-Drawn Spaces*, 1998; *BIPED*, 1999; *Loops*, 2001–2008), Bill T. Jones (*Ghostcatching*, 1999, and *22*, 2005), Trisha Brown (*how long does the subject linger on the edge of the volume …*, 2005), and Wayne McGregor (*Choreographic Language Agent*, 2007–present, and *Stairwell*, 2010). The group's contributions to these pieces frequently take the form of digital projections that are based on motion capture of the dancers' movements, and that are shown either alongside or independently of the performances. Never exact recordings, the projections, which employ digital manipulation, and often artificial intelligence, present new iterations of the performances while capturing their formal qualities and overall trajectory. Since they are digitally simulated, the projections are by no means drawings in the traditional sense of a hand making marks on paper, yet they share a striking resemblance to the hand-drawn form (for instance, the process by which shapes appear on the screen evokes the act of drawing and the movement of the hand going back, erasing, reworking, and building up a composition).

* * *

PAUL KAISER Although I'm speaking in my own voice, I'm also speaking from ideas by the people with whom I collaborate a lot, notably Marc Downie and Shelley Eshkar, and obviously the choreographers that we've had the incredible opportunity to work with over the years, unexpectedly.

NADIA PERUČIĆ What is your background?

PK My original background was in experimental film, which I started doing even as a teenager. I've also been interested in writing. I studied film history in college, as well as art history. Sometime after that, I started volunteering in a school for severely learning disabled children and I liked it so much that I got a Masters, and taught for almost 10 years. It was at that point that I started paying close attention to the way children draw. This was in the mid-80s, when the computer became accessible, so for the first 10 years my computer work was with children, building stories with them on the computer. The collaborations that I did with them are remarkably similar to all those that I've done ever since, and are completely connected to the way that I work now. What I discovered was that the ideas that were sparked between minds were more interesting than the ones held by themselves. The kids would be engaged in these private acts, but actually it was only when they started collaborating with me or one of their peers that the richness of their ideas became apparent, probably because of the mirrors, or views we provided on them.

I learned how to collaborate from my students, and they also showed me less consciously what was interesting about drawing. In particular, I started to think of drawing as a performance, and that's the connection to dance, I suppose. When they drew, they would enact their drawing. There was often muttered narration, sound effects, and explosions, and also it was very gestural. Given my film background, there was something filmic about it also, because they would keep changing their position with regard to their eyes. So they would be really close for certain things, and then they'd back way off to do something else.

NP How do you see your collaborations now? When you were working with Wayne McGregor on *Stairwell*, it seemed to be a continuous exchange of ideas, where he would do a movement, then look at how you digitally rendered it, then create another movement in response to that.

PK That's correct, it was iterative. It was a very weird system that we created to capture him. It was a kind of motion capture, but it was of our own invention, and the idea was to actually try to capture the whole body with its thousands of points (typically in motion capture, you capture just the joints). So on the one hand, fantastic, if you can do that well, but on the other hand, it makes many mistakes. For example, if his arm is on the floor, and he picks his arm up, for a moment, the algorithms will mistake part of the floor for a part of his body, and it will lift, which we love. McGregor started to see that as a possibility, and his whole choreography and performance in the stairwell was an attempt to essentially mimic in his movements the shapes of this crazy stairwell.

NP So you're working with the creative process throughout.

PK The whole way through, and the dancers are, too. It's never just a translation of existing stuff. If you know what it's going to be, it's not interesting. I don't know much about dance, and in a way that helps. In fact, one of our rules of collaboration is that the areas of expertise shouldn't overlap. That's why collaboration is interesting, but if we were all too similar it's boring, and it doesn't work, and it's full of conflict.

NP In terms of your collaborations being varied, how did your involvement with Merce Cunningham (*Hand-Drawn Spaces*) and Bill T. Jones (*Ghostcatching*) at around the same time come about?

PK Merce gave us two of his dancers, whom he supervised, and we worked with them, but never from an existing dance. I mean, we don't record dancers. At the same time, I wanted to work with someone who's the opposite of Merce. Someone who was very concerned with the particularly of the body, and of identity, and I was also interested in someone whose movement was very much about muscles—curves and ripples of the muscle—as opposed to angular. So that led us to Bill T. Jones. We recorded both *Hand-Drawn Spaces* and *Ghostcatching* in the same motion capture studio on the same day. But the circumstances weren't ideal: the studio had a hard concrete floor, and the longest the computer could capture was maybe 25 seconds. One of the things that Merce said at the time, which I strongly believe in is, you can only make work when there are limitations. So he was fine with it. There are no big leaps in the piece, and you know that's that. Bill on the other hand, is very adversarial, he almost acts out rebellion in everything he does, rather self-consciously if I may say so, and he was sort of defiant. He said: "You can never capture my movement. I can do this, or I can do that. This is terrible. Are you trying to steal my soul?" It was like ghost-catching, which is where the name came from, and as he was improvising, he just sort of got wilder and wilder as if taken over by the piece, and he was doing all of these things where he was rolling and sweating too much, and the motion capture things were coming off, and it was great.

NP In the Jones piece, you see his musculature, or you don't actually see it, but its presence is apparent. Whereas the Cunningham piece looks more schematic and the bodies more stick figure-like. Was this deliberately mediated on your part, or was it translated that way through the computer?

PK Well in most cases it was mediated, but in one case we expressed Bill's body with these beautiful virtual drawings with more continuous lines that Shelley made. With Merce's piece we kept pushing it more toward greater abstraction, and greater calligraphic precision. We just didn't want to do the same thing twice, and the only reason to work with two such different choreographers is to make two very different pieces. So *Ghostcatching* is narrative, it's psychological, it's fraught with identity and questions of identity. Also, at the end of *Ghostcatching,* his figure is multiplied into this odd-linked-multiple-bodied-creature, and there's this horrifying view of the future, essentially. So it's a very different piece from Merce's, which is really just about motion.

NP What about your work with Cunningham on *BIPED*, and the portrait of his hand motions, *Loops*?

PK We did *BIPED* on the heels of that. When we finished *Hand-Drawn Spaces*, Merce invited us to do a piece with him. In fact that was our pattern of collaboration with him, back and forth. And this was a much more traditional, "non-collaboration," collaboration in that we didn't see the work, or hear the music until the dress rehearsal. We had this idea of motion capturing parts of the dance, and he was all for it. The funny thing was, he gave us so little material. We went into the motion capture studio, and I was expecting quite a lot, and he gave us almost nothing; just a few phrases. I said, "Well can you at least give us some stepping motions?" So he created a few stepping motions on the spot, but I mean we really got a tiny amount of the *BIPED* material. So we combined it with some of the older *Hand-Drawn Spaces* material, and we made a lot of attempts to vary it through representation, which we did.

While we were doing *BIPED*, even before that, we were very conscious of the fact that we'd been sitting in the motion capture studio with one of the really great performers of the 20th century, but we weren't able to capture him. We then learned that you could do finger capture where you have sensors on the forearm and hand, and we captured Merce performing *Loops*. The idea was that the points of the hand would connect as much by cat's-cradle-like relationships as by anatomical ones, and that each point could act almost independently to make small local decisions as to how it would appear. We also wanted it to be in sort of a hand-drawn style. For part of the sound, Merce read from the diary he kept as a 17-year-old first visiting New York for three days. The original version of *Loops* ran in real time. So the piece never repeated. It was in fact a live piece. It was his last live piece. He never set it on anybody else, except this virtual being.

NP Was this the artificial intelligence part of it?

PK Yes, so the way it works is, the captured data point, say this tip of the finger, has the following ability: it can decide how it's going to connect, and in what line style it's going to connect to some other point.

NP So there are a certain number of variations that it can continually do.

PK Yes, and the most interesting thing is this: if at this point it decided to connect with its nearest neighbor, then the tip of this forefinger might actually be closest to the middle knuckle of the pinky on the other hand. This is all Marc's brilliance.

Loops is, for me, a deeply moving portrait of Merce, because it shows motions that he's never set on anybody else, and you hear his voice, and you have this amazing encounter of the very different ages. The words of a young man read by an old man is really an amazing thing, especially because it's obviously exactly the same person, even though locutions are dated here, and the enthusiasm is different.

NP Since OpenEndedGroup began working in a particular cultural moment, the mid-1990s, has your idea of open-endedness changed with advances in technology and evolving ideas about open source systems in general?

PK When we came up with that name it was really a play on words, because yes, the code we have is open source, but what is much more important to us is that we never start a work knowing what it will be in the end. So it goes back to the point I made earlier about how we would never work on an existing dance by Merce. We wanted it to be an open-ended exploration where none of us knew what it was before we did it.

NP What would you like your next project to be?

PK A lot of things I think about tend to have to do with childhood. In almost every talk I give on dance, I make the following opposition and say that on the one hand, one kind of height of beauty is the extremely disciplined and beautiful dancer, who has mastery over her movements. To my eye, an even more extreme version of beauty is that of a toddler. When a toddler moves across the room it's the most beautiful motion I know of. So why is that? There are two reasons for that. One is that they will never do the same thing twice because they're learning it, they haven't mastered it yet. Secondly, the way I put it, their thought is happening not in their head, but within their whole body. So at any given moment as they are sort of Frankensteining their way over, you can feel the thought going into this elbow over here, or this pinky, and it's all live with awareness, with registration of the action, attempts, false attempts, falling, and the whole thing is so present, and there's no way that you can act that out.

I know a lot of the choreographers (including the ones that we work with) try to inject that kind of uncertainty into their dancers, but it's still staged. It's not the same thing at all. So that's something I've been obsessed with trying to do forever, a toddler project. We now have the perfect one. You record the kids in 3D straight video, but then you have a virtual creature learning their motions. So the same way that they're learning, you also have this virtual thing learning at the same time. It would be so beautiful.

Selected Bibliography

Alain Badiou, "La danse comme métaphore de la pensée," in Alain Badiou, *Petit manuel d'inesthétique*, Le Seuil, Paris 1998, p. 91–110

Sally Banes, *Terpsichore in Sneakers: Post-Modern Dance*, Wesleyan University Press, Middletown (CT) 1980

Anne Bénichou (ed.), *Recréer/scripter–Mémoires et transmissions des œuvres performatives et chorégraphiques contemporaines*, published following the study days *Documenter, recréer… Mémoires et transmissions des œuvres performatives et chorégraphiques contemporaines* held in Montréal (May 2–4, 2013), "Nouvelles scènes" series, Les presses du réel, Dijon 2015

Philip Bither, Trisha Brown, and Peter Eleey, *Trisha Brown: So That the Audience Does Not Know Whether I Have Stopped Dancing*, exh. cat., Walker Art Center, Minneapolis (MN), 2008

Carole Boulbès (ed.), *Femmes, attitudes performatives, aux lisières de la performance et de la danse*, published following the international conference *Femmes, attitudes performatives* held at the Centre culturel André-Malraux, Vandœuvre (November 21–22, 2012), "Nouvelles scènes" series, École nationale supérieure d'architecture de Nancy/Les presses du réel, Nancy/Dijon 2014

Gabriele Brandstetter, *Tanz-Lektüren. Körperbilder und Raumfiguren der Avantgarde*, Fischer, Frankfurt 1995

Gabriele Brandstetter and Marta Ulvaeus, "Defigurative Choreography: from Marcel Duchamp to William Forsythe," in *TDR–The Drama Review*, vol. 42, no. 4, The MIT Press, Cambridge (MA) 1998, p. 37–55

Gabriele Brandstetter, "Choreography as A Cenotaph: The Memory of Movement," in Gabriele Brandstetter and Hortensia Völckers (eds.), *ReMembering the Body*, Hatje Cantz, Ostfildern 2000, p. 102–132

Gabriele Brandstetter and Sibylle Peters (eds.), *De figura. Rhetorik – Bewegung – Gestalt*, Fink, Munich 2002

Gabriele Brandstetter and Christoph Wulf (eds.), *Tanz als Anthropologie*, Fink, Munich 2007

Gabriele Brandstetter, "Schnittfiguren. Intersektionen von Bild und Tanz," in Gottfried Böhm, Gabriele Brandtsetter, and Achatz von Müller (eds.), *Figur und Figuration. Studien zu Wahrnehmung und Wissen*, Fink, Munich 2007, p. 13–32

Tobias Burg (ed.), *Zeichnung als Prozess. Aktuelle Positionen der Grafik*, exh. cat., Museum Folkwang/Kehrer, Essen/Heidelberg 2008

Cornelia H. Butler, *Afterimage: Drawing through Process*, exh. cat., The Museum of Contemporary Art, Los Angeles 1999

Cornelia H. Butler and Catherine de Zegher (eds.), *On Line. Drawing Through the Twentieth Century*, exh. cat, The Museum of Modern Art, New York 2010

Mathieu Copeland and Julie Pellegrin (eds.), *Chorégraphier l'exposition/Choreographing Exhibitions*, Les presses du réel, Dijon 2013

Marco Costantini (ed.), *En corps: Lausanne et la danse*, exh. cat., Musée historique, Art & Fiction, Lausanne 2012

Bojana Cvejić and Anne Teresa De Keersmaeker, *Carnets d'une chorégraphe: Fase, Rosas danst Rosas, Elena's Aria, Bartók*, Rosas/ Fonds Mercator, Brussels 2012

Bojana Cvejić (ed.), *"Rétrospective" par Xavier LeRoy*, Les presses du réel, Dijon 2014

Jane C. Desmond (ed.), *Meaning in Motion. New Cultural Studies of Dance*, Duke University Press, Durham and London 2006

Aurore Després (ed.), *Gestes en éclats. Art, danse et performance*, Les presses du réel, Dijon 2016

Richard Etlin, "Aesthetics and the Spatial Sense of Self," in *The Journal of Aesthetics and Art Criticism*, vol. 56, no. 1, Wiley-Blackwell, Hoboken (NJ) 1998, p. 1–19

Susan Leigh Foster, *Reading Dancing: Bodies and Subjects in Contemporary American Dance*, University of California Press, Berkeley 1986

Simone Forti, *Handbook in Motion*, The Press of the Nova Scotia College of Art & Design, Halifax 1974

Jan-Philipp Frühsorge, Angela Lammert, Carolin Meister, and Andréas Schalhorn (eds.), *Räume der Zeichnung*, Akademie der Künste/Verlag für moderne Kunst, Berlin/Nuremberg, 2007

RoseLee Goldberg, "Performance: The Art of Notation," in *Studio International*, vol. 192, no. 982, July–August 1976, p. 54–58

Markus Heinzelmann and Matthias Winzen (eds.), *Gegen den Strich. Neue Formen der Zeichnung*, exh. cat., Staatliche Kunsthalle/ Verlag für moderne Kunst, Baden-Baden/Nuremberg 2004

Ann Hutchinson Guest, *Choreo-graphics. A Comparison of Dance Notation Systems from the Fifteenth Century to the Present*, Gordon and Breach, London 1989

Emmanuelle Huynh, Denise Luccioni, and Julie Perrin, *Histoire(s) et lectures: Trisha Brown & Emmanuelle Huynh*, Centre national de danse contemporaine/Les presses du réel, Angers/ Dijon 2012

Adnen Jdey (ed.), *La Part de l'Œil*, special issue: "Ce qui fait danse: de la plasticité à la performance," no. 24, Brussels 2009

Claudia Jeschke, *Tanzschriften. Ihre Geschichte und Methode: die illustrierte Darstellung eines Phänomens von den Anfängen bis zur Gegenwart*, Comes Verlag, Munich 1983

Caroline A. Jones, *Sensorium. Embodied Experience, Technology, and Contemporary Art*, The MIT Press, Cambridge (MA) and London 2006

Rosalind Krauss, *Line as Language. Six Artists Draw*, exh. cat., The Art Museum, Princeton University, Princeton 1974

Laurence Louppe (ed.), *Traces of Dance: Drawings and Notations of Choreographers*, Dis Voir, Paris 1991

Laurence Louppe, *Poétique de la danse contemporaine*, Contredanse, Brussels 2004

Christine Macel and Emma Lavigne (eds.), *Danser sa vie. Art et danse de 1900 à nos jours*, exh. cat., Centre Pompidou–Musée national d'Art moderne, Éditions Centre Pompidou, Paris 2011

Christine Macel and Emma Lavigne (eds.), *Danser sa vie. Écrits sur la danse*, Éditions Centre Pompidou, Paris 2011

Felicia McCarren, *Dancing Machines. Choreographies of the Age of Mechanical Reproduction*, Stanford University Press, Stanford 2003

Helen Molesworth (ed.), *Dance/Draw*, exh. cat., The Institute of Contemporary Art/Hatje Cantz, Boston/Ostfildern 2012

Heike Munder and Raphael Gygax, *Between Zones. On the Representation of the Performative in the Notation of Movement/ Zwischenzonen*, exh. cat., Migros Museum für Gegenwartskunst, JRP | Ringier, Zurich 2010

Jean-Luc Nancy, *Le Plaisir au dessin*, exh. cat., Musées des Beaux-Arts/Hazan, Lyon/Paris 2007

Julie Perrin, *Figures de l'attention: cinq essais sur la spatialité de la danse*, Les presses du réel, Dijon 2013

Catherine Quéloz (ed.), *Yvonne Rainer, une femme qui … Écrits, entretiens, essais critiques*, JRP | Ringier/Les presses du réel, Zurich/ Dijon 2008

Janelle G. Reinelt and Joseph R. Roach, *Critical Theory and Performance*, The University of Michigan Press, Ann Arbor 2007

Dee Reynolds, *Symbolist Aesthetics and Early Abstract Art*, Cambridge University Press, Cambridge 1995

Dee Reynolds, *Rhythmic Subjects. Uses of Energy in the Dances of Mary Wigman, Martha Graham and Merce Cunningham*, Dance Books, Alton 2007

Susan Rosenberg, "Trisha Brown: Choreography as Visual Art," in *October*, vol. 140, Spring 2012, p. 18–44

Pascal Rousseau, "Figures de déplacement. L'écriture du corps en mouvement," in *Exposé – Revue d'esthétique et d'art contemporain*, no. 2, 1995, p. 86–97

Eva Schmidt (ed.), *Je mehr ich zeichne. Zeichnung als Weltenwurf/ The More I Draw. Drawing as a Concept for the World*, Museum für Gegenwartskunst/DuMont, Siegen/Cologne 2010

Ellen Schwart (ed.), *Tracking, Tracing, Marking, Pacing*, exh. cat., Pratt Institute, New York 1982

Noémie Solomon (ed.), *Danse–An Anthology*, "Nouvelles scènes" series, Les presses du réel, Dijon 2014

Noémie Solomon (ed.), *Danse–A Catalogue*, "Nouvelles scènes" series, Les presses du réel, Dijon 2015

Hendel Teicher (ed.), *Trisha Brown: Dance and Art in Dialogue, 1961–2001*, exh. cat., The MIT Press, Cambridge (MA) 2002

Paul Valéry, *Degas Danse Dessin* [1938], Gallimard, Paris 2008

Catherine de Zegher (ed.), *The Stage of Drawing: Gesture and Act. Selected from the Tate Collection*, exh. cat., Tate Publishing/ The Drawing Center, London/New York 2003

All websites cited in the footnotes of the present volume were accessed and verified in November 2016.

Index of Names

M

N

O

P

R

S

T

V

W

Y

Acknowledgments

We would like to express our warm thanks to the artists and the authors, as well as Catherine Aguilar, Paolo Amaldi, Kathrin Bentele, Guillemette Bolens, Lionel Bovier, Fae Brauer, Kathleen Breembosch, Tarramo Broennimann, Edouard, Frances and Laurent Burkhalter, Yves Christen, Chiara Corazza, Lisa Darms, Mariama Diagne, Maria Luisa Diaz de Leon Zuloaga, Clément Dirié, Clovis Duran, Nicolas Eigenheer, Roger Fayet, Hans Galle, Dario Gamboni, Irene Gerogianni, Gwenaëlle Gilliéron, Sophie Glidden-Lyon, Caterine Gualco, Annabel Guérédrat, Diana Hammer, Ji-Yoon Han, Benjamin Ambrosius Heinz, Tomoko Hiraoka, Margaux Honegger, Pia Karaspuro, Christelle Khoury, Sibylla Klein, Petra Krausz, Claire Lamotte Clert, Noemi Lapzeson, Nicolas Leuba, Marcella Lista, Clare Manchester, Rainer Michael Mason, Sana Masood, Sarah Möller, Michael Nock, John O'Toole, Eléonor de Pesters, Inge Pieters, Géraldine Piguet-Reisser, Christian Roy, Ivan Ruet, Margo Running, Zoé Seiler, Francesca Serrati, Kirsten Tanaka, Hendel Teicher, Simona Travaglianti, Jason Underhill, Michel Vust, Peter Welz, Juliane Wieland, Mariel Williams, and Maja Wismer.

Sarah Burkhalter & Laurence Schmidlin

Imprint

EDITORS
Sarah Burkhalter & Laurence Schmidlin

ESSAYS AND INTERVIEWS
Gabriele Brandstetter, Sarah Burkhalter, Pauline Chevalier, Anne Teresa De Keersmaeker, Julie Enckell Julliard, Mark Franko, Katrin Gattinger, Magali Le Mens, Laetitia Legros, Anna Lovatt, Nolwenn Mégard, Robert Morris, OpenEndedGroup/Paul Kaiser, Nadia Peručić, Catherine Quéloz, Robin Rhode, Laurence Schmidlin, Yvonne Rainer, Susan Rosenberg, Katia Schneller, Alexander Schwan, Alan Storey, Cindy Van Acker, and Catherine Wood

EDITORIAL COORDINATION
Clément Dirié, with the collaboration of Kathrin Bentele and Margaux Honegger

COPY EDITING AND PROOFREADING
Clare Manchester

TRANSLATION
Sarah Burkhalter (from French to English): introduction; John O'Toole (from French to English): Pauline Chevalier, Julie Enckell Julliard (essay), Laetitia Legros, Cindy Van Acker, Laurence Schmidlin; Christian Roy, with Sarah Burkhalter (from German to English): Gabriele Brandstetter

DESIGN CONCEPT
Gavillet & Rust, Geneva

DESIGN
Nicolas Eigenheer, Nicolas Leuba

PRINT AND BINDING
Musumeci S.p.A., Quart (Aosta)

TYPEFACE
Genath (www.optimo.ch)

PHOTO CREDITS
p. 4: Courtesy of Simone Forti and The Box, Los Angeles; p. 16: Courtesy of Yvonne Rainer; p. 28: 2017, ProLitteris, Zurich; p. 46–47: Bibliothèque nationale de France, département Bibliothèque-musée de l'opéra, RES-68; p. 60: © Trisha Brown. Courtesy de Sikkema Jenkins & Co., New York; p. 74: Collection of The Museum of Modern Art, New York. Committee on Drawings Funds. Acc. no.: 19.2011.4. © 2017. Digital image, The Museum of Modern Art, New York/Scala, Florence; p. 88: Courtesy of Alan Storey. Photo: Ashley Judge, 2008; p. 100: Production: Le Fresnoy, Tourcoing, 2007 and 2008. © Laetitia Legros et Le Fresnoy, Tourcoing, 2007 and 2008; p. 112: Courtesy of Anna Halprin and the Museum of Performance + Design, San Francisco. Photo © William B. Heick; p. 130: The Judson Memorial Church Archive. MSS 094; Box 1; Folder 39; Fales Library and Special Collections, New York University Libraries. Courtesy of Philip Corner; p. 148: © 2011 Yi-Chun Wu/ The Museum of Modern Art (IN2143.1). © 2017. Digital image, The Museum of Modern Art, New York/Scala, Florence; p. 164: Production: Cie Greffe, Genève, and Festival Électron, Geneva. Courtesy of Cie Greffe, Geneva, and Cindy Van Acker. Photo: Isabelle Meister; p. 174: © Peter Welz Studio, Berlin; p. 182: Courtesy of The Channa Horwitz Estate and Ghebaly Gallery, Los Angeles. Photo: Robert Wedemeyer; p. 192: Courtesy of Helena Almeida and of The Leal Rios Foundation, Lisbon. Photo: João Biscainho; p. 208: Collection and courtesy of Robin Rhode and Lehmann Maupin, New York and Hong Kong © Robin Rhode; p. 218: Courtesy of OpenEndedGroup (Shelley Eshkar and Paul Kaiser)

This book is supported by the Polygraphie Danse & Dessin association.

It also benefited from the generous support of

FLUXUM FOUNDATION

Fonds général de
l'Université de Genève

As well as of Anne-Shelton Aaron, Janet Briner, Frances Burkhalter-Carroll, and other donors and foundations who wish to remain anonymous.

PUBLISHED BY
JRP | Ringier
Limmatstrasse 270
CH–8005 Zurich
T +41 43 311 27 50
E info@jrp-ringier.com
www.jrp-ringier.com

IN CO-EDITION WITH
Les presses du réel
35, rue Colson
F–21000 Dijon
T +33 3 80 30 75 23
E info@lespressesdureel.com
www.lespressesdureel.com

ISBN 978-3-03764-469-0 (JRP | Ringier)
ISBN 978-2-84066-917-3 (Les presses du réel)

Distribution

GERMANY AND AUSTRIA
Vice Versa Distribution, www.vice-versa-distribution.com

FRANCE
Les presses du réel, www.lespressesdureel.com

SWITZERLAND
AVA Verlagsauslieferung AG, www.ava.ch

UK AND OTHER EUROPEAN COUNTRIES
Cornerhouse Publications HOME
www.cornerhousepublications.org

USA, CANADA, ASIA, AND AUSTRALIA
ARTBOOK | D. A. P., www.artbook.com

For a list of our partner bookshops or for any general questions, please contact JRP | Ringier directly at info@jrp-ringier.com, or visit our homepage www.jrp-ringier.com for further information.

Documents Series 24:
Sarah Burkhalter &
Laurence Schmidlin (eds.)
Spacescapes
Dance & Drawing since 1962

This book is the twenty-fourth volume in the "Documents" series, dedicated to critics' writings.

The series was founded by Lionel Bovier and Xavier Douroux.

A French edition of this book is also available.

Also available

DOCUMENTS SERIES (IN ENGLISH)

John Baldessari, *More Than You Wanted to Know About John Baldessari*
ISBN 978-3-03764-192-7 (JRP|Ringier) [*Vol. 1*]
ISBN 978-3-03764-256-6 (JRP|Ringier) [*Vol. 2*]

Raymond Bellour, *Between-the-Images*
ISBN 978-3-03764-144-6 (JRP|Ringier)
ISBN 978-2-84066-513-7 (Les presses du réel)

Joshua Decter, *Art Is a Problem*
ISBN 978-3-03764-195-8 (JRP|Ringier)
ISBN 978-2-84066-621-9 (Les presses du réel)

Gabriele Detterer & Maurizio Nannucci, *Artist-Run Spaces*
ISBN 978-3-03764-191-0 (JRP|Ringier)
ISBN 978-2-84066-512-0 (Les presses du réel)

Christian Höller, *Time Action Vision*
ISBN 978-3-03764-124-8 (JRP|Ringier)
ISBN 978-2-84066-396-6 (Les presses du réel)

Hans Ulrich Obrist, *A Brief History of Curating*
ISBN 978-3-905829-55-6 (JRP|Ringier)
ISBN 978-2-84066-287-7 (Les presses du réel)

Hans Ulrich Obrist, *A Brief History of New Music*
ISBN 978-3-905829-190-3 (JRP|Ringier)
ISBN 978-2-84066-619-6 (Les presses du réel)

Igor Zabel, *Contemporary Art Theory*
ISBN 978-3-03764-238-2 (JRP|Ringier)
ISBN 978-2-84066-573-1 (Les presses du réel)

Hans Ulrich Obrist, *The Czech Files*
ISBN 978-3-03764-387-7 (JRP|Ringier)
ISBN 978-2-84066-760-5 (Les presses du réel)